MEDIEVAL STRUCTURE: THE GOTHIC VAULT

JAMES H. ACLAND

MEDIEVAL STRUCTURE: THE GOTHIC VAULT

UNIVERSITY OF TORONTO PRESS

©University of Toronto Press 1972
Toronto and Buffalo
Printed in Canada
ISBN 0-8020-1886-6
ISBN microfiche 0-8020-0226-9
LC 72-76769

CONTENTS

The walling in and roofing over of space is what architecture is all about. To discover how man gained proficiency in this balancing of material against gravity we must do more than examine the great monuments and impressive temples. In the primitive structures of early man and in the vernacular of the evolved cultures, generations of craftsmen devised ingenious and practical uses for the everyday materials of building. Good sense imposed by the necessary limitations of money and effort ensured that these anonymous buildings would exhibit a spare economy and an obvious structural logic.

As a necessary background for a study of medieval architectural structure, I have summarized the technical achievements of primitive builders. From these ingenious expedients local carpenters and masons evolved vernacular modes of building in Europe and around the Mediterranean. Early in my studies of Gothic vaulting it became evident to me that the meteoric success of Gothic builders owed much to their intelligent use of local traditions. The complexity of the medieval cathedral church and the civic hall was an elaboration of a limited yet logical set of structural themes. This grammar of structure, the essential bedrock of architecture, emerges from the work of cultural anthropologists, arguing from the rich and confused matrix of a society in being, and from the elegant detective work of the archaeologists, studying the traces of vanished cultures.

If the architect is to give physical form and visible statement to the utilitarian needs as well as the highest aspirations of man, if the building is to be more than an expensive toy, economy in the use of material and logic in the use of structural techniques is essential. Architecture is far more than the playful and enchanting evocation of theatrical effect by the use of decorative detail, mechanical gadgetry, and exhibitionism in structure. It is a deadly serious matching of human effort and will against the needs for adequate shelter of a world population. Much talk about the economy of abundance in which we live in the western world today cannot conceal the inefficiency and ugliness of the contemporary city; the large part of the world's population are ill-housed masses who live in desperate and foetid slums untouched by rebuilding and progress. Although we can put transistor radios in the hands of stone-age savages we often seem quite incapable of intelligent and rational analysis of the basic processes of building for man and his family.

The persistent failure of speculative builders in our towns to achieve a livable environment suggests the need for a thorough rethinking of our modes of building. As an architect, I believe that we must make every reasonable effort to ensure that the archaeological and anthropological evidence for early and vernacular building be used as a tool for research into the physical and planning problems faced by communities today. Much of our overwrought technology and our wasteful gadgetry can be done away with if we properly read the lessons of history and prehistory. Our new-found mobility has come just in time to let us glimpse something of the diverse heritage of existent neolithic cultures before they vanish forever.

The medieval play with structure which was so characteristic a part of the Gothic experiment was a peculiarly European achievement. A clever and theatrical professionalism came about because Europe during the Middle Ages was the meeting ground of two cultures and two traditions. When the builders of the north attempted to translate their predominantly timber architecture into permanent masonry, or when they tried to superimpose the stone or brick dome of the desert south upon the open walling of temperate Europe, they were forced to devise highly sophisticated structures. But when they and their clients tired of the extremism of exaggerated monuments they reverted to vernacular sources for new programmes of building which could bypass the illogic of extreme solutions. Within the four centuries of the Gothic experiment the builders kept turning back to indigenous local themes which could once again enliven and enrich their monuments.

I suggest that the contrast between shell surfaces and skeletal frames in this book is more than a useful tool for historical analysis. Our engineers use one or both of these techniques in their rocket shells and space capsules. Design alternates between the rigidity of triangulated space frames and the economy of curved shells. Though working with different materials and at a different scale, our engineers and architects encounter problems analogous to those faced by medieval masons.

Initially my interest in the Gothic came from the vision of the web of stone wedged into the sky: from that moment many long years ago when I hopped over the tailboard of a Canadian army truck en route to Belgium, and saw the towers and buttresses of Amiens soaring above the ruck and rubble of the town. Later at Cologne I was struck by the obdurate strength of the crazy cathedral fabric of medieval and nineteenth-century stone which remained substantially intact despite direct hits by bombs, while about it steel and ferroconcrete structures lay in twisted wreckage.

In one way or another the preparation of this book has extended over fourteen years. I tend to favour direct personal examination of structures and this has entailed much travel. The help, encouragement, and assistance which so many have freely proferred during these trips have lightened what has at times seemed to be an insuperable task. It would be manifestly impossible to thank all who have contributed in some degree to the evolution of this book but I would like to give special mention to those who proffered advice, encouragement, and salutary words of warning during the initial study of Central European Gothic. It was in the pages of John Harvey's *Gothic World* that I first saw examples of the characteristic ribless cellular vaulting of Saxony, Bohemia, and the Baltic. He proved to be most helpful, suggesting contacts and outlining an itinerary. His interest in Spain stimulated a study of Iberian Gothic, a topic of particular interest to me because of the rich late medieval tradition of sixteenth-century Mexico. Professor Felipe ma Garin at the University of Valencia was good enough to essay an accurate chronology of ribless vaults in Spain.

In Saxony Dr Löffler at the Institut für Denkmalpflege at Dresden not only sent an excellent guide to these prismatic vaults but took me on a jaunt in an elderly DKW through the mining towns of Saxony to visit some of the buildings under renovation and reconstruction. In Prague Mrs Miroslava Gregorová, representing the Union of Czechoslovak Architects, arranged travel and contacts during my first visit to 'eastern Europe. My particular thanks go to Miss Eva Strnadová in Prague who made available her unpublished study of the Bohemian diamond vault and was good enough to turn over to me the critical results of her research, along with photographs and drawings. John Fitchen of Colgate University was unsparing in criticism and constructive in suggestions which were to give order to the initial manuscript.

The effort to pull together archaeological, historical, and technical data from widely disparate sources and divergent disciplines has made this a difficult book to write. Ian Montagnes' patient and perceptive commentary and knowing critiques have brought form and order to the text. He helped change the manuscript from a sketch, to a study, and then to a consistent theme. To William Rueter, for his eminently readable layouts, and to Prudence Tracy for a final tightening of the manuscript, go special thanks. Without support from the University of Toronto for research, travel and study time the book could never have appeared. The Canada Council has generously helped defray the very considerable costs of publication.

JAMES H. ACLAND
Toronto, 12 April 1972

The choir, St Etienne, Beauvais

FRAME, MASS, AND SHELL

1
PRIMITIVE FRAME

The pattering of raindrops on naked skin is a disagreeable experience, sufficiently uncomfortable to motivate man to seek or improvise shelter. Using an overhanging rock ledge, a handy tree frond, a thatch of grass or reed, or a hide stretched over a few sticks, early man created a roof to protect himself and his family from the chilling rain or torrid sun. He deliberately modified a portion of his natural environment to suit it to his needs and wishes.

Architecture is shelter. No roof ... no building. At its very root and source, architecture always has been the shaping of packages of space which insulate or isolate the occupant from undesirable facets of environment while admitting desirable attributes. The filtrable membrane of the structure must be adapted to a wide range of conditions, in some cases excluding cold air and yet permitting the entry of sunlight, in others isolating the occupant from heat or cold while permitting the movement of fresh air. The more effective this screening out or selection from aspects of the environment becomes, the less need there is for mechanical or artificial adjustment of the internal environment. For example, a window wall facing to the south can be a most efficient thermal trap capturing the heat of the sun during the winter – but in the summer it must be shielded from direct sunlight or the interior becomes a low grade solar furnace. In a hot damp climate the continuous movement of air becomes essential for comfort. The wall disappears and the building becomes little more than a parasol roof. Extreme heat or cold in desert regions are best countered by insulating walls which are opaque to thermal transmission.

In general, builders devised two contrasting structural techniques to meet these demands. In one, the frame tradition, characteristic of the northern forests, the structure evolved as a skeletal fabric carrying a skin or membrane adjusting to climatic need and functional demand. In the other, the mass and shell tradition, common around the shores of the Mediterranean and in the Middle East, a dome or shell vault was placed over massive walls. The continuously curved surfaces of the shell ensured structural stability. The frame is vertebrate, with a skeletal armature, the shell invertebrate with a homogeneous external surface which functions as both structure and insulation. Vernacular frame was rectilinear and open, looking out to light and air. The characteristic urban expression of the type was the frame and gable house packed in rows along the streets of the medieval town. Windows or 'wind eyes' invited the refreshing winds of a temperate summer and could be opened to the warming low rays of the winter sun.

In contrast, the massive wall fabrics employed in the south lent themselves to a tradition of compressive shell masonry, making structural use of interlocking curved surfaces to create an overarching dome or vault. Such use of reconstituted earth – whether in the form of rammed earth, rubble masonry, or brick – proved an economical and logical expedient in insulating the interior from hot,

OVERLEAF *The mass wall, Guanajuato, Mexico*

The frame wall in Belgium: Ghent. A changeable climate encouraged the invention of a range of complex valved shutters hung in a light structural cage.

dry, desert winds and blazing sunshine. As well, it was a mode of building well suited to desert regions where building timber was in short supply. Mass was centripetal and inward looking, turning deliberately away from the blinding glare and hot winds of the southern street. The characteristic urban expression of the type was the heavy walled cube looking in to a cool and sheltered courtyard, as in Greek, Roman, or Middle Eastern housing.

To grasp properly the nature of structural evolution we must disabuse ourselves of the notion that one sunny morning an inspired neolithic mason messing around with stones and mortar suddenly invented the arched vault. This heroic or cataclysmic concept of invention does less than justice to the nature of technological process, which is a social and joint effort slowly advancing from the tried-and-true, customary mode of operation by slight adaptations to minor changes. The tentative and halting application of such small variations can lead, in time, to major and revolutionary developments, but it is almost invariably an empirical process moving step by step from the known to the unknown.

The mason or carpenter facing a collapsed structure would inevitably ask himself 'Why did it fall down? What went wrong?' The response: a modification here, a change in coursing there, or a better interlocking of timbers. Structural failure or deformation was so ready a measure of the success or failure of the building that the early builder could argue from this firm ground of empirical experience to modify the fabric. He felt, rather than calculated, the behaviour of material, imputing to inorganic matter muscular pulls, pressures, and deformations analogous to those he could sense in his own body. That this 'animation' of inanimate matter is demonstrably false is beside the point. This neuromuscular empathy for the behaviour of elastic materials worked. Surprisingly enough, it still works: not always, but often enough to enable us to move on to the next step and the next decision. Men have built thin shell vaults of masonry for centuries, indeed millennia, but only in the last decade have we had the precise mathematical tools and the digital computer to verify their behaviour.

The extraordinary burst of creative building in Europe from the twelfth to the fifteenth century which we today call the Gothic, is best explained in relation to its roots in the customary day by day modes of building current in Europe at the opening of the Middle Ages. Too narrow a focus upon great monuments, ceremonial structures, and impressive temples can conceal the main line of architectural achievement. The primary thread of evolution in building is to be found in the relatively humble

houses along the street and in the utilitarian farm buildings and shelters in the countryside. Good sense informed by limitation of money and effort ensured that these anonymous buildings would exhibit a spare economy and structural logic too often concealed beneath mannered furbelows in the so-called great monuments. The essential continuity of building for man is to be found in the logic of climatic control, the economy of structural utility, and the adjustment of space to social need. The over-specialized dead ends of building, the famous monuments and symbolic creations, may have summed up the aspirations of a narrow class or the dream of an elite, but in so doing they became the dinosaurs of architectural evolution, so elegantly adapted to a particular ecological niche that they could not be adapted to any other purpose. They remain as museums and galleries independent of the thrust of evolutionary change in the city.

A

In the hot, wet jungle, walls disappeared and the roof became a steeply pitched umbrella.

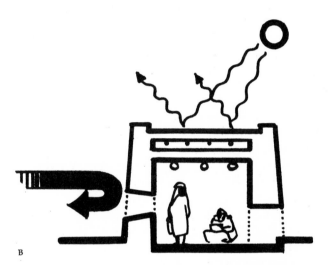

B

Builders in the hot, dry desert constructed heavy insulating walls with small openings. Flat white roofs reflected the heat of the sun.

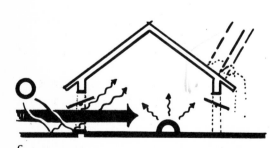

C

In cold, wet (so-called temperate) climates builders had to compromise between winter and summer demands. Dry insulating walls became variable membranes capable of being opened to light and air.

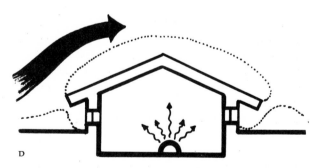

D

Builders in the cold, dry northern deserts used double walls, double ceilings, and snow covered roofs to trap air as an insulator.

Early man had to build with readily available local materials – canes and grasses, leaves and twigs. From these pliant and insubstantial materials he had to create a relatively permanent and structurally rigid unit. He did it by interweaving them to cover, vault, or span a useful space. At first he may well have simply tied together the tips of canes, leaving the roots embedded in the ground. In this snug little arbour, a dome or roof springing directly from the ground, he created a protected equable environment by using natural materials adapted with little change to his needs.

Where it was available, wood must have early been favoured as a material for building. Strong in tension, resistant to shearing across the grain, in thin sections it can absorb considerable bending without failure. Its light porous structure, cellular and fibrous, makes it comparatively easy to shape. Nonetheless it is difficult to cut across the grain. Even with a razor-sharp steel axe or offset saw, cutting through a twelve-inch log is a laborious process. Primitive man had only chipped or polished stone axes, rudimentary saws which he made by setting obsidian flakes or animal teeth into shafts of wood, and sandstone grinding blocks.

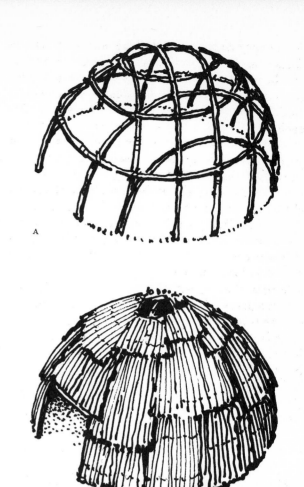

Early builders devised a light skeletal frame to carry a sheathing skin. Paleolithic round hut: A *skeleton,* B *skin*

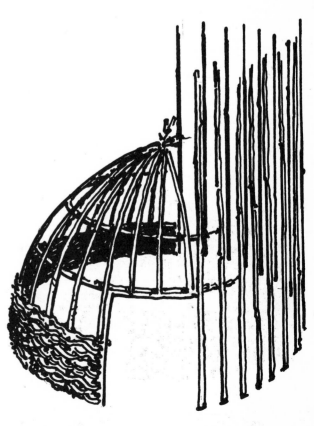

Saplings were tied together or interlaced to carry a sheathing of leaves, grasses, or hides. South African Xhosa hut. (after Walton)

In the very first structures there was, in truth, no distinction between wall and roof. With no tools to cut heavy timbers or rigid poles, the primitive builder of necessity made a structure which was all roof. It was a hemispherical or cylindrical lattice shelter of flexible withies or saplings interlaced to create a rigid basketweave fabric. At its simplest it was akin to the tiny woven dwelling of twigs and leaves still built by the forest pygmies of the Congo basin. In the more elaborate examples, a structural shell of interwoven wicker laced through a framework of saplings carried a sheathing of leaves, bark, woven mats, or hides. There was a clear separation between structure and sheathing, each composed of materials best adapted to its special role.[1] In the structural shell or grid, the redundancy of elements ensured that loads were evenly distributed throughout the fabric so that the failure of any one piece did not affect the whole. Although primitive, the round hut was a remarkable structural device. In it man learned that it was possible to create a rigid domical fabric by interweaving pliant withies and saplings, that double curvatures in a lattice dome gave the most stiffness in the least material, and that gravitational forces were most economically met by interlocking all elements of the building into warped and curved surfaces disposed against the pull of gravity.

Herdsmen and hunters adapted the little round hut to use as a demountable shelter. The Great Plains Indians of North America reduced the hut to a cone of wooden poles lashed together only at the top. The taut membrane of animal skins pegged tightly about the frame held the structure firm by counterposing tensile stresses in the cover against the compressive strength of the poles. Tartar tribesmen in Central Asia devised a demountable hut in which a scissors trellis of pivoted sticks carried a cone of poles socketed into a wooden ring.[2] They lashed felted mats over the framed lattice to create a warm and effective temporary shelter in a demanding climate. Most important, the entire yurt could be broken down and folded together into pack loads for rapid movement.

NOTES

1 J.M. Fitch *American Building* (Boston 1948) 165
2 J.M. Fitch and D.P. Branch 'Primitive Architecture and Climate' *Scientific American'* (December 1960) 133–44

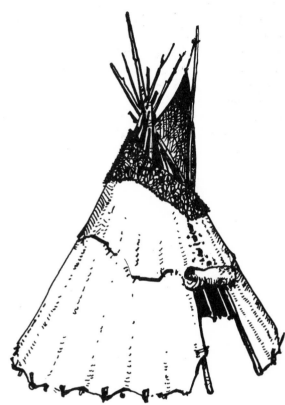

Long after the round hut was abandoned by settled agriculturalists, nomads continued to use it as a temporary shelter. In the Comanche Tipi, Plains Indians covered the poles with a buffalo hide, with an adjustable smoke vent at the apex.

The Masai of South Africa built hide-covered conoid huts with vertical walls to gain more useful interior space. (after Brodrick)

Through Tibet, Mongolia, and Siberia, Mongol nomads invented the yurt, a collapsible scissors trellis and interlocked cone of rafters which could be carried by pack animals.

The paleolithic round hut was easy to build but very limited in size. Where more space was needed, the hut was changed to a barrel-vaulted long house, as in the Iroquois wigwam. It still could be built of light saplings tied or interlaced together, but, because it was only a singly curved surface, it was not as rigid as the doubly curved shell of the round hut. Evidently there were limits to the strength possible in so thin a structure.

As early as 15,000 BC migratory hunters in Europe had discovered that turfs and earth were excellent insulators.[1] They buried the simple round hut in a shallow excavation, building up a wall of turfs about the framework. The light saplings of the domed roof they covered with animal hides. Little

more than cramped and smoky shelter, this primitive pit house became the source for the elaborate earth lodges of Europe, Asia, and North America.

By 6000 BC with an armoury of improved cutting tools, finely chipped flints, and polished blades, neolithic men could now wrest timbers from the forest. Fine cutting and shaping was laborious, but by girdling trees to kill them and using fires to help bring them down, builders had a well-nigh inexhaustible supply of structurally rigid poles. With these components, three to six inches in diameter and some sixteen feet long, they could lash together assemblages sufficiently strong to carry insulating turfs over the roof. No longer a mere overnight shelter, the building became a permanent focus for communal activity during the long cold winter. The peeled-pole, earth lodge became a characteristic artifact of early farming communities in the north.[2] As a sheltered workplace and barn for animals and men it contributed to the growth of arts and technical innovation.

Given the rigid pole, neolithic builders could extend their spans, by adding vertical posts, to shelter an extended family group. In the developed earth lodge, the posts were disposed in a square about the central fireplace. Cross beams nesting in branched forks of the posts carried the upper ends of the rafters, which formed a rough cone covered with turf. There was no need for refined shaping of the timbers – a laborious process with polished stone or bronze tools – because the weight of the roof locked the frame into position. With the kayak, the sled, the harpoon, and the bow, the earth lodge survived until recent years to testify to the remarkable mechanical and structural ingenuity of neolithic hunters.

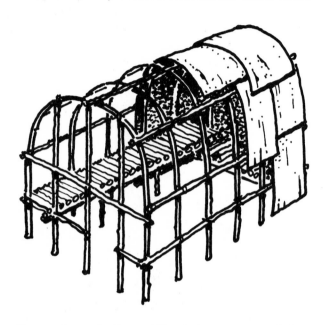

Eastern forest Indians of North America extended the round hut into a lashed frame barrel vault and covered the wigwam with sheets of bark. (after John White, 1588)

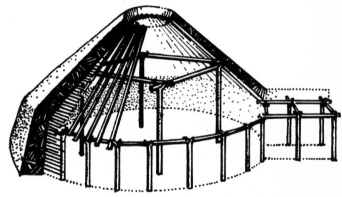

The doubly curved surfaces of the round hut could be built of slender flexible canes and saplings by paleolithic man.

In the forested north, neolithic builders using better tools could cut poles to create a rigid cone of rafters in the pit house.

Searching for warmth and insulation they buried the hut in the ground, covering the rafters with turfs and sods. Intermediate supports extended the roof span. In the characteristic earth lodge a square of posts braced a cone of pole rafters: Hidatsa lodge in the plains of North America.

In the subpolar regions of the open tundra and the sparse forest of the taiga, the Lapps of Finland adapted whale ribs and jawbones (or, when available, birch poles) to create four arched braces framing a smoke vent and carrying an insulating cover of turf: a form very similar to the Eskimo summer earth lodge. The Yakut of Siberia devised a deeply buried earth lodge with revetted walls to shelter against the cold. Japanese neolithic builders in the northern islands took this Siberian prototype earth lodge from Sakhalin to create the Tateana hut. Projecting the rafters above the basic cone of insulating turf, they began that emphasis upon intersecting roof planes which was to become such a major element in Japanese architecture.

NOTES

1 John Bradford 'Building in Wattle, Wood and Turf' in Singer, Holmyard, and Hall *A History of Technology* (Oxford 1957) I, 299–301

2 The earth lodge can be found from England to Finland, across Siberia to the Japanese islands, and in the great plains of North America. Each of these variants has a cone of rafters resting on a four-square grid of posts in a shallow depression. Robert H. Lowie *Indians of the Plains* (New York: American Museum of Natural History 1963) 34–8; Arthur Drexler *The Architecture of Japan* (New York 1955) 18–19; Kaj Birket-Smith *Primitive Man and His Ways* (English translation, Odhams Press 1960, Mentor Books 1963) 114–15

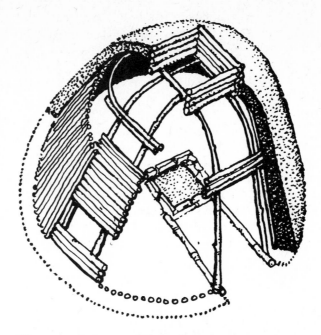

The nomadic Lapps of Finland used a square of curved whale bones or birch poles to carry the pole and turf cover. (after Manker)

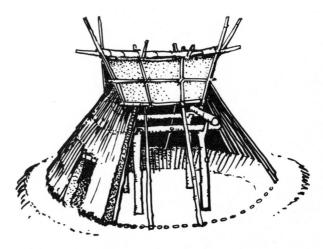

The neolithic builders of northern Japan added a sheltering cap over the smoke vent in a region of . heavy rain. The extended pole rafters carrying this cap became a striking element in later Japanese architecture. (after Drexler)

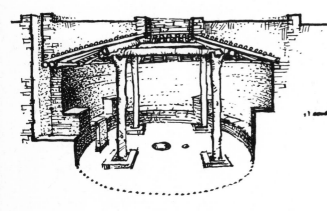

In New Mexico the deeply buried earth lodge eventually became the ceremonial Kiva, dedicated to the earth spirits.

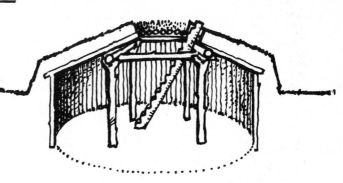

At Kamchadal, Siberia, the Yakut buried the earth lodge with pole walls to contain the earth. (after Brodrick)

When agricultural techniques and animal hus-
bandry were introduced into Europe about 2500 BC,
the early farmers soon found that they needed extra
space to store grain and crops. Though the circular
earth lodge sheltered animals as well as men, it was
a form difficult to expand. Size was limited by the
length of poles available for rafters. The Neolithic
farmers met this new need by repeating the central
square of supports used in the earth lodge, to create
an elongated regular plan. The section through this
long house of the north is identical to that through
the earth lodge, but the repetitive bays allowed in-
definite expansion for storage. The frame was, as in
the past, made of lashed poles. Earth berms were
banked up against the low walls of split logs or
interwoven wattle.[1] The builders set the butt ends
of the long tapering poles into the berms and braced
them over the two rows of posts. Over the rafters
they placed a close mesh of light horizontal purlins
to carry the thatch, turf or bark roof.

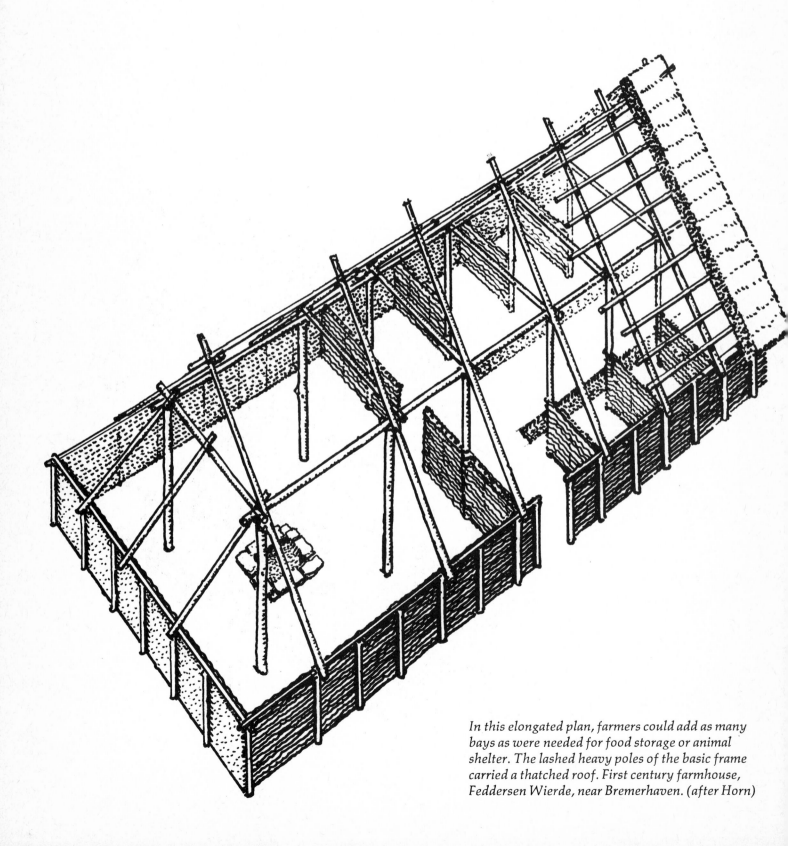

*In this elongated plan, farmers could add as many
bays as were needed for food storage or animal
shelter. The lashed heavy poles of the basic frame
carried a thatched roof. First century farmhouse,
Feddersen Wierde, near Bremerhaven. (after Horn)*

Over the long reaches of prehistoric time the stubborn conservatism of Neolithic builders ensured a continental dispersal of a few building forms. Their hard-won competence was based upon a very few technical devices. The lashed pole, woven cane, and tied thatch structures could be adapted to a wide range of climates and social demands. In Kyushu and the southern Japanese islands early builders copied the elevated frame huts of the islands of the South China Sea to create huts with high pitched roofs to shed the unceasing rain, platforms above the water and wet ground which ensured a dry living space, and walls left porous to allow the movement of air. As in Europe, the structural elements of these walls and roofs became the decorative motifs for a later monumental architecture. In Japan rocks and logs tied over the roof to hold down the thatch against high winds were translated in the Shinto temples into decorative roof combs called katsuogi and projecting rafters developed into pierced chigi.

NOTES
1 Walter Horn 'On the Origins of the Medieval Bay System' *Journal of the Society of Architectural Historians* 17, 2 (1958)
2 Arthur Drexler *The Architecture of Japan* (New York 1955) 18–19

Around the South China Sea, the lashed frame house perched on a platform was dry and airy in a hot and humid climate. Lashed frame Takayuka Hut, Kyushu, Japan, AD 200. (after Drexler)

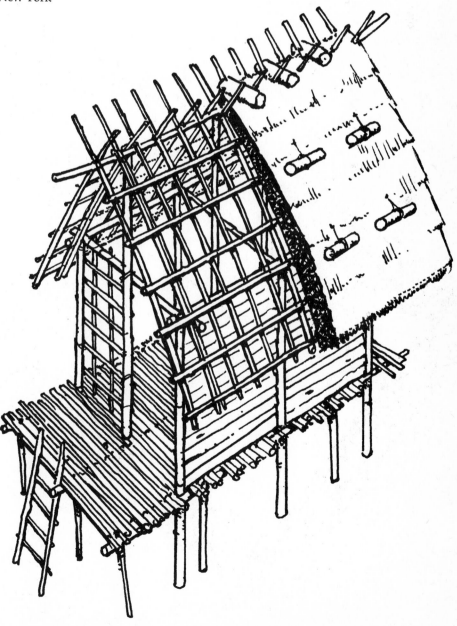

The tightly lashed shell of poles carrying a protection of thatch or turf gave adequate insulation in the north but was subject to rapid decay. Moisture penetrated into the rafters, lashings rotted away, and the bark or sheathing became damp and mouldy in a short time. With only a central vent as a flue and one entry opening, the long house of the north tended to be dark, damp, smoky, and uncomfortable. The solution was to use the same basic plan but construct it of heavier timbers so that openings could be placed between the supports. To build a true frame of this type required better tools than the bronze axes and polished stone celts of the Neolithic. Only about 700 BC when iron tools became generally available in Europe, do we begin to see the emergence of carefully fitted framed structures in wood.

The peasant farmers exploited the new efficiency of iron axes and adzes to shape and model whole logs and develop a new form of structure. They set up vertical posts, cut with grooves into which were hammered tongued logs, and thus created a rigidly braced grid wall.[1] No longer was it necessary to tie the building fabric together with complex and delicate lashings. Shaped timber connectors did the job better and were more lasting. Later builders learned to dispense with the heavy log or plank infills between the posts. They put up an open framed grid of timbers, mortised and tenoned at the joints to ensure rigidity. The apertures could then be left open as windows or doors or they could be filled with panels of woven wattle and daubed clay, effectively separating structural frame and sheathing skin.

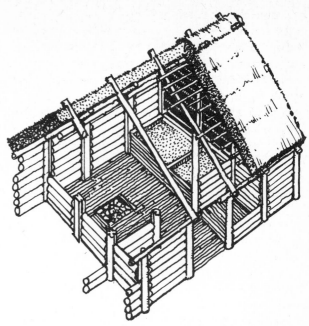

With iron tools builders could cut and shape timbers to interlock the elements in a rigid cage. At Biskupin, Poland, about 700 BC they grooved the heavy posts to take tenoned logs.

When they obtained iron tools, the Haida on the west coast of North America built plank houses in which they used the characteristic square of internal posts of the earth lodge.

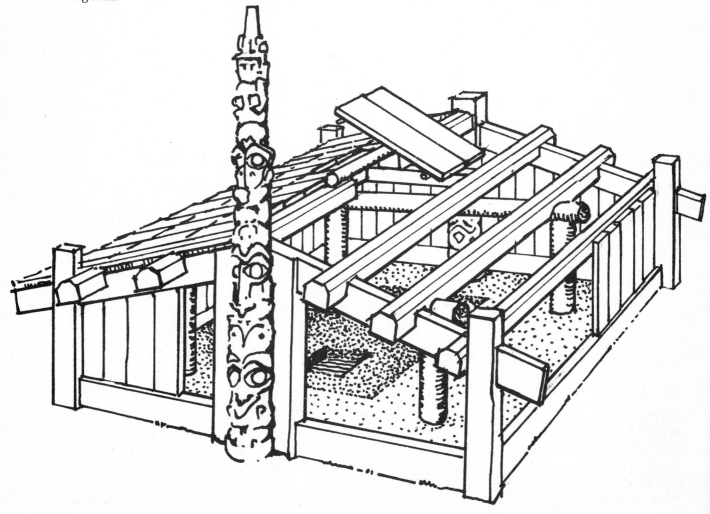

Along the northwest Pacific coast, the Haida and Kwakiutl Indians devised plank houses of cut and split timbers when they obtained iron tools. As with European carpenters, they changed from round earth lodges to rectangular houses supported by internal posts.

In this frame tradition characteristic of the north, the carpenter tended to envisage buildings as skeletal fabrics from which he could hang a wide range of sheathing materials. The very nature of wood was such that it suggested a spare linear approach to design to take full advantage of the stiff pole and rigid beam. Timber structures suggested a geometry in which long linear elements are fastened together to create a cage. The space was defined by its edges and its angles, not by its surfaces and masses.

But a price had to be paid for this sparse and elegant geometry. The structure was only as strong as its connectors. To make best use of the pre-shaped, precut timbers the carpenter had to tie, pin, or socket the separate elements into a rigid whole. Some joints were subject to pressure, others to tensions, and still others to flexure or rotation. The carpenter's design reflected this preoccupation with lines, forces, and joints. In the frame tradition he built in repetitive bays, with clearly defined linear accents and with a concentration of detail in the connections between elements.

NOTE
1 The Iron Age village of Biskupin in Poland, preserved by the flooding of a peat bog in 700 BC, is an entire community of well-built planned houses constructed as warm refuges against the northern winter, using this technique. Geoffrey Bibby *The Testimony of the Spade* (New York 1956) 384–94; J. Kostrewski 'Biskupin' *Antiquity* 12 (London 1938) 311

Framed wood was the normal mode of building in medieval Europe. Centuries of experience in cutting and shaping of timber led to the elegant vocabulary of frame and panel used in the deanery of Winchester Cathedral.

In this fortified Iron Age village at Biskupin the peasant farmers built houses, defensive walls, and watch towers of carefully interlocked logs.

The rigidly framed and tightly braced skeletal structure carrying panels of sheathing was characteristic of western Europe. But it would be an oversimplification to assume that this was the only technique of wood building which the new iron tools made possible. In the north and east, where terminal coniferous forests gave an abundance of easily worked soft wood, the Iron Age builders often turned to massive walls of logs placed vertically or horizontally. But the vertical posts and staves, though simple to erect, were subject to dry rot where they were embedded into the ground.[1] In time it was found necessary to introduce horizontal sills of wood or masonry to stop penetration of the moisture into the vertical logs. Once this was done the combination of a horizontal sill with a horizontal plate at the top of the staves made this a variant of the rectilinear frame.

More useful, and longer lived, was the wall of horizontal logs interlocked at the corners to form a heavy timber crib. The first such houses were of peeled logs only roughly notched at the corners; they required heavy chinking between the logs to ensure a tight wall. Later, logs were grooved on the underside, and in time were adzed to rectangular or shaped profiles to seal against wind and weather. Eventually the interlocks at the corner intersections were devised to shed water to the outside. In regions where a continental winter climate places a premium upon an economical insulating winter wall, the log wall has had a continuing application up until our own time.[2] In it wood is used as a dry insulating mass wall in which there is no distinction between structure and sheathing. It is a typical response in areas where the recent cutting over of forest land for new agriculture provides a surplus of usable timber.

NOTES
1 Thomas Paulsson *Scandinavian Architecture* (London 1958) 32
2 G.H. Hamilton *The Art and Architecture of Russia* (London 1954) 103–7

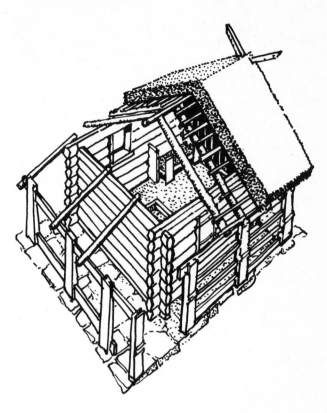

With iron tools builders could cut heavy logs to interlock at the corners in a horizontal crib of timbers. In the 'stuga' farmhouse in Norway, the logs sheltered by the heavy roof gave a dry insulating wall in a damp and cold climate. (after Lundberg)

In palisade or stave construction vertical posts were driven into the ground and tied at the top as in this early stave church on the island of Gotland.

In the Huneborstel House at Braunschweig, built in 1536, the strongly accented bays and diagonal wedges emphasized the braced frame structure.

This storehouse from Virserum, Småland, Sweden, has horizontal planks notched at the corners.

Roughly shaped logs with corner interlocks were used to carry an upper framed hayloft in this barn in the Norsk Folk Museum, Oslo.

Logs cut to an elliptical section gave maximum width and adequate insulation. This Norwegian log storehouse was raised on stone piers to avoid dry rot.

The carpenters built the Maison Kammerzell at Strasbourg with a high-pitched gable front and covered the essentially medieval timber frame with Renaissance detail.

2

MASS WALL AND CORBEL ROOF

From hut, to pole lodge, to framed house and great hall, the carpenters of Europe followed a consistent structural theme. Their response was firmly embedded in the local tradition of building. It was an intelligent adaptation of local resources to a particular climatic demand. But of course it was not the only possible early answer to the problem of shelter. The restless ingenuity of man kept breaking through established craft techniques. In different regions, in response to other social demands and meeting quite different climatic extremes, builders evolved other responses to architectural structure.

The linear skeletal tradition of the northern builders evolved from the basketwork armature of the primitive round hut. In the south, another adaptation of the round hut led to heavy massive walls and shell roofs. When primitive builders first plastered the wicker frame of the hut with a shell of daubed clay, for protection from the desert sun and dry winds, they took the first step towards masonry buildings.

At first, the wooden armature functioned as a reinforcing mesh. Not only did it make the process of construction easier, because clay could be built up about the frame, but it also took care of pulling or tensile stresses and shock loads as does steel in ferroconcrete construction today. Nontheless the mixture of wood and clay had disadvantages. The wood tended to rot and, as the clay dried out it shrank away from the lattice of wood.

Eventually primitive builders began to erect the walled cylinder of the hut without reinforcing, by piling up wads of moist clay in rough coursing. Usually straw, grasses, or hair were mixed with the clay to give it greater strength. The result was a remarkably efficient mass wall, 'cheap as dirt,' ideally suited to desert conditions where wood was in short supply. Given the structurally rigid drum of rammed earth, the roof became an independent fabric. Each tribe tended to devise its own type, some emphasizing ventilation and others massive insulation against the heat of the sun.

When primitive men first plastered the walls of a round hut with clay they devised the first masonry structures. This T'aung hut in Basutoland has a cylindrical clay wall for insulation and a thatch roof for venting. (after Walton)

OVERLEAF *The maximum span in the trulli of Apulia is under 20 feet; for extra room, another domed compartment would be added.*

In time, mass walls were built directly of clay, with only a mixture of straw to minimize cracking, as in this drum hut at Kordofan, Sudan. (after Brodrick)

In regions where good building timber was scarce the value of the few sound structural timbers and the short life of clay walls led to the reuse of beams. Rather than cut the beams to suit the cylinder of the round hut, man began to let the spans dictate the shape of his buildings. Eventually the rectangular earth wall hut became a characteristic structural form of the early towns. Not only was it more efficient in the use of scarce wood; its shape was better suited to the need for compact multiple dwellings in the tight defensive settlements of the early agricultural revolution.

Earth walls laid with rough clay coursing or rammed into shape between a wooden framework demanded a weather-resistant finish. A fine clay grout or finish coat smeared over the rough surface would retard leaching by rain but required annual renewal. The early discovery of gypsum plasters and the setting characteristics of burned lime provided the ideal solution. Earth walls were painted with a distemper of plaster or stucco which, while not permanently resistant to water, could withstand several seasons of weathering. Such a technique led inevitably to rounded edges and softly modelled profiles as progressive weathering and the addition of one protective layer after another modified the initial geometry of the structure.

At Taos Pueblo, New Mexico, the finish coats of clay wash have softened the hard angularity of the cubes into the subtly curved profiles characteristic of earth wall structures.

About the fourth millenium BC, man began to search for building materials more permanent than wadded clay. In the alluvial river basins he cast sun-dried bricks in wooden moulds. With these rectangular units he could lay a true wall with accurate coursing and with a better bond. Very early the brick assumed approximately its present mass and general shape. Although proportions have varied, the brick has always reflected its basic constructional role: a convenient load for one hand freeing the other for trowelling and mortaring.

From the potters, builders in brick early learned the advantages of firing which converted the water-soluble clay to a ceramic which could resist weathering for centuries. When cemented into place with lime mortar, bricks became a major element in the evolution of building. Their small size and the strength of the mortar bond combined to create walls of a relatively homogeneous mass. The cohesion of the mass was such that the builder could now begin to experiment with forms which carried the masonry over the span in vaults or domes.

In regions where outcropping sedimentary rocks weathered to oblong rectangular blocks, the builder had no need to go through the laborious process of shaping and firing bricks. He had ready at hand permanent weather-resistant building components ideally suited for the coursed and interlocked masonry wall. Indeed, in the high upland plateaus favoured by early farmers, clearing of stones from the fields for agriculture encouraged the peasant farmer to make use of this waste material in shelters and huts.

In brick buildings and in coursed fieldstone huts the early constructors found that it was possible to step out slightly course by course with a corbelled or cantilevered projection. Over a narrow passage or a circular space this could be extended in a steep curve until the projecting stones met at the crown. Evidently there was always the danger that straight lengths of walling would overturn before the meeting at the top, but where a circular form was used to create a corbelled dome the technique worked admirably.

The projection of each individual block was more than counterbalanced by the weight of the block above. The horizontally coursed corbel vault was ideally suited to the round plan, because any tendency for the whole wall to fall inwards was countered by the horizontal arched ring created at each course. Here the builders, although they were as yet unaware of the principles of true arched construction in the vertical plane, were making use of the wedging principle of the true arch with every course they laid in the horizontal plane.

Early builders projected one course over another to make a cantilevered or corbelled arch of flagstones. These corbelled projections with flat courses worked admirably in circular buildings.

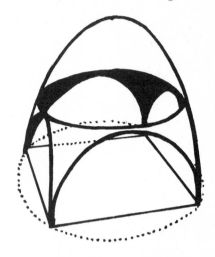

The small flat stones of limestone regions adapted easily to corbel construction. In Apulia, the 'heel' of Italy, the local masons built 'trulli' in which conical corbel domes were set over square plans.

In the more recent examples of these 'trulli' in Alberobello the masons have not hesitated to use wedged true arches over doors and openings, but, to avoid the expense of centering, they continue to build corbelled domes over the main span.

In Apulia, the heel of Italy, the local limestone breaks naturally into small flat flags. Using it with great skill, the local builders modified and refined the late neolithic corbel vault during the middle ages to develop a surprisingly versatile yet logical use of local materials.[1] At Alberobello and in the surrounding countryside most buildings were of 'trullo' construction, and there are still masons who can build corbelled domes.

In these 'trulli,' the pointed domes have been built with two masonry shells.[2] Inside, roughly dressed flagstones are laid up in horizontal courses to create a steeply pitched concave profile. Structurally stable, because of the compression ring action of the horizontal circles of stones, these corbelled domes can span up to twenty feet, but average just under fifteen.

Over this structural core the masons placed a rubble and mortar seal as a bed for the thin flagstones of the roof. These roofing flags pitch down to shed water. The system is weathertight, structurally sound, and a useful insulator against the heat of the summer sun. Most important, these heavy masonry roofs can be built up, ring by ring, without the need for expensive and complex timber centering during construction.

The round conoid of masonry was adapted to square room shapes by projecting segments of the corbelled vault down into the corners of the room. What the masons did, in essence, was to cut away vertical facets from the ellipsoid of the dome. The triangular. segments of corbelling which made the transition from the circle of the dome to the square of the room were an early use of the pendentive surface.

In recent centuries the masons used true arch construction in the arches between rooms, over the side cubicles, and above entry doors, to hollow out the heavy supporting walls. Nonetheless, because of its constructional advantages they continued to use the corbelled dome over the major spans. They attained functional diversity in farmsteads and houses by adding one corbel vaulted room to another. The contrast between the limewashed vertical walls of the living accommodation and the staccato pointed profile of the beehive roofs topped by decorative caps creates a distinctive and effective urban texture, based upon the logical application of a structural motif.

NOTES
1 Minnio Castellano 'La Valle dei Trulli' *Architectural Review* (December 1960) 420–2
2 Edward Allen *Stone Shelters* (Cambridge, Mass. 1969) 77–131

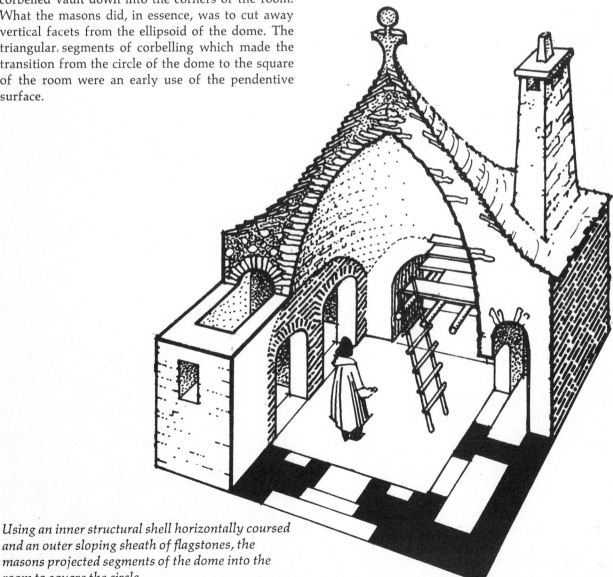

Using an inner structural shell horizontally coursed and an outer sloping sheath of flagstones, the masons projected segments of the dome into the room to square the circle.

In southern France and in Ireland the principle of the horizontally coursed corbelled shell was applied to rectangular plans. Masonry gables were created so that two singly curved, or flat, sloping surfaces came together in a ridge.[1] The technique worked, after a fashion, but the numerous failures of these structures point to the fundamental weakness of corbelling with flat courses. The central portion of the ridge is often found collapsed for, without the restraining action of the horizontal arch ring as used in the round form, weathering, wind, and earth tremors eventually upset the delicate balance. Evidently what was needed to ensure the stability of a longitudinal or tubular vault of masonry was the application of some principle of construction which could brace or wedge the stones into position. The answer eventually discovered was to pitch the coursing and so convert the corbelled roof to a true vault with voussoirs, that is, wedge-shaped stones which would press and lock into position.

Until the radiating or canted courses of true arch construction were used, the corbelled arch remained limited to short spans and, preferably, circular plans. As with the peeled-pole, earth lodge, a limited technology dictated the continuing use of the primitive round plan. Nonetheless, the two advantages inherent in this system of construction ensured its continued use well into recent years in the Mediterranean basin. No centring or formwork was required to set up the roofs, a particular advantage where timber was in short supply. And because the horizontal coursing of the corbelled vault exerted little or no thrust at the haunching or footing, there was no need for heavy buttresses or braces for the wall.

At Gordes, in the Provence, the limestone hillsides have eroded to provide an abundant supply of small flat flagstones. Here, the local masons built rectangular corbelled huts with pointed barrel roofs, locally known as 'bori.'[2] Like the trulli, these structures were constructed with an inner shell of horizontally coursed limestone flags. Over this structural core they set an outer layer of flagstones, embedded in mortar and sand, pitched to shed water. The steep pitches and narrow spans of from eight to ten feet minimized the danger of collapse. Nonethe-

less the builders were aware of the instability of longitudinal corbel vaults and countered it by introducing stone tenons to tie across the upper portion of the span.

On the Irish coast Christian monks from the eighth century AD made use of the same techniques in building their oratories.[3] But here the structures were to be used as chapels and required spans of up to fifteen feet. The monks ran into trouble. Many of the roofs of the early monastic buildings have collapsed. That of the Gallarus oratory, while still standing, has a pronounced inward bow at the centre: only the careful coursing and interlocking of the stones has forestalled failure.

NOTES
1 F. Henry 'Early Monasteries, Beehive Huts and Dry Stone Houses' *Proceedings of the Royal Irish Academy* 58, section c, 3 February 1957) 148–9, 153
2 Pierre Desaulle *Les bories de Vaucluse région de Bonnieux* (Paris n d)
3 H.G. Leask *Irish Churches and Monastic Buildings* (Dundalk 1955) I, 21–5

Careful interlocking of the stones in each course has held the vault secure against saddle failure in the 'bori' of Gordes in Provence.

Longitudinal barrel vaults with horizontally coursed corbel walls tended to fail at the saddle.

In time the Irish monks introduced ties at the apex of corbelled vaults and braced the outer shell with true arch construction inside. St Kevin's, Glendalough, County Wicklow, Ireland

The persistent failure of longitudinal corbel vaults along the crown must have been a constant challenge to the early mason. Steepening of the pitch, a heavier lower wall, mortared joints, and carefully cut interlocking stones all helped to a degree but did not entirely solve the problem. Evidently there was something wrong with horizontal coursing in the vault. The occasional perceptive individual may have experimented with a few bricks or blocks on a board or inclined plane. He would have encountered the principle of wedging under load, which locked the bricks into position. But this is conjecture; all we know is that the first arched vaults that have been discovered are over culverts in the Akkadian palace at Eshnunna, Mesopotamia, built in the third millenium BC.[1] They are of sloped or canted coursing, constructed as if bedding planes in a corbel vault had been slightly tipped.

With canted coursing the early masons could lay up the rings of brick without extra support or centering. The adhesion of the mortar was sufficient to hold the bricks in place on the inclined plane during erection. In these ingenious structures masons could correct the obvious deficiencies of the corbel vault without losing the considerable constructional advantage of a vault which could be laid without centering. Such vaults have a long history. Self-centering brick vaults of this type were built over the storage areas of the Ramesseum at Thebes from 1292 to 1125 BC and today villagers along the Nile and Berber masons in the Sahara use precisely the same construction in the vaulted roofs of their huts.

Not only was the canted vault a remarkable structural innovation, but it gave the designer freedom to suit the vault to differing room shapes. Once he had firmly grasped the basic principle involved, that it was possible to reach out into space by building out inclined and curving courses of masonry or brick, he could shape the vault to his architectural demands. Square, oblong, or polygonal rooms could now be spanned by building out intersecting bands of canted coursing to meet at the crown. Truncated barrel vaults, cloister vaults composed of curved segments rising to the crown, and shallow domes set into square compartments now could be built of thin shell masonry rather than with heavy and cumbersome corbelling.

The combination of brick with a tenacious lime mortar entered the folk tradition of building in the Mediterranean and the Middle East, to become a primal source for the mass and thin-shell architecture of the South. So efficient is this ancient mode of vaulting that, in the Mediterranean and in Mexico today, brick and tile masons can compete in price and speed against the builders of contemporary ferroconcrete shells. They have no need for expensive framework, their vaults set up faster, and they use steel only around the edge to resolve thrusts.

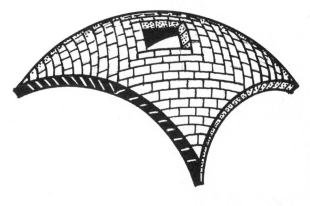

The Catalan vault can be adapted to cover a square room by building out canted courses from the corners.

The advantage of the canted barrel vault is that it can be laid up without temporary centering. Mexican masons continue to build these Catalan vaults today as in this instance at Guanajuato.

If the radiating stones, or voussoirs, are laid up at a canted angle they will wedge into position creating a true arch, as in these canted barrel vaults over drains at Khorsabad, Mesopotamia.

This use of moderately flattened bedding of the courses, which enables the vault to partake of the advantages of both the corbel and the wedged vault, has continued in use in the Mediterranean basin and the Middle East until today. The thin-shell brick domes and vaults of Byzantine architecture, the great spans of Sassanian palaces, and the lofty domes of Iranian Muslim mosques would never have been realized without the use of these arched corbels in the canted vault. By reducing thrust, facilitating erection, and minimizing centering this technique conferred an unparalleled flexibility upon the brickmason.

NOTE
1 Seton Lloyd 'Building in Brick and Stone' in Singer, Holmyard, and Hall *A History of Technology* (Oxford 1954) I, 472

Masons can step out with coursing built parallel to the sides to meet at the crown, as in this instance at Guanajuato.

3
DOME AND SHELL

In the doubly curved surface of the lattice-shell hut early builders made intuitive use of the rigidity inherent in warped planes. Long before physicists and engineers had devised theories to explain the behaviour of these complex shells, men had made practical use of their properties. In the same way, the vault was not invented overnight as the result of a rational analysis of the behaviour of arches and shell surfaces. Instead, practical men, dissatisfied with the evident limitations of earlier methods of construction were searching for ways to lighten their labour. Laziness was the goad, encouraging innovation.

The carpenter was a craftsman whose particular skill lay in the deft locking together of linear elements into a rigid cage; the mason was a sculptor manipulating masses and planes. The carpenter brought loads to a precise and determinate focus. His fundamental problem was the joint or fastening. The mason by instinct and training tended to disperse the loads and thrusts generated by vaulted shells into massive, heavy supports. His special challenge was the reduction of point loads, and his enemy was needless weight.

Masons early found, from the stark evidence of failure in their fabrics, that heaviness of construction in the span often led to deformation or collapse of the building. Of course the walls could be thickened to soak up and disperse these loads and thrusts but this made difficult the introduction of windows and doors.

For millennia masons built arches, vaults, domes, and thin-shelled fabrics of masonry without having analyzed correctly the precise nature of the reactions involved. Indeed it is only in recent decades that an adequate theory applicable to thin-shell vaults has been devised. Nonetheless, by a judicious process of trial and error, an empirical examination of deformations and failures, and a common-sense adjustment to the behaviour of the material, they created subtle and sophisticated fabrics which have only been equalled in recent years.

To better understand the problems faced by the mason it would be helpful to analyse some of the forces generated in structural elements. Remember that primitive builders and medieval masons did not have the advantages of these analytic techniques. They had to proceed step by step, meeting each problem as it arose by arguing from their own individual sense of muscular tension or pressure to achieve rough and ready approximations and rules of thumb.

First – and so obvious that it is often overlooked – stability is required in a building. The structure must stay put: it must remain static and fixed in position. Essentially, all buildings are static machines in which a complex interplay of forces balance out to a condition of equilibrium. All building materials deform or strain to some small degree under load. The designer's problem is to devise systems which can hold this elastic deformation within acceptable limits so that it does not become an irreversible movement. The elastic adjustment of material to load, which can redistribute forces within the machine of the building to achieve a new static balance, is the factor of safety which makes possible our structural achievements.

OVERLEAF *The rich mosaic and fresco on the internal walls and curved surfaces form a sharp contrast with the severe external geometry of this church at Thirsa in Greece.*

Today we can diagram with some accuracy the flow of forces within a simple structural element. Indeed it is possible actually to see the loading patterns by studying clear plastic models under polarized light. In this technique, precisely scaled model sections of a structure are cut from an epoxy plastic plate.[1] The model is loaded to simulate conditions in the actual structure. The loaded plastic is softened by heating it in an oven, allowing it to strain or deform in response to the loading. Slow cooling will lock these deformations in so that they can be accurately measured. The internal configuration of stresses can be inferred from the light interference or fringe patterns which can be seen when the model is viewed in polarized light. These multi-coloured bands relate to the stresses in the structural section. If we can assume that structural materials are elastic: that is that they can deform up to certain limits without cracking or failure, and that they are homogeneous and isotropic: that they strain equally in all directions, we can argue directly from the behaviour of the plastic model to the situation in a large structure.

In a beam, resting on two supports and carrying only its own weight, each support will press back vertically with a force equal to half the weight of the beam. Within the beam, as it flexes downward in response to its own weight, the top surface will be compressed and the lower surface elongated. If we trace the lines of pressure, represented by heavy dark lines in the diagram, we find them concentrating near the surface, and this is just where the maximum shortening occurs. The dotted lines, tracing the route of tensile or pulling stresses, concentrate at the middle of the lower surface, and this is where stretching is at the maximum.

There are other forces generated within the beam by the loading. The concentration of forces at the support introduces a vertical shear or punching effect to slice off the beam at the support. As the beam bends, horizontal shear, tending to separate the upper and lower surfaces by sliding action, combines with vertical shear to create a diagonal line of potential failure just inside the support. This shows up in the plastic material of the model as closely spaced interference lines. The value of the model is that remedial action can be taken before construction to strengthen this area or the beam can be redesigned to reduce the concentration of stresses at this point. In a composite ferro-concrete beam the appropriate response to this concentration of loads is literally to stitch the material together by introducing steel loops into this area over the support to hold the concrete together. The support could also be redesigned to avoid this narrow focussing of stresses and thus avoid the need for extra reinforcing steel. The cracking of the lower surface of the concrete beam under flexure can be avoided by introducing steel bars into this lower fibre, again stitching together the threatened area. If there is sufficient vertical space in the design, it might pay to give the beam an upward bow, that is, make it into a compression arch to suppress completely these tensile stresses. Because wrought iron could only be produced in small pieces, suitable only as ties or cramps, the medieval builder gen-

erally avoided the use of metal tension elements in his design, preferring to redesign into forms which would generate only compression forces.

NOTE
1 Robert Mark and Richard Alan Prentke 'Model Analysis of Gothic Structure' *Journal of the Society of Architectural Historians* 27, 1 (1968) 44

Light interference patterns showing stress in a plastic model beam under polarized light

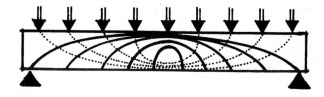

Lines of pressure and tension in a beam

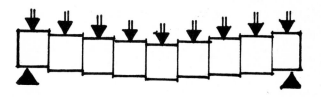

Vertical shear in a beam

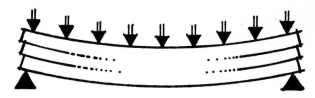

Horizontal shear in a beam

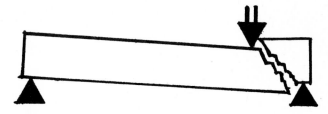

Shear failure near support

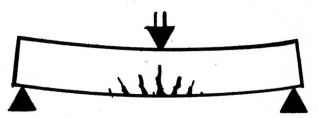

Bending failure over two supports

Evidently the simple rectangular beam is a wasteful, if convenient, device for horizontal spans. In wood, which works well both in compression and tension, it is used because logs are long and narrow. Because of its elastic strength, wood can deflect or bend under loading and then snap back into position after the load is removed: an ideal material for beams.

But stone is quite a different matter. Most stones are strong in compression but relatively weak in tension. The granular or crystalline structure of stones makes them subject to fracture in the lower surface when used as beams. Masonry beams can span only short distances, so that the masonry builder had to make use of a new principle.[1]

Examination of the lines of tension and pressure in the beam suggest possible responses. If the designer is using a material strong in tension such as a cable or chain, he may concentrate alone upon the lines of tension, shaping his material to follow precisely the most economical line. He then can dispense entirely with material under compression. The suspension bridge and the suspended tent use just this principle. A uniform flexible cable hung from two supports falls in a catenary curve, which is close to a parabola, but the engineer must devise some means to counterbalance the strong pull at either support. In essence, the weight or mass of material taken out of the beam must be introduced as an anchor beyond the support.

Or, if the designer is working with a material strong in compression alone, such as brick or stone masonry, he can reverse the procedure. Envisage a chain hung in suspension. Weld the linkage together and reverse it and you have a compression arch precisely suited to absorb uniformly distributed loads. Such an extremely slender arch would tend to buckle but the same line traced out in compression masonry makes an economical span. If the load, that is the weight of material in an arch, is uniformly distributed, the line of pressures traces a catenary curve. Historically, most arches were not built with catenary or parabolic curvatures. As a result they had to be built with needlessly heavy stones, to keep the line of pressure within the arch ring. Notice how the line of pressures in the semicircular arch ring swings close to the top surface at the crown. This weakens the structure because the eccentric thrust tends to allow the keystone to drop, thrusting out the adjacent stones. The pointed Gothic arch created by the intersection of two arcs had a distinct advantage because the shape of the arch more closely approximated to that of a reversed catenary curve.

As with the suspension cable there is a price to be paid for the economy of the arched span. The diagonal thrusts generated by the wedging action of the compression arch have to be restrained at the points of springing, that is, the abutments from which the arches spring. As with the gable where two rafters lean against one another, the springing must be rigid enough to take both the weight of the structure and the horizontal thrusts generated by the wedging action. A tension member holding together the supports, as in the string of a bow, can solve the problem, or the supports can be made so heavy that they can guide the thrusts safely to the ground.

NOTE
1 R.J. Mainstone 'The Springs of Structural Invention' *Journal of the Royal Institute of British Architects* 70, 2 (1963) 57–70

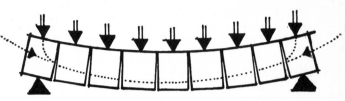

Beam bending and opening of lower surface in tension

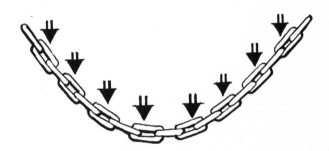

Tensile structure alone: a chain suspended from two supports conforming to line of tension in a catenary curve

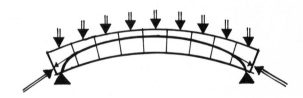

Compression structure alone: a masonry arch wedged into position along line of compression in a reversed catenary curve

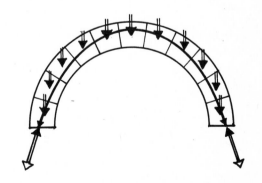

In the semicircular masonry arch the line of pressure does not conform to the shape of the arch and therefore the crown tends to fall while the sides buckle out.

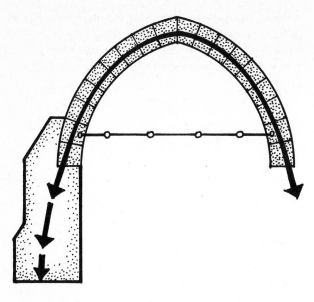

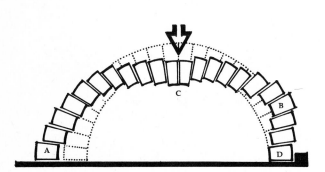

Though the pointed Gothic arch better fits the ideal line of pressure, if too acutely pointed the crown tends to rise while the sides fall inwards. (Similar to saddle failure in pointed corbel vaults)

But there was more to the problem of the vault than thrusts at the springing alone. What exactly happened to the individual wedged stones, the voussoirs in the arch ring, when the arch deformed under loading? If we assume that there is no friction between the individual stones, so that they can easily slide one against the other, it is evident that the crown of a semicircular vault will fall, pressing out the springing at A, or if that is secure as at D, it will squeeze out the voussoirs at B. But this is a theoretical case. The gritty stones of an arch cling tenaciously to one another. Rather than slide they will usually rock or rotate about hinging points of failure. In this more usual case the crown will depress as a unit, pushing out and rotating the haunching voussoirs. Medieval builders were long aware of this bursting action of the lower courses of an arch or vault and took appropriate measures to restrain it long before a theory of graphic statics had been devised.

In a semicircular arch where the stones can slide the crown C will fall while the sides B are pressed out above a secure springing D or at the springing itself A.

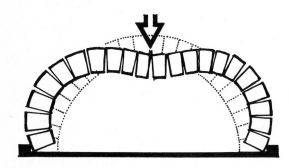

More normal is the rotational deflection of the stones during failure.

Narrow compression arch rings, spanning from pier to pier, were but one aspect of the vaulting problem. To roof a space without permanent masonry the designer had to multiply and interlock these individual arch rings in vaults or domes. In so doing he created curving surfaces in which individual arch rings would brace and stabilize one another in much the same way that the light flexible units of the lattice hut mutually stiffened and reinforced each other. The complex shell surface of the masonry vault was a form exceedingly difficult to analyse but one which possessed an inherent rigidity because of its curving shape. Before isolated arches were built and long before formal theory of voussoir action was devised, men were building vaulted surfaces which in one way or another recognized the bursting forces at the haunching, the diagonal thrust at the springing, and the need for as light a crown as possible.

The tools and layout or measuring devices available dictated the final form of the vault. However complex the final form, the modes of layout and the sequence of construction had to be simple enough to be used readily by the masons on the job. A working platform with the plan of projection of the vault marked out upon it, a curved wooden template to ensure the desired curvature, and plumb bobs to place accurately the curve over the plan were the mason's simple but effective devices. Accurate control of the final shape of the vault demanded that rotation or translation of the template curve evolve in accordance with a simple measurable rule.

By rotating a generating surface, the template, about a vertical axis the builder was able to trace out and control a wide range of curved surfaces suited to a circular plan. Domes traced out by the rotation of an arch-ring about a vertical axis were remarkably stable building forms. The interlocking of vertical and horizontal curvatures created rigid surfaces remarkably resistant to deformation. If the template curve was concave, its rotation created a surface in which the two interlocking curvatures were in different directions. The flaring tulip-shaped conoid is an example of this form which was frequently used in medieval vaulting.

The generating curve or template can be moved or translated along a predetermined trace, which in turn can be straight or curved, to create a whole new range of curved planes useful in vaulting. Here the builder took a curved wooden template and slid it along his working platform to trace out the curve of his vaulted surface or, more directly, he re-used his wooden centering, moving it along the span as the work progressed. The simplest of these translational surfaces was a tubular form traced out by a semicircle moved in a straight line. This barrel or tunnel vault was a form of single curvature, that is, it could be rolled out flat without deformation, and as such was not as rigid as segments of a dome or doubly curved surfaces.

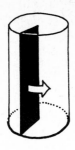

To trace out the form of his vault the mason rotated a template about an axis.

The generated surfaces could be given any curvature desired by shaping the template to elliptical or concave curvatures.

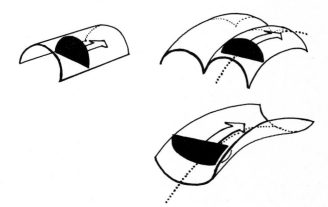

For longitudinal barrel vaults the mason shifted or translated the template along a straight or curved path.

Of the armoury of plane surfaces generated by geo-metric displacements, the hemisphere or dome had so long and so consistent a use that it could warrant a book in itself. It always remained an acceptable alternative to the barrel vault, where a circular or central plan suggested a simple hemisphere of masonry. The dome was peculiarly well adapted to buildings in which heavy walls or continuous but-tressing gave a firm support to the shell. As such, it is not surprising that the early experiments with domes and refined use of it in monumental struc-tures first were carried out in the Mediterranean basin and in the Middle East.

The beehive corbelled hut was the source for the dome. When builders first began to cant in, or tip, the coursing of beehive huts they made the critical structural transition to rigid voussoir domes. Each horizontal ring of masonry, as it was added, was wedged into position as a self-sustaining compres-sion ring held in static equilibrium. This meant that at any point in the rise construction could be stopped to leave an eye or opening for light. As with the canted barrel vault, it was customary to dip the coursing sufficiently to ensure some wedging action and yet keep the pitch flat enough so that at least the lower two thirds of the dome could be built without centering or framework.

The dome with canted coursing was a com-promise between the corbelled flat-coursed dome and the hemisphere with voussoirs radiating from the central point of the springing line. Too flat a coursing and the dome would fail in the same man-ner as a corbelled dome; too steep a pitch, and the mason would then have to use involved and expen-sive wooden formwork. In this judicious com-promise between the precise structural rigidity of the radiating voussoir dome and the constructional advantages of the canted form, the mason tended to rely more and more upon small stone or brick con-struction with thick mortar joints which would lock on setting into a comparatively rigid monolithic shell. As each ring of masonry and mortar set, it set into, not only a compression ring, but a tension ring dependent upon the strength of the mortar bond.

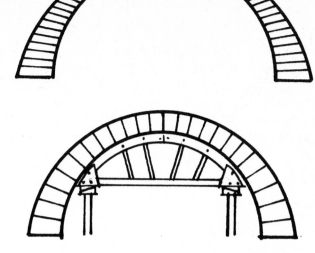

The first domes were developed from beehive corbelled domes by slightly canting the courses. Later domes with steeply pitched radiating joints required centering.

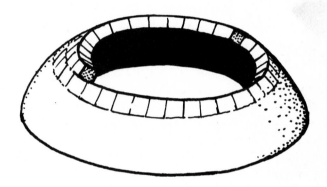

Each ring of masonry in a dome is a structurally stable compression ring.

Regardless of how the coursing was laid up, there were basic static problems to be met in the design of a dome. Examination of the forces generated within its surface will make clear the behaviour of more complex vaults. The dome possesses a great advantage over the single vertical arch ring: each vertical arch ring is braced into position by the wedging action of the horizontal rings. It is this cutting of two forces across one another which makes the doubly curved shell so useful a structural device.

If the dome is built with a steep pitch following a catenary curve, then the problem is simple. The vertical forces travel down well within the shell of the dome to emerge as diagonal thrusts at the base where they can be met by a tension ring or heavy buttresses. But when the dome is built with a comparatively flat profile, that is, as a hemisphere or ellipse, as each horizontal ring is added the crown as a whole tends to fall. The upper rings push out the lower.

Historically a number of expedients were used to minimize or counterbalance these bursting forces just above the haunching. Almost invariably the dome was built thinner at the crown, and occasionally very light materials such as pumice or hollow tiles were used to lessen the weight at the crown. Buttressing or walling was carried well up beyond the springing of the dome. By the sixteenth century a light and economical solution was found by introducing a tensile girdle built into or around the masonry. Tied timber rings, chains, cables and, finally, reinforcing steel bars were introduced as tensile hoops countering these forces and thrusts. The Greeks and Romans used bronze or wrought iron cramps or ties in masonry building to tie stone to stone where particularly difficult structural problems were met. Masons during the Middle Ages continued this tradition but it was not until the Gothic that consistent use was made of tension bars and tensile hoops to counter the thrusts of domes and vaults.

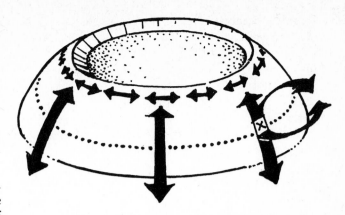

The double curvature of the dome with interlocking compression rings makes it a very rigid form.

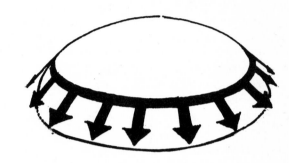

Heavy loads at the crown will generate bursting forces just above the haunching.

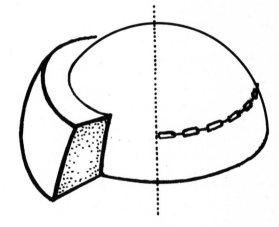

These bursting forces can be countered by loading down the shell with heavy buttresses or by introducing a tension ring or chain.

From the analysis of the thrusts generated by a domical shell it becomes clear that the particular problem faced by the architect was the resolution of the radiating thrusts encircling the dome. When a long-span dome was to be perched upon a comparatively high masonry substructure this became no mean feat.

Evidently a heavy cylindrical drum of brick or stone masonry could be built to soak up the thrusts and carry them safely to the ground. But this was wasteful of material and labour and made no provision for openings for light and valves for movement. At a smaller scale this problem was faced by the builders of the trulli: how to support the dome of masonry on piers or isolated supports to allow freedom of movement and the penetration of light and air. Their response was to introduce relieving arches within the heavy walls over the door openings.

Exactly this technique was used for the design of the supporting walls for monumental domes. The drum wall was cut into segments so that it became a ring of heavy piers, linked by broad transverse arch rings, tunnel vaults, or spherical shells. With these devices the continuous peripheral thrust and the heavy gravity loads of the dome could be safely channelled down to isolated pier supports.

In the Pantheon in Rome, erected from AD 120 to 124 by the Emperor Hadrian, these principles were applied to attain a span of 142 feet. A rigid drum of brick and concrete, carved and hollowed out with niches and passageways, precisely concentrated the weight of the dome upon heavy piers, which were hidden on the exterior by the continuous sheathing of brick.

In the lower two thirds of the domed construction the masons laid shallowly canted courses of brick-work flooded in a heavy bed of cement mortar, taking advantage of the reduced thrusts and minimal centering of canted coursing, as well as tieing the whole complex together with a cement which had considerable tensile strength. To further reduce the weight of masonry in the lower courses of the shell they coffered the shell, creating a lacework of intersecting ribs. In the upper portions of the dome lightweight pumice stones completed the coursing to the open eye.

Eventually the engineers of Imperial Rome used mass concrete to span the great crowd containers built for public recreation and ceremony. Lime and gypsum mortars require oxygen for their setting and therefore cannot be used as a binder or cement in mass concrete. The Romans devised a concrete in which the binding cement was made of 'pitsands' and volcanic dust from Puteoli (Pozzuoli). These silicon oxides, which had been dehydrated in the heat of volcanic action, hardened, when mixed with water and slaked lime, into a material as durable and waterproof as many stones. By mixing sand, small pebbles, and stone chips with this hydraulic cement, the Romans invented the first building material that could be poured into a mould to assume any shape desired. They took full advantage of this new material to cast immense monolithic caps of concrete over the baths and public structures of Imperial Rome. Job techniques were rationalized to make

best use of unskilled slave labour, so, although the technique was wasteful of material and labour, it was economical in its reduction of the skilled labour necessary to the job. In addition, the monolithic cast dome, because of the cohesive strength of the concrete, reduced thrusts about the periphery.

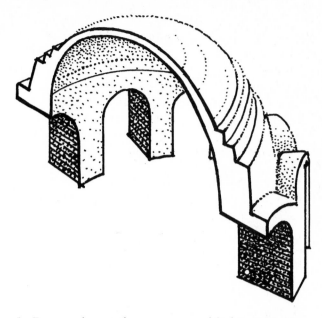

In Roman domes the masons used light pumice in the crown to reduce thrust. Heavy poured concrete at the springing and relieving arches distributed the thrusts to piers.

Roman tile and concrete dome springings at Hadrian's Villa, Tivoli, AD 124, show the cohesive strength of Roman concrete.

But volcanic sands and dusts were a rare building resource and so elsewhere in the Roman Empire builders had to continue to cope with shell structures exerting a pronounced thrust. As well, the acceptance of Christianity brought about a demand for complex churches in which there were specific and architecturally distinct areas for clergy and laymen, which could turn to the magic focus of the altar. In a masonry structure these complexities meant that the dome or vaulting had to be carried on isolated pier supports disposed along a linear nave. What was needed was a structural device which could act as a transition between the diffused pressures of the dome and specific point supports. The mason had to gather together the thrusts and gravity loads of the dome to direct them safely to the walls or supports.

The trulli of southeastern Italy employed a perfectly feasible mode of squaring the circle of the

In the Imperial Palaces on the Palatine Hill Roman engineers used concrete and tile vaults to carry the ornate marble decoration. (after Choisy)

dome by corbelling or bracketing out horizontal coursing from the corner. Or, an arch ring, called a squinch arch, set into the corner, converting the square to an octagon, a plan easily adjusted to the circle of the dome as in San Giovanni degli Eremiti at Palermo, where stepped squinch arches carry the tall lantern domes. In Greece and Sicily the masons often introduced a 'trompe' or small half-dome surface behind the squinch arch to create a more effective transition to the square.

But there was a more direct way to solve the problem. The dome could be squared by simply extending it down into the corners of the square compartment. In this case the diameter of the dome was made greater than the span of the room, so that a spherical square segment could be, as it were, chopped out of the whole dome to fit it neatly into the square. In this technique, the dome became a shallow section of a sphere, carried by four pendentive surfaces, the pendentives being the four curved triangular projections at the corners.

After the first experiments at Ravenna and Constantinople it became evident that the pendentives did not need to be of the same curvature as the dome. The masons began to erect hemispherical domes on the circular springing provided by the four pendentive surfaces. A more spacious interior and a more dramatic external profile resulted. During the later phases of Byzantine it became customary to raise a small dome over the pendentive supports on a pierced drum or lantern, flooding the interior with light.

With squinch arches or pendentives Byzantine brickmasons had a structural vocabulary capable of effecting the transition between the dome and its supporting piers, barrel vaults, and quarter domes.

By the ninth century Byzantine architects began to use cross-in-square plans. In these a dome perched on a drum of pierced masonry was supported on four piers at the intersection of barrel-vaulted compartments. Here the pendentives made an ideal transition between the circular lantern drum and the curved shells of the barrel vaults. This basic cruciform shape was expanded into a square plan by introducing minor domes or vaults into the corners.

Masonry fill or ballast introduced over the pendentive surfaces counterbalanced bursting forces and diverted the thrusts of the dome and lantern safely into the transverse barrel vaults.

The cross-in-square plan, with major dome on drum, transverse barrel-vaults set against the pendentives, and subsidiary domes or vaults in the corners, was so firmly rooted in the traditional architecture of the Mediterranean that it outlasted the framed Gothic of the medieval north. Finding its rebirth in Italy, as Byzantine masons and architects fled from the Turkish conqueror, it was the source for the renaissance of the Mediterranean tradition of building in the fifteenth century.

At San Giovanni degli Eremiti, built from 1132 at Palermo, masons used stepped squinch arches to carry the dome.

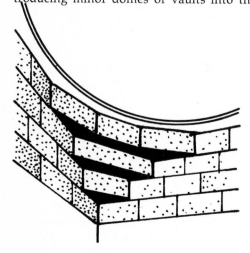

Where hydraulic cement concrete was not available late Roman builders went back to the principles of the squared corbel dome to make the transition between square room and hemispherical dome.

The lantern domes at Palermo, projecting above the roof, were pierced for lighting.

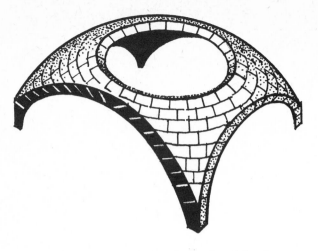

The simplest way to square the circle of the dome was to project the domical pendentive surface into the corner.

With barrel vaults, pendentives, drums, and domes of brick, Byzantine masons evolved the characteristic cross-in-square plan.

In St Theodore at Mistra in Greece the masons perched the dome and drum over the intersection of two barrel vaults.

4

BARREL VAULT

In Spain and France the tubular barrel vault, rather than the dome, became the prime structural element in early church architecture. In this preference for rectangular buildings, there is more than a suggestion that builders were translating into masonry the long halls and rectilinear cages of the timber vernacular. The earlier corbelled vaults had shown just this same contrast: domical 'trulli' in the south, rectangular 'bori' in the north.

In answer to the search for a fireproof, monumental, shell roof Romanesque masons built continuous half-barrels of masonry running along the nave of the church, and terminated them in a half dome at the apse.[1] The simple barrel vault gave a powerfully ordered spatial focus to the ceremony at the altar end. Only where the transept crossed the nave did the masons occasionally employ a dome or lantern, and here they used it to emphasize the importance of the choir, where the facing rows of clergy or monks officiated at the ceremony of the mass. The hierarchic sequence of space in the linear plan suited the western liturgy and ceremony, and, most important, it was an additive mode of building capable of expansion along the spinal axis.

The emphasis upon movement and circulation during the service, characteristic of the western liturgy, demanded a linear flow of traffic from the altar. With the growing cult of relics and the adoration of individual saints, each enshrined in a specific chapel, a secondary circulation developed which was quite independent of the main choir and nave areas and required a distinct architectural expression. Until the eleventh century, these secondary chapels were placed as projections from the transept. There they interfered with the ceremonies at the main altar. Eventually they were grouped off an ambulatory surrounding the choir, to create the characteristically complex 'chevet' of the late Romanesque and the early Gothic. Linked to the aisles and the transept, the ambulatory became a girdle of circulation for visiting pilgrims separated from the main body of the church. Initially the masons covered this ambulatory with a curved barrel vault which excluded light. The search for a more flexible type of vaulting which could be adapted to the chapel entries, to clerestory windows, and to the closely spaced columns around the choir led in time to experiments with rib and panel construction in the Gothic.

NOTE

1 Vincente Lampérez y Romea *Historia de la Arquitectura Cristiana Espanola* (Barcelona and Madrid 1930) I, 343–52

The strong severe order of the longitudinal barrel vault focussed attention upon the altar. At Silvacanne, France, the interior is dark with no windows along the nave.

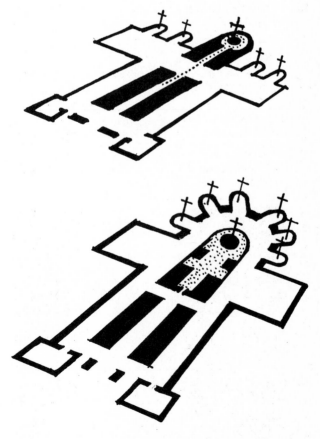

Eleventh-century churches required extra chapels which were at first grouped along the transept. In the twelfth century the architects devised an ambulatory around the choir with projecting chapels.

OVERLEAF *A longitudinal barrel vault over the choir of St Foi, Conques (c 1130), was opened to light and air at the crossing by introducing a ribbed lantern carried on squinch arches.*

The continuous barrel vault was crude, clumsy, and heavy. Nonetheless, the logic of its form, which so powerfully expressed the hierarchic focus upon the altar, ensured its continued use in the Christian church. In the south of France and on the Spanish coast, where brilliant sun and blazing skies placed a premium upon shade and shelter, the barrel vault was a thoroughly practical device. But in the north of Europe cold wet winters and cloudy skies demanded a more open structure to capture every fugitive ray of sunlight. This functional demand was met by three centuries of sustained technological invention which converted the dark heavy tunnel of the early Romanesque church into the elegant cage of the Gothic cathedral.

Despite the disarming simplicity and conceptual unity of the barrel vault, masons had to exercise considerable ingenuity to adapt it to the complex needs of the church. The continuous shell of the barrel had to be carried on piers between nave and aisles. The thrust of the vault had to be carried over the aisles to be restrained at the heavy external walling. Somehow or other openings had to be pierced through the shell of the vault or through the heavy walls to light the cavernous interiors. Above the curved ambulatory, the thrusts of the half dome and the vault of the choir had to be brought out to piers between the apsidal chapels.

The barrel vault was nothing more than the translation of an arch along a linear axis. With a shell surface curved in only one plane, it was structurally less rigid than the dome. Along its entire length continuous thrusts and loads had to be channelled to the pier supports and to the external walling. Unlike the dome, its top could not be pierced for lighting. If the mason cut openings at the springing, he would be weakening the very area subjected to all the thrusts and loads of the material above.

The barrel vault exerted a continuous diagonal thrust along the lines of springing on either side, so that the bursting forces tending to displace the voussoirs along the side of the vault were continuous along its entire length. Any eccentric loading which would deform the vault laterally was countered only by the thickness of the shell and not by the shape of the vault.[1]

Evidently, diagonal thrusts could be countered by introducing a tension tie of timber or metal across the opening. If placed one third of the way up the curve this tie would counter the bursting forces. This expedient was occasionally used, as in the upper narthex of St Philibert at Tournus, where transverse timber tie beams were locked into longitudinal timber plates set in the masonry. But, because of its aesthetic disadvantages, this device was never used in the principal vaults of the nave.

Without a transverse tension tie the vault had to be thickened along the haunching. The weight of all this ballasting material was carried on the piers of the nave arcade. Despite this mass of material, continuous thrusts still had to be carried over the aisle to the external walls. Little wonder that the provision of adequate lighting was the central problem for early Romanesque designers.

NOTE
1 John Fitchen *The Construction of Gothic Cathedrals* (Oxford 1961) 42–5

A barrel vault exerted a continuous thrust along its sides.

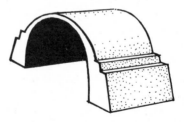

Usually the thrusts were dissipated in the heavy mass of the haunching and the supporting walls.

In rare instances, the masons used timber ties to restrain the thrusts of the barrel vault.

At St Nazaire, Carcassonne, the masons created an open hall with heavy barrel vaults resting on alternating supports.

The first step to lighten the barrel vault was taken well before AD 1000 as masons began to introduce transverse arch rings of carefully cut masonry below the rough rubble shell of the barrel. This broke the continuous sweep of the vault into a repetitive series of panels which could be related to the bay system of piers or heavy columns set along the nave. It must be emphasized that this use of the banded barrel vault did not focus loads upon the points of suspension. The vault still exerted a continuous thrust along the restraining wall, necessitating heavy haunching and buttressing, but the stiffening arch rings made possible a general reduction in the overall thickness of the curving shell. Most important, it made it possible for the masons to conceive of each bay as a structural unit designed in isolation.

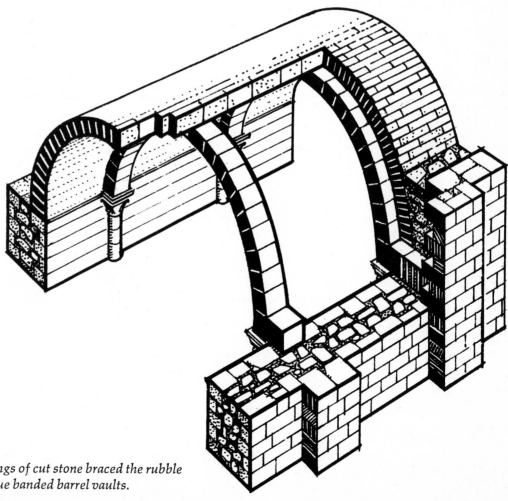

Transverse arch rings of cut stone braced the rubble shell in Romanesque banded barrel vaults.

During the Middle Ages Spain was an embattled frontier between feudal Europe and dynastic Islam. There, Frankish and Germanic adventurers met with and were challenged by the classical learning and new science of the Arab world. This meeting and conflict of cultures made Spanish Christian architecture the most experimental in all of Europe before AD 1000.

The climate of Spain, dictated by a region of high upland plateaus, was Mediterranean during the summer with blazing sun and hot searing winds, and yet the winters, of bitter cold and snow, were continental European. The mountain ranges were heavily forested, providing abundant supplies of excellent building timber. Here the two traditions of

building, the winter hut of wood and the summer shelter of masonry, interacted to create the modal themes of the medieval culmination.

Two buildings will serve to demonstrate the virility of imagination shown by builders in this peninsula: the ninth-century Santa Maria de Naranco and the eleventh-century pilgrimage centre at Santiago de Compostela.[1]

In Santa Maria de Naranco, built near Oviedo from 842 to 850, the unusual plan – without aisles or an altar focus, and with loggias or balconies at either end and a side entry – suggests that it was designed as a royal palace or audience hall although the building reverted to monastic usage in the tenth century. The Asturian builders took the long linear

In Santa Maria de Naranco, Galicia, Spain, built from 842 to 850, the masons braced the side walls with buttresses on the exterior and arcades in the interior, to take the thrust of the barrel vaults.

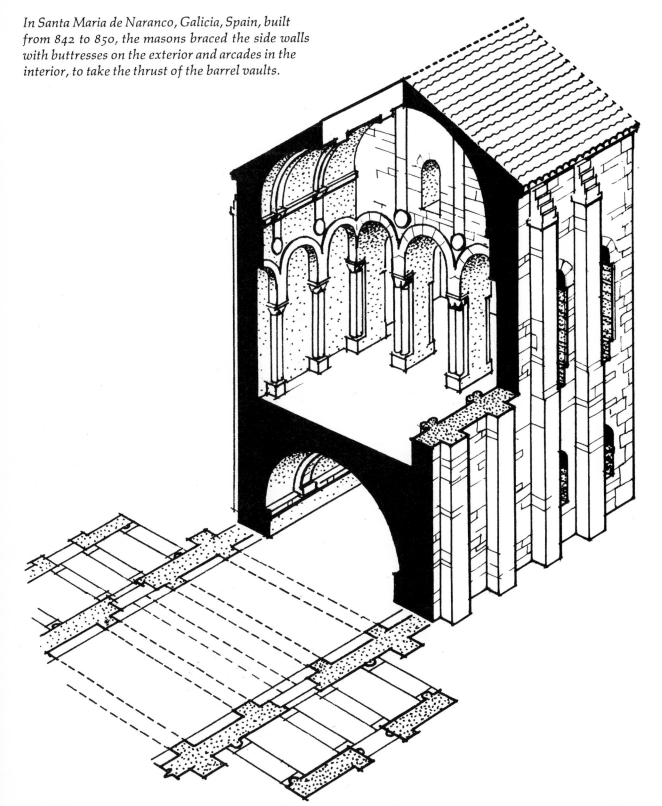

Germanic hall of framed timber and translated it into permanent masonry. In so doing they established a fruitful link between the masonry mass and shell tradition of the south and the articulated frame of the north.

In place of framed bents of timber they used masonry arcades and banded barrel vaults. In both the upper and the lower halls cut-stone arch rings projected from the rough rubble shell of the barrel to break the continuous masonry shells into rhythmic bays. Pilaster buttresses on the external walls were projected at each bay to create a striking vertical accent. The detailing, as might be expected for the time, was crude and heavy, with the banding arch rings sprung from decorative modillions set into the wall, but the intent is clear – to devise a masonry structure in which repetitive panels and sequential frames create a strong rectilinear vocabulary. In this, Santa Maria de Naranco signalled a decisive break away from the continuous-shell surfaces and heavy planar walling of the Mediterranean tradition. Here in embryo were the elements of the later Romanesque and the Gothic: sequential, additive structural bays disposed along a linear axis, and a clear distinction between structural frame and segments of sheathing wall.

But Santa Maria de Naranco was exceptional in that the vault had only to cover a singly boxy space with no aisles. How were these elements: barrel vault with banding arches, pier arcade, and buttresses, to be adapted to the complex ritual demands of a great church?

During the tenth and the eleventh centuries masons hit upon a wide range of diverse regional responses to this new theme in building. In the effort to restrain the continuous pressures of the barrel vault and to carry them safely across the aisle to the external walls and buttressing, they used full height aisles or aisles split in half by a gallery. Both semicircular barrels and quadrant barrels abutting against the main vault were employed, but always the critical problem was the piercing of this assemblage of continuous shells and walls to obtain adequate lighting for the ceremonial space of the nave.

At Santiago de Compostela, the masons introduced galleries in the aisles. Rather than attempt to squeeze clerestory lighting between the quadrant barrels of the gallery and the nave barrel, they relied upon light bouncing from the floors of gallery and aisle to light the nave. In the intense sunlight of Spain the system works. The thrusts of the barrel were met by quarter or quadrant barrels leaning against the main shell. In turn these quadrants were braced into position by external buttresses, linked at the top by arches. Nave piers and buttresses were

An aisle and gallery butting against the barrel vault helped to brace the high vaults in position at St Foi, Conques.

At St Trophîme, Arles, continuous quadrant barrel vaults over the high aisles, built 1170–80, restrain the thrusts of the high vaults.

stabilized into position by the deck of the gallery carried on cross vaults. Through the device of transitional arcadings and isolated buttresses the continuous thrusts of the vault were brought to resolution at the point buttresses, freeing the wall from a structural role. Now the wall could be pierced for lighting without weakening the basic frame.

The piers flanking the nave were no longer squat chunks of masonry. Their surfaces began to be modelled, with attached shafts carrying the arches above. A gallery with its own range of windows bounced light up to the underside of the nave barrel vault. Aisles spanned by small cross vaults became a part of the main assembly space in the church and functioned as circulation feeders to the nave.

In place of the rather clumsy and shallow buttresses at Naranco, the buttress piers were linked by blind arcades and were stepped back to the walling with its deeply chamfered window openings. As was customary in the south, where rainfall was comparatively light and frost action little problem, the tile roof was laid directly on a light fill placed over the vaulted surfaces.

NOTE

1 Kenneth John Conant *Carolingian and Romanesque Architecture 800–1200* (Penguin Books 1959) 44–5, 99–102

Quadrant barrels over the galleries and cross vaults over the aisles braced the monumental nave piers of Santiago de Compostela in Galicia.

Where the need for large windows was not the critical element in design, as in southern France, the monumental simplicity of the barrel vault ensured its continued use long after northern builders had turned to other expedients. Throughout Provence, at the mouth of the Rhône, churches and abbeys were built with longitudinal barrel vaults well into the twelfth century. To reduce the thrusts they were often constructed with pointed profiles as in St Trophîme at Arles and at the Abbey of Senanque. Occasionally the gallery was suppressed and the aisle was extended almost the full height to create a pillared hall interior, introducing clerestory windows above the aisle, as at St Trophîme. Their cramped location and tiny size reflect the fundamental unsuitability of the barrel vault to clerestory lighted churches. The haunching of the aisle vaults had to be high enough to take the thrusts of the main barrel, leaving little leeway for windows.

More successful were those buildings in which, as at Santiago de Compostela, the walls were opened between the piers well below the vaulted surfaces. At the abbey of Montmajour and in the church of 1173 at Agde in the delta of the Camargue, this technique led to structures of great simplicity and strength. Not only were they intelligent responses to the climatic demands but, in the confused religious and dynastic turmoil of the south of France, they could act as fortified bastions and strong points. At Agde, Montmajour, and at Aigue-Mortes the twelfth-century churches were topped by crenellations for firing slots and projecting machicolations for defence. It was only necessary to pierce vertically through the external arches between piers to create openings through which projectiles could be dropped on the heads of attackers. The severe, masculine, and defensive strength of these structures set a pattern for the resurgent catholicism of Paris when the cathedral was built at Albi in the fourteenth century.

The quadrant barrels over the aisles at St Trophîme, Arles, leave little space for clerestory windows.

In the late twelfth-century abbey at Senanque the barrel vault and supporting arcades are pointed.

Where the church had to double as a fort, nave wall arcades were projected as defensive machicolations, in St Etienne, at Agde, 1173.

With a barrel vault running longitudinally along the nave, windows could only be introduced below the springing of the vault creating a shadowed ceiling. The builders needed radically new disposition of the vaulting to flood the entire interior with light. Burgundian masons in the eleventh century occasionally set barrel vaults transversely across the aisle so that windows could rise to the full height of the vault.

Just this arrangement was used over the nave of the abbey church of St Philibert at Tournus. With this neat and ingenious expedient the transverse barrels were carried on arch rings swinging across the nave. Except at the end, where the thrusts were met by the crossing dome and the frontal tower, each barrel pressed against its neighbour, effectively cancelling out the thrusts. With no need for heavy external buttressing along the flanks of the building, windows could be as large as desired. The total effect in the interior is splendid. The building is bright, cheerful and open, in complete contrast to the darkness of most eleventh-century structures.

The tentative and experimental nature of eleventh-century structure becomes evident as we trace the changes to the vaulting in this church. Evidently dissatisfied with the darkness of the longitudinal barrel vaulted choir of 979, the monks turned to primitive cross vaults over the aisles, in the cloister and in the narthex. But they were as yet unready to use the cross vault over the high nave. Instead they or their mason hit upon the expedient of transverse barrels and in the longitudinally barrel-vaulted ceiling of the upper narthex they used tensioned timber ties. Evidently their mason must have been a de-

signer with a pronounced flair for structural innovation. His concern was to find ways in which the pressures of curving vaulted planes could be resolved without using heavy walls and massive buttresses. His responses were direct and simple: timber ties and counterposed barrels, but these expedients were little used during the later Romanesque and the Gothic.

Except for the nearby church at Mont St Vincent, some isolated instances in Switzerland, and the aisle vaulting at Fountains Abbey in Yorkshire, the transverse barrel was rejected. Evidently the very sharp distinction between each bay made necessary by the introduction of low transverse arch rings came into conflict with the search for forms which would offer no impediment to the aesthetic eastward focus on the altar. Despite the structural logic of the transverse barrel, the future of vaulting lay in the progressive refinement of the cross vault. For that we must turn to the experiments being carried out in northern France and England.

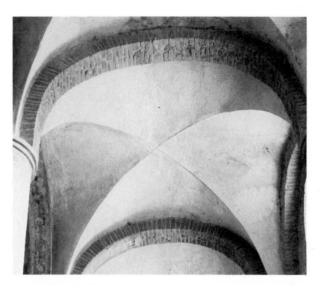

As in banded barrel vaults, the masons separated each bay of the aisle with masonry arch rings at St Philibert.

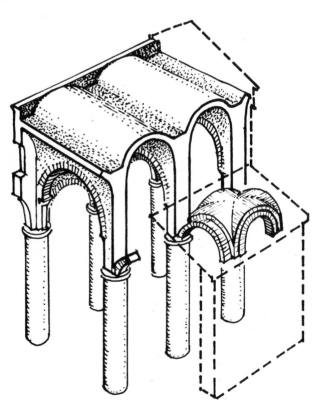

In masonry structures the transverse shell barrels were carried on arch rings swung across the nave. At St Philibert, Tournus, the eleventh-century builders used cross vaults over the aisles, and transverse barrels over the nave.

The vaults of the cloister at St Philibert show the layout difficulties encountered in early cross vaults. Elliptical profiles and awkward springings betray a tentative response to a novel structural problem.

The upper narthex chapel at Tournus still has the timber tie bars which take the thrust of the longitudinal barrel vault.

The culminating achievement at St Philibert, Tournus, was the high transverse barrel vault over the nave.

5
MEDIEVAL TIMBER FRAME

During the long slow centuries of the early Middle Ages in northern Europe, wood remained the dominant building material. As the broadleaf and coniferous forests were cut to make way for agriculture, the baulk of timber, the pole, the plank, and the peg were combined and recombined with growing skill and sophistication to solve a host of technical problems.

The peremptory demands of incessant warfare led to a refinement of Roman siege machinery, with mangonel and catapult increasing in range and weight of projectile. The need for metals dug from ever deeper mines forced the invention of geared assemblies for hoisting and pumping. Animal, wind, and water power sources were pressed into service to crush, grind, and carry material. At the waterfront port, improved derricks and hoists were devised to load the ships, while shipwrights embarked upon that long series of refinements and adjustments which converted the long boat of the north to a serviceable oceangoing merchant craft, the Hansa cog. In this dawn of European technology the carpenter was in the forefront of technical invention, using cordage, wooden poles, and timber gearing to control and manipulate energy in response to the demands of peace and war.

Before AD 1000 court and castle, monastery and abbey, town and fortified wall were rough timber constructions. After AD 1000 this new technical skill began to be reflected in the increasing scale and technical artistry of building. The timber-framed structure became a carefully interlocked rigid frame suitable for monumental structures.

As the single-masted Hansa cog – a shell of wood which was a timber vault in reverse – evolved into the three-masted carrack of 1500, the internal structure had to be braced and trussed to take the racking stress of wave action. (after Landström)

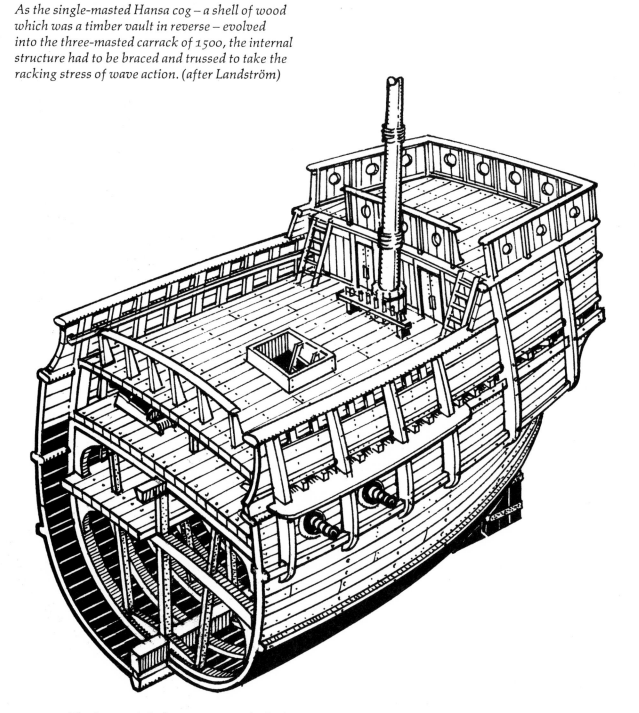

OVERLEAF *The frame of the house was interlocked with mortise and tenon joints to make it rigid. Newport, Hertfordshire*

The special problem which plagued early builders was the attainment of rigidity within the cage of linear elements. They quickly found that a simple linear cube was perilously unstable until some means had been found to lock the members into position. At first the posts were embedded in the ground to make the structure resistant to mechanical shock, winds, or earthquake loads. This worked temporarily but the posts had only a short life because the alternate wetting and drying of the butts in the ground led to rapid decay.

The sloping diagonals of the roof rafters in the Germanic long house were ideal to brace the rectangular grid of posts and beams into position. With their butts resting on the ground and tied at the purlins and at the ridge, these pole rafters converted the structure into a rigidly braced triangulated figure.

The rectangle can deform by hinging at the joints, but the triangle is not subject to such deformation. This is the principle of the truss: a braced configuration of triangulated elements. In the truss the joints can be hinged or free to rotate because the triangles convert all loading to tension or compression along the lines of the members. The raftered roof with a tie at the base is the simplest form of truss. The pair of rafters, leaning one against the other, can be taken as the limiting case for the arch, reducing it to two wedged elements.

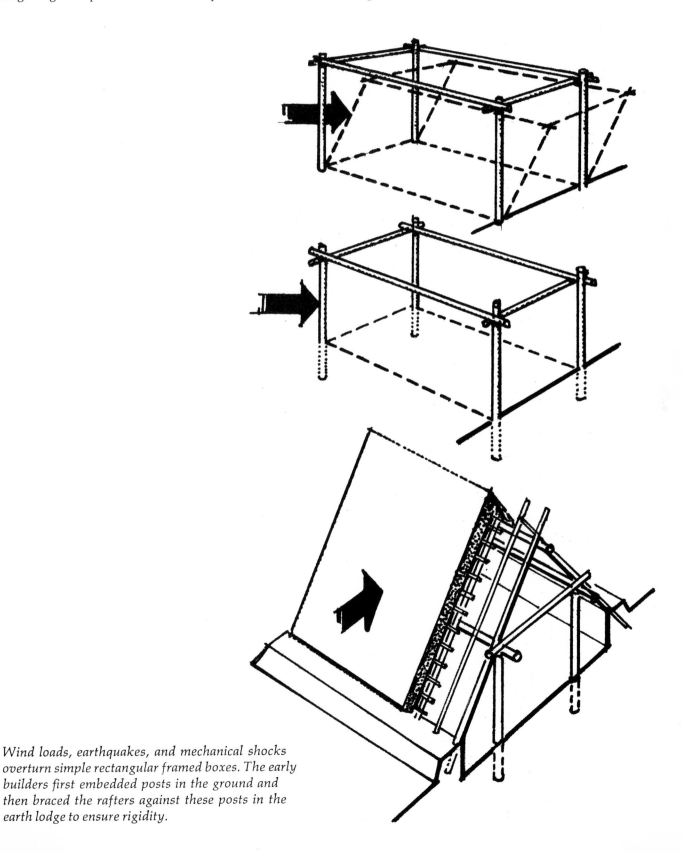

Wind loads, earthquakes, and mechanical shocks overturn simple rectangular framed boxes. The early builders first embedded posts in the ground and then braced the rafters against these posts in the earth lodge to ensure rigidity.

Raftered roofs springing directly from the ground very neatly solved the problem of rigidity, but once the roof came to be perched on a framed box entirely above ground level some means had to be found to lock the joints together. Before iron tools made it possible to cut and interlock linear timber elements, the builders had to rely upon complex cord or hide lashings to ensure a firm joint. Lashed frame huts which are faithful echoes of neolithic modes of construction continue to be built today. A Mayan hut at Mulchic, Yucatan, built by the caretaker of an excavation site, shows exactly the problems faced by the early builders.

The builder supported his principal rafters on posts resting on stone sills. This would be unstable were it not for the wall panels of lashed vertical cane, plastered on the inner surface, which braced the posts longitudinally. The rounded ends of the

hut provided further rigidity. He tied the tops of the walls together by setting cross beams into sockets on the tops of the posts. Setting rafters with crutches on these ties he lashed the rafters securely to a ridge pole at the top. For further strength a collar tie was introduced part way down the rafter. Without the rigidly braced fabric of the roof the walling would be quite insecure. The weak point in the design is the link between roof and wall. If a diagonal brace were introduced between tie beam and post the entire fabric would become a completely braced system. But this would reduce headroom in the hut and would be an unnecessary refinement in a temporary hut. Once the post and cane wall is fully plastered as is customary in Mayan huts, it gains more than sufficient rigidity for long use.

Primitive builders continue to use poles lashed to create rigid triangles. The roof of this Mayan hut, at Mulchic, Yucatan, sheds rain but allows the free movement of air to keep the hut dry.

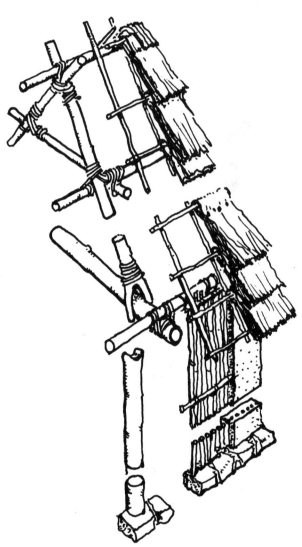

The lashed-pole, thatched-roof assembly

After AD 1000 the monasteries, no longer mere refuges from the perils of tribal invasion, become a prime source for our knowledge of contemporary technical skill. In the new open Europe of the eleventh century these complex communities became inns for travellers, factories for the production of goods, and depots for the distribution of the products of field and forest. By the thirteenth century the tithe barns of the monasteries had grown into large framed timber halls and weathertight, secure warehouses.

It is instructive to compare a tithe barn built in the thirteenth century with the lashed assemblies of early houses and barns. A thousand years of building evolution have left the basic form essentially unchanged – a hall with aisles on either side, and a steeply pitched timber roof tying the three elements together under a single gable – but there has been a marked improvement in the craft of carpentry. In place of lashed poles, butt joints, and rough and ready framing, the medieval tithe barn is constructed of carefully shaped and interlocked timbers, keyed together to create a rigidly braced continuum.

The tithe barn of the Abbey of Beaulieu at Great Coxwell, Berkshire, was built about AD 1230 with rigid frames of oak disposed in large square bays along an interior 152 feet in length.[1] The new emphasis upon a rigid articulation of the elements into braced and keyed frames by the use of diagonal braces is most evident in the care taken to avoid deflection or movement of the posts. Because the posts were set on pedestals of masonry to protect them from moisture, there was a special need to guard against overturning. Longitudinally the posts were braced by double tiers of raking struts, cut with mortises and pegged with dowels to the roof plate.

Transversely across the span the posts were joined by tie beams with a lap dovetail joint in which the wood is cut to lock together, and then raking struts were socketed into the angle to create rigid portal frames. Finally the posts were braced against the external fieldstone wall pieces. Because the major frames were roughly 20 feet apart, some means had to be found to introduce subsidiary supports. Between each frame the carpenters introduced crucks or long arched braces of timber inserted into the fieldstone wall and wedged against the roof plate. Long raking struts were then introduced to key the wall plates to the posts and comparatively slender roof rafters, 4 inches by 5½ inches, locked the entire assembly into a rigid unit. Finally the roofers attached the stone slates with wooden pegs over the laths and rafters of the roof.

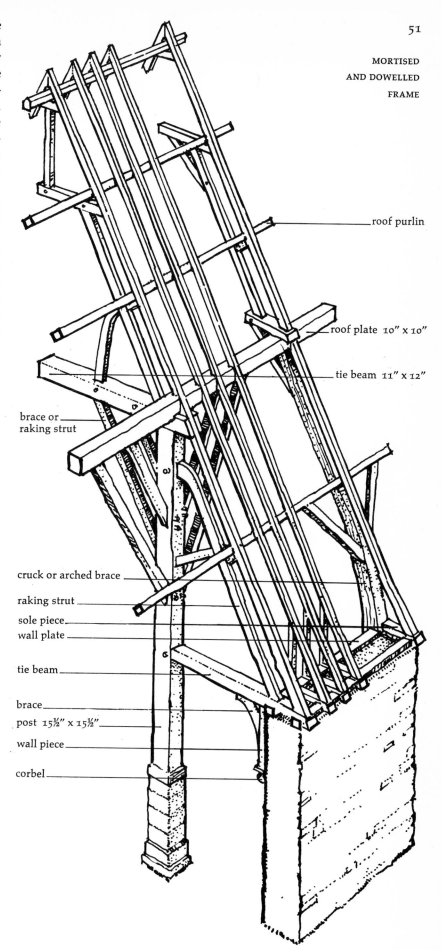

roof purlin

roof plate 10" x 10"

tie beam 11" x 12"

brace or raking strut

cruck or arched brace
raking strut
sole piece
wall plate
tie beam
brace
post 15½" x 15½"
wall piece
corbel

About 1230 carpenters used alternating braced frame and arched and braced crucks to ensure rigidity in the Tithe Barn of the Abbey of Beaulieu at Great Coxwell, Berkshire. (after Horn and Born)

In this purely utilitarian storage barn the essential continuity of the timber tradition of the northern builders becomes evident. The monks and their carpenters refined and polished the technical execution of the fabric without diverging from forms rooted in prehistory. A rhythmic bay system of supports, the resolution of stresses around sharp corners, the concentration of loads upon slender supports, the interlocking of elements into rigidly framed skeletons: these were the elements which led to the superb achievements of later Gothic and early Renaissance carpenters. Indeed, it was this structural ingenuity and refined disposition of static material into linear skeletons which emboldened the masons of Europe to break free of the tyranny of the heavy wall, to create tenuous skeletal fabrics of stone in the Gothic cathedral.

NOTE
1 Walter Horn and Ernest Born *The Barns of the Abbey of Beaulieu at its Granges of Great Coxwell and Beaulieu-St. Leonards* (Berkeley 1965)

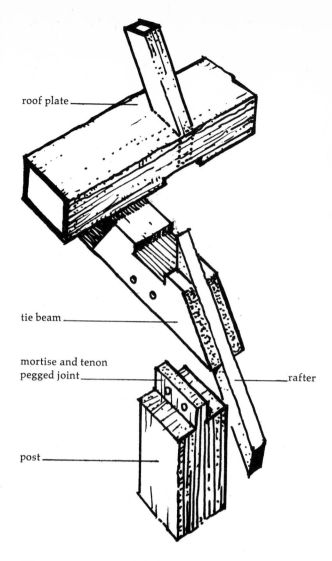

roof plate

tie beam

mortise and tenon
pegged joint

rafter

post

The post, rafter, and tie beam intersections were mortised and pegged together. (after Horn and Born)

In the great Coxwell Barn comparatively simple lap or mortise and tenon butt joints were held together with hardwood dowels. Essentially this was a pin-jointed truss. When the footings settled, the wind gusted, or the structure shifted, a large part of the forces acting upon a joint were concentrated upon the narrow profile of the wooden peg. In time the pegs would wear, and with continued flexing of the fabric they were likely to shear. The joint clearly would be strengthened if its elements were cut so that the forces were transmitted directly by wedging action, with the pin used only as a clamp holding the pieces of wood in position. In two barns built at Cressing Temple, Essex, the carpenters used lapped joints, together with connections wedged or splayed to resist the pulling apart of timbers. So carefully interlocked were the members that it is possible to reconstruct with some precision the sequence in which the structures were raised.[1]

In the Barley Barn, built about 1200, principal posts and roof plates were fitted together on the ground with their raking struts in place and then were swung vertically into position on the post plates. In the centre bays transverse straining beams were tenoned into the posts and transverse tie beams were dropped into position on top of the roof plates. Diagonal braces were set into the sides of these transverse horizontal members and a lapped raking strut, pegged in from the side, tied the whole frame into a rigid triangulated truss. The carpenters braced the wall posts into the principal posts and placed long scissors rafters so that they lapped right across the mainspan assembly and the collarbeam. It only remained to socket in the rafters to create an extremely rigid, tightly meshed structure.

The refinements of carpentry used in the joints of these two barns point to a very accomplished level of technical skill at the height of the Middle Ages. Evidently this was not the work of monks turning an amateurish hand to problems of building and construction but rather the achievement of professional builders trained in their craft and experimental in their technique.

Though similar in basic form, the Wheat Barn, built about 1275, shows, in detail, the rapid evolution of structural skill which occurred in the thirteenth century. Its carpenters devised secret notched joints to hide the complexities of wedged splays behind a superficially simple surface profile. In the interlock between the transverse tie beam and the wall plate, for example, an ingenious splayed lap dovetail ensured that thrusts would be taken by the shoulders of the dovetail and not by the dowel. Rafters were keyed to the transverse tie beams with concealed splayed mortises wedging the rafter firmly into position against eccentric loads. In the raking struts secret notched laps interposed a hidden shoulder against forces tending to pull the brace from its socket.

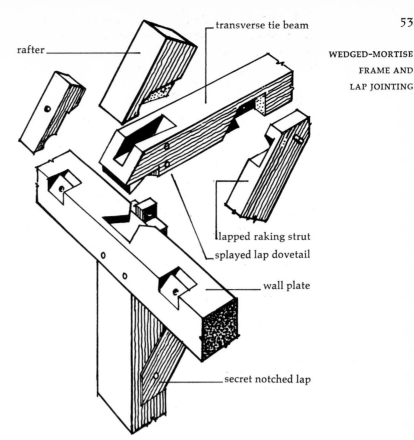

rafter

transverse tie beam

lapped raking strut

splayed lap dovetail

wall plate

secret notched lap

The carpenters of the Wheat Barn built at Cressing Temple, Essex, about 1275, cut hidden splayed dovetails to lock the joints together. (after Hewett)

In the frames of the Barley Barn at Cressing Temple double rafters and a cross truss were so interlocked with pegged and dovetail joints that it is possible to reconstruct the sequence of erection. (after Hewett)

Some reconstruction was necessary in several external bays of the Wheat Barn about 1500. The carpenters added projecting jowls to the wall posts to strengthen the link to the transverse tie, with a hidden lap dovetail locking tie and plate together. By this time long experience with the problems encountered in the design of decoratively detailed hall and church timber roof structures had accustomed the builders to the use of curved members, which emphasized the continuity around the corner which was their prime objective.

The carpentry of these purely utilitarian barns points to the persistent effort by medieval builders to pare away excess structure. By reducing the framing to a series of widely spaced, long-span portal frames or trusses, they emphasized the separation between structural skeleton and sheathing skin. The concentration of loads upon the isolated points of support freed the interior for efficient use, and made possible a more open plan and (where desired) a window wall.

NOTE
1 Cecil A. Hewett 'The Barns at Cressing Temple, Essex' *Journal of the Society of Architectural Historians* 26, 1 (1967) 48–70

In later adaptations to the Wheat Barn at Cressing Temple, added about 1500, the carpenters used complex hidden mortises and splayed wedges for the curved braces. (after Hewett)

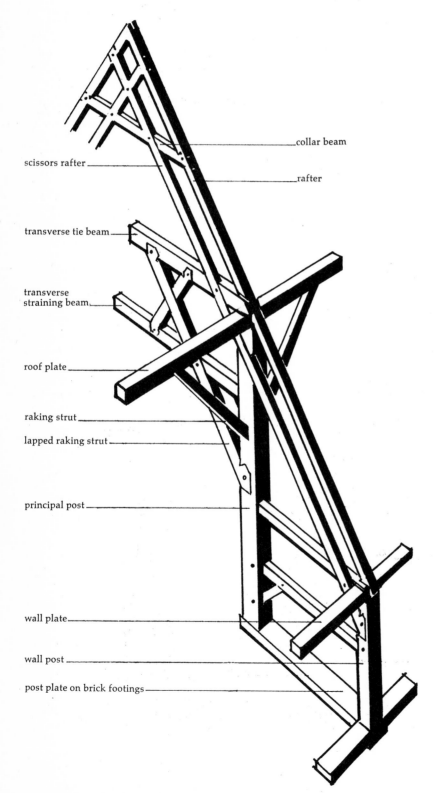

collar beam

scissors rafter

rafter

transverse tie beam

transverse straining beam

roof plate

raking strut

lapped raking strut

principal post

wall plate

wall post

post plate on brick footings

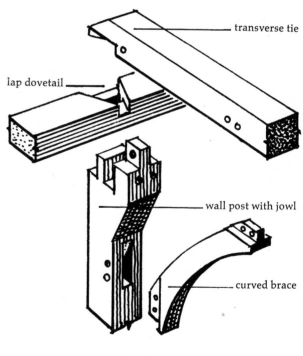

transverse tie

lap dovetail

wall post with jowl

curved brace

The timber roof developed for barns was adapted to protect the masonry vaults of the great cathedrals in northern countries from snow and rain. Sprung from wall to wall, it closed in the nave of the major churches early in their construction and made possible the completion of vaults under shelter. The master carpenters who built trusses used all the devices and interlocking carpentry detailing that we have seen in the construction of barns to create rigid frames resistant to wind loading and settlement stresses. The steep pitch of the roof, usually between 54° and 57°, was a logical response to the demands of a rainy northern climate.[1] The steeper the pitch, the less chance there was of water seeping back through the overlapping slates, and the more effectively the truss could carry the considerable weight.

Because the roof truss of the great cathedral churches was ultimately destined to be concealed above the vaults it could be designed for structural purposes alone. Usually a splay of scissors struts fanned out from the points of support on the clerestory wall. Wherever possible, long overlapping straight members locked the truss into a rigid frame.[2] The heavy transverse tie beam served several purposes. In its normal capacity it effectively countered the tendency of the rafters to spread at their footings. It also acted as a compression brace, resisting the pressures the flying buttresses exerted on the walls until the vaults could take the stress. In addition the permanent timber structure of the roof was so divided that it could be used as a support for working platforms and scaffolds during the process of construction.[3] The windlasses and devices for hoisting heavy stones or bells, illustrated in contemporary manuscripts, were carried on these ties. Here we see an instance of the close integration of the work of the carpenter and the mason in the north.

NOTES
1 John Fitchen *The Construction of Gothic Cathedrals* (Oxford 1961) 26
2 John Fitchen 'A Comment on the Function of the Upper Flying Buttress in French Gothic Architecture' *Gazette des Beaux Arts*, series 6, 45 (February 1955) 69–90
3 Fitchen *The Construction of Gothic Cathedrals* 28

In the north of Europe architects protected the delicate fabric of vaulted shells against snow and ice by erecting huge mortised and pegged wooden frame roofs over the masonry structure. Reims cathedral. (after de Baudot)

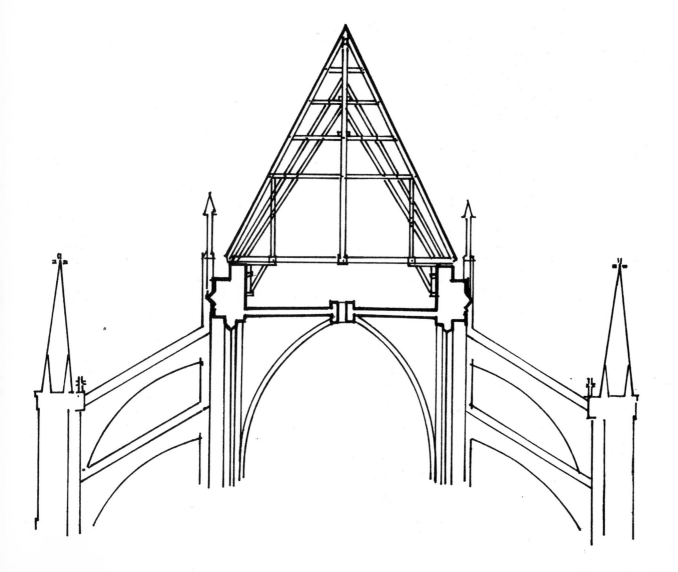

The evolution of exposed timber roofs followed a somewhat different course. In the guild halls and parish churches of the newly prosperous medieval towns, the burghers may have been hesitant to embark upon the expense of a masonry vault, but they did insist that the underside or soffit of the roof should be a handsome cover. The carpenters rejected tie beams despite their structural advantages, because the tie reduced head room and created a complex busy interior. Initially one or another variant of the scissors truss with a collar was favoured instead, creating clear height and a spacious effect. Where desired the underside could be cased with boarding in a simple decorative treatment as in Eye church, Suffolk, or the nave of Ely cathedral.

The steeply pitched roof lent itself admirably to this technique but from the fourteenth century, as lead began to replace slate as a sheathing, the builders had to cope with the tendency of lead to flow or creep when laid up at too steep an angle. Roof pitches flattened to such an extent that the roofs were concealed behind the parapets of the wall.[1] To achieve adequate strength in a shallow truss they had to accept an exposed tie beam running across the nave at the springing.

A new approach was needed. The carpenters made a virtue of necessity by emphasizing the tie beam as the dominant element in the design. Over the slightly cambered heavy tie they introduced a king post and a lattice of vertical struts carrying the purlins and rafters. Curved braces springing from the walls acted as corbel brackets reducing the effective span of the tie. What they achieved was a shallow but rigid wooden truss using heavy elements and a wide spacing to simplify materially the complexities of the earlier roofs.

English carpenters attained such skill at a decorative manipulation of these structural forms in timber that they were able to design timber trussed roofs which copied the patterns of medieval masonry vaulting. To economize, they used timber as if it were stone. Where there was some doubt about the ability of an existing Romanesque wall to take the thrusts of new masonry vaulting the designer could use wood members as ribs and planks as panel infill to simulate the pattern of stone vaulting. The scissors or king post structure of the truss was hidden above the decorative panelling.

NOTE
1 William C. Wachs 'Historical Geography of Medieval Church Architecture' (unpublished PH D thesis, University of Cincinnati 1961) 84

The scissors truss with collar was used to extend the volume of the room up into the trussed space.

Under the low pitches made possible by the use of lead sheathing the carpenters in the fourteenth century exposed the rigidly framed tie beam trusses as decorative embellishments. (after Bond)

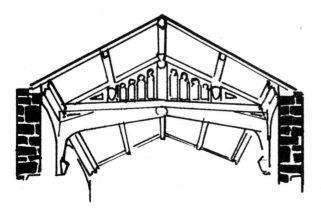

Usually the scissors truss was concealed by a decorative wood sheathing as in the nave at Ely cathedral.

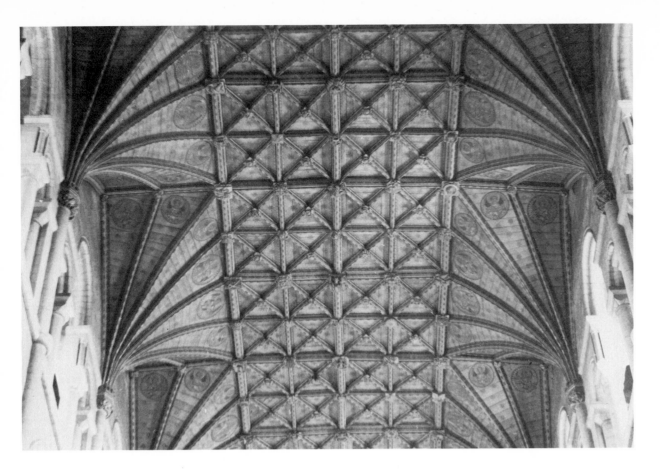

*Over the choir at Peterborough cathedral the trussed
timber was cased to simulate a vaulted masonry
roof.*

*In the choir at Winchester cathedral the timber truss
copied the masonry vaulting over the nave.*

Before the thirteenth century medieval builders emphasized long straight timber members in their trusses.[1] This was perfectly logical because the straight compression strut is best suited to withstand buckling or torsion. But in the alternate bays of the Great Coxwell tithe barn the carpenters used long curved blades or 'crucks' for their braces. There is a certain structural illogic to this because the curved member in compression has to be made heavier for a given load than a straight strut.

In this instance they appear to have looked back to the curved members of cruck barns. With the new pointed-arch detailing of Gothic masonry everywhere triumphant, they seized upon this element, the curved cruck or arch-brace, as the ideal device to unify the design of masonry arches and timber trusses into a consistent vocabulary of design, pull-ing the work of the carpenter and of the mason into aesthetic unity. The cruck, the curved brace of timber characteristic of construction in the north and west of England, developed from the curved member of the Welsh hafod or summer house used by sheep herders.[2] Similar in its basic form to the Ukrainian cruck huts of Russia, the hafod was a demountable hut constructed of saplings embedded in the ground and tied together at the apex.

In time this technique was translated into a permanent structure with heavy curved blades resting on masonry footings. A collar tied the arches together at the apex and a mortised tie beam projected through the curved arches to secure a framed vertical wall. This fusion of framed and arch-braced elements became a characteristic English contribution to timber construction in the Middle Ages.

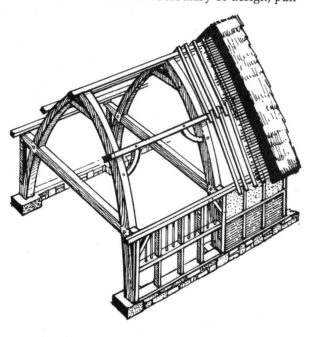

The long curved bents or blades used in arched braced timber roofs were derived from the frequent use of 'crucks' or curved braces in barns.

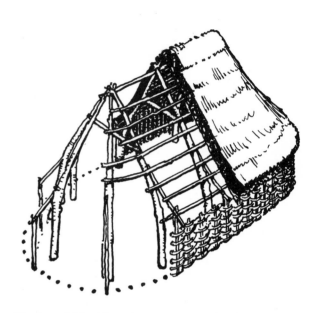

The 'cruck' had long been used in primitive barns and shelters throughout Europe to replace straight rafters, as in this Ukrainian peasant hut.

The original wattle and daub plasterwork in this cruck construction at Monks Kirby has been replaced by brickwork.

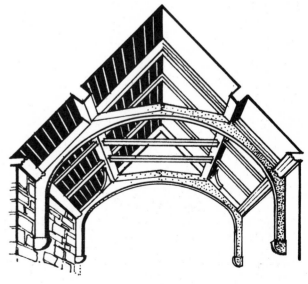

When the cruck was adapted to arch braced roof construction it gave a rigid connection to the wall. St Mary's, Leicester (after Cox and Ford)

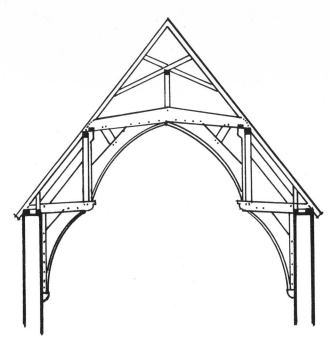

In the hammer-beam truss, arched braces stepped out from corbelled brackets to extend the span: Pilgrims Hall, Winchester, 1325–6. (after Wood)

The cruck was initially introduced into the exposed timber roofs as a device which would brace the rafters and collar beam of a truss against the supporting walls.[3] The arch-braced roof, as at St Mary's, Leicester, was satisfactory for short spans. While not as rigid as the trussed structures of the great tithe barns, it avoided the visual complexity of scissors, raking struts, and ties.

But for spans of thirty feet or more, some multiple curved elements were necessary. The hammer beam was invented to meet this problem. The key element was the sole piece on which the truss rested. Carpenters, by the fourteenth century, began to cantilever this hammer beam into the interior to act as a bracket from which a secondary timber arch could be swung over the nave.[4]

In an early hammer-beam truss at Pilgrim's Hall, Winchester, carpenters locked the projecting hammer beam into the wall by a curved brace. From this bracket vertical posts rose to a collar which tied the rafters together. By mortising in curved braces between the collar and the bracket, they were able to achieve the effect of a series of corbelled arches stepping out over the span. A redundant king post was introduced at the apex, an element which was dropped in later designs. In actual fact, the strength of the structure lay, not in the principle of corbelled bracketing, but in the careful mortising of the elements into a rigid triangulated truss.

The carpenters at Ely cathedral embellished the hammer beam truss brackets with carved angels.

A scissors truss would have been more economical of labour and material, but by this time the carpenters were attempting to rival the fretted fantasies of late Gothic masonry architecture. At Wetherden, Suffolk, the double hammer-beam truss became an elaborate display piece. The thrust and flow of forces within the structure took second place to sculptural enrichment and theatrical carving. In Gothic design mason and carpenter traded ideas and interchanged techniques. For the mason, this traffic in concepts of building was an advantage because it freed him from the dominance of sheer mass: for the carpenter, this interchange was not quite so advan-

tageous. Too often it led to aberrations in which the essentially linear and skeletal qualities of wood construction were lost in the effort to equal the plastic virtuosity of the mason.

NOTES
1 Francis Bond *Gothic Architecture in England* (London 1906) 559
2 F.H. Crossley *Timber Building in England* (London 1951) 110
3 Bond *Gothic Architecture in England* 563
4 Margaret Wood *The English Medieval House* (London 1965) 314

At times the projecting brackets of hammer-beam trusses added little to the structural stability: Double hammer beam at Wetherden, Suffolk, c 1500.

In the church at Needham Market, Suffolk, the hammer-beam brackets carry posts which were elongated to provide clerestory lighting.

The long tradition of timber construction in the north came to fruition in two outstanding engineering efforts during the fourteenth century: the octagon and lantern at Ely cathedral and the Great Hall of Richard II at Westminster.

After the fall of the Romanesque crossing tower at Ely cathedral in 1322, William Hurley, the King's Master Carpenter, opened the central space into an irregular octagon with a diameter of 70 feet.[1] From the eight masonry piers he projected triangulated timber brackets based upon the principle of the hammer beam-truss to carry the delicate lantern of timber.[2] Arched braces under these brackets became ribs carrying timber-vaulted panels, and the lantern was pierced with wooden tracery to flood the crossing with light.

In the Great Hall of Richard II at Westminster Palace, 1395–6, with a span of 67½ feet, Hugh Herland, the Master Carpenter, sprung hammer beams from points low on the side walls. This in itself would have proved insufficient to carry so great a span and he introduced long curved arched braces which rigidly locked the framework into position. The elaborate traceries carved in the spandrel openings of the truss relate the design to the masonry work of the walls by Henry Yvele and brace and stiffen the entire fabric.

NOTES
1 Geoffrey Webb *Architecture in Britain in the Middle Ages* (Penguin Books 1956) 123A, 127
2 John Harvey *Gothic England* (London 1947) 58

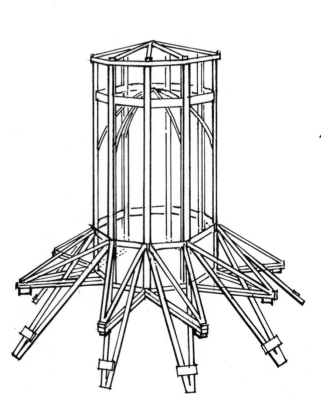

William Hurley devised triangulated timber brackets to carry the delicate lantern of wood over the octagon at Ely, 1328.

At Westminster palace Hugh Herland built a long-span, composite, arched brace and hammer beam truss between 1328 and 1340. (after Webb)

By the thirteenth century, millennia of building with wood had laid a firm base for the medieval flowering of art and architecture. Timber was used not only for the hidden constructions of roof and truss; it also determined the basic pattern and module of design along the street. Builders, with an eloquent and sophisticated vocabulary of framed elements in timber ready to hand, created streets and squares in the urban texture which were humane in scale and keyed to the pattern of daily life. The customary, deep rooted, mode of building with wooden frame was a technique equally applicable to house or guild hall, parish church or warehouse.

The carpenters of medieval Europe evolved a method of construction from the vernacular of timber framing which was both economic and flexible. To build a frame first and then to sheath it has always been a logical and systematic mode of building operation which clearly distinguishes between the structural skeleton and the weather resistant skin. With this technique, materials of construction could be used to their best functional advantage. The four-foot panel of sheathing and the sixteen- to twenty-foot span of the heavy timber beam set an over-all structural scale keying all buildings into a consistent unity.

Despite the ever present danger of fire this mode of building continued well into the seventeenth century. Royal edicts and municipal proclamations thundered in vain against the continuing use of timber frame. Eventually building in wood was superseded, not because it was dangerous, but be-

In Goslar, Germany, long after Renaissance had superseded the Gothic, builders continued to use medieval framing.

The repetitive bays of timber construction were easily adapted to house, warehouse, or shop along the narrow streets of the medieval town. At Kings

Lynn, the long overhang of the Hanseatic warehouse contrasts with the fire-proof brick wall of the foreground seventeenth-century structure.

cause timber became so expensive, as the forests were cut away, that, of necessity, builders were forced to turn to permanent masonry materials.

Country barns and farmhouses could be built to be as wide as was structurally or economically feasible, but in the new towns building space was at a premium. The narrow constricting girdle of expensive fortified walls surrounding the medieval town forced medieval builders to create multistorey cages fronting on the street. In a northern climate they rejected the centripetal courtyard plan with rooms looking inward to a court and instead increased the density of habitation in the town by going high.

Along the street on long narrow plots the carpenters built four- and five-storey houses with common party walls. The dressed square-timber

beam of ten to twelve inches, when closely spaced, could span up to twenty feet without undue deflection. This structural determinant established the basic plot width for the single family house. To gain needed extra space they added a floor or expanded to the rear.

The long narrow plan placed a special premium upon generous window openings; the grid of timber fore and aft was opened to light and air by the use of strip or row windows extending at each floor across the facade. The fireplace and kitchen flues of brick or masonry tended to move from a central location under the ridge to the party walls so that they could be built independently of the timber frame. Party walls were constructed of timber frame with heavy infills of brick and plaster to retard the

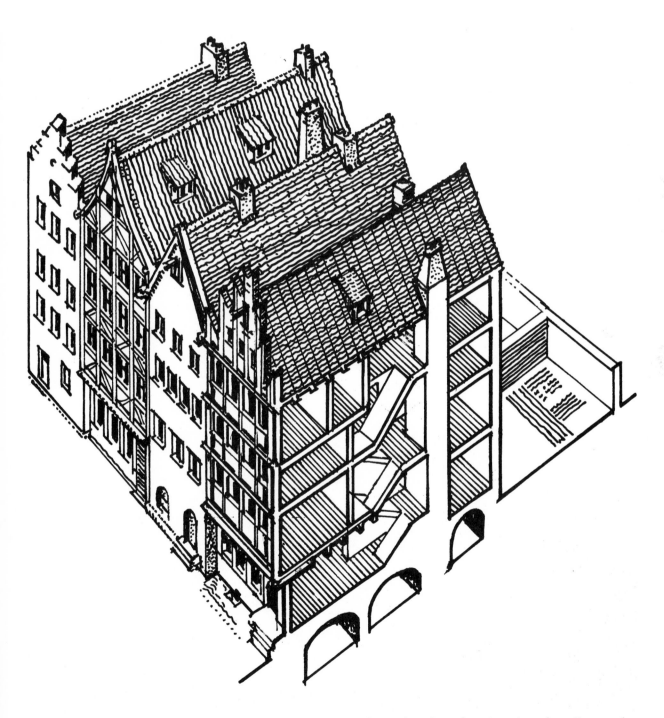

In the medieval row housing of northern Europe the buildings looked out to the street and garden for light and air. Side corridors and stairs led to the rooms.

In Ghent, Antwerp, Amsterdam, and Lübeck, the successful traders of the Hanseatic League erected substantial warehouses and residences with long strip windows to let in light and air. Grasleie, Ghent

At Landshut in central Europe the German burghers imposed strict building regulations on the size and scale of new structures to attain a uniform street facade of fireproof materials.

spread of fire. Over these long narrow buildings it was most economical to run the roof ridge along the full depth. Each building presented a gable to the street which became a decorative headpiece for the structure with diverse and varied architectural detail.

The densely packed, tall, narrow row houses of medieval Europe proved to be so successful a response to the climate, and so logical an expression of the needs of a merchant economy, that they continued to be built well into the early years of the nineteenth century. Waves of stylistic influence beat against this indigenous local mode of building with only superficial effect: despite the change to party walls of load-bearing brick, and a facing of brick, stucco, or stone, on the façade, the basic plan remained little altered. The need for adequate penetration of light into the interior demanded an open glass screen wall. In the north, throughout the Renaissance and well into the Baroque, the wall facing the street, in its detail and in its composition, remained a frank reinterpretation of the fundamental logic of the cage and curtain-wall vocabulary of northern Europe.

Until the second world war the core of most German towns remained medieval in scale. At Ulm the narrow-fronted, gabled houses pressed close in below the minster.

The generative principle of northern European architecture has been building as a structural frame sheathed with a weather-resistant material. The distinction between skeleton and skin, between gravity frame and functional sheath, has been the dominant design motif. From paleolithic beehive shelter to neolithic earth lodge to Iron Age framed hut, builders in the north of Europe progressively modified, refined, and articulated their structures in such a fashion that each component frankly stated its structural role or its functional necessity.

Posts and beams, braces and trusses conformed to an inherent logic. Roofs proclaimed their role as independent covers sheltering occupants, structure, and walls against rain and snow. Walls became filtration membranes with doors as circulatory valves, and windows expanded to let in light and solar heat. Where the wall had to function as an insulating partition or a fire break, panels of brick or plastered lath were set into the heavy timber frame.

This mode of building was not restricted to northern Europe. In other regions with similar climatic demands builders devised similar forms. But only in Europe was this tradition energized by continuing contact with North African, Mediterranean, and Middle Eastern influences. In Europe's tortured history as a battleground between east and west, north and south, the vernacular local tradition of building in frame was forced to monumental scale as it met and fused with the Mediterranean themes of shell dome and mass wall.

Mediterranean mass wall at Cordoba, Spain, turning inwards to a shaded courtyard.

Baltic medieval brickwork opened out to light and air. Van der Gruut house, Bruges, 1465–70

FRANCE

6
FOLDED SHELLS

The dynamic of a Christian faith, intolerant, ego-centric and embattled, provided the focus and pivot for the new society emerging in the north of Europe. The wave of Islam, which had engulfed the Mediterranean basin and the Middle East, forced Christianity to find a new home and a new base in continental Europe. Turning away from the remnants of classical culture, abandoning the exhausted hillsides and rocky promontories of the Mediterranean, Christian monks and clerics carried the faith into the forests of central Europe, along the Atlantic and Baltic shore, and up the broad and fertile river basins.

In this reshaping of the Christian tradition to a Frankish and Germanic pattern in a new homeland, architecture and the allied arts emerged as the physical expression of a new and aggressive culture. As Mediterranean modes of building were grafted upon the root stock of northern European technique, the carpenter of the north and the mason of the south traded ideas, each modifying and adapting their particular skills to new demands and new problems. Two vernacular traditions, frame and mass, merged in the Gothic. The extreme specialization and narrow adaptation of the timber-framed tradition of the north became a more spacious concern with per-manence and monumentality. The sombre weight, elusive surface, and plastic mass of the southern tradition of building was invigorated by a new concern with precision and elegant structural invention. The cross-fertilization of these two disparate approaches to building led to a hybrid vigour in design. The immediate result was the Gothic cathedral, the end product, a technical sophistication and a command of men's labour and material which have become the imperative dynamic of our modern world.

Three critical stages mark the emergence of this medieval achievement. In the search for more light, masons changed from the smoothly modelled and curved shell surfaces of dome and barrel vault to acutely folded shells of masonry. Emphasis upon the groin or fold led to the use of a rib at this intersection. Finally the heavy massive containing wall disappeared, as point supports and buttresses carried the localized thrust of the rib to the grade level. By the opening of the thirteenth century masons had learned how to compose all three of these motifs into a new architectural summation. They supported folded shells on delicately ribbed cages, and propped the airy fabric into position with skeletal buttresses.

The massive wall of the south: a continuous shell of masonry with only minor openings and shallow arcaded reveals. The west front tower, St Philibert, Tournus.

The strutted and ribbed cage of the north: masonry reduced to a skeletal fabric in the Sainte Chapelle, Paris.

OVERLEAF *With folded and arched masonry plates the medieval designer created delicate shell structures. Crossing, San Vincente, Avila*

The barrel vaults and domes of the Byzantine and the Romanesque were perfectly adequate structural devices where heavy walls and massive supports gave continuous restraint to the pressures generated by a curved shell surface. When large window openings cut the walls into a range of piers some means had to be found to concentrate these diffuse loadings into specific points of support. At first the masons folded the vaulted surfaces to direct the loads and stiffen the fabric.

To envisage the structural advantages of sharply folded surfaces it helps to examine the mode of deformation of a simple barrel vault restrained along two sides. A load at the top will depress the crown so that the sides will bulge or burst out. This is easily demonstrated by using a curved sheet of paper. Of course, the entire curved sheet or plane can be made so thick that it is rigid enought to counter this load. The early Romanesque builders did exactly this when they built heavy barrel vaults. But this clumsy weight was wasteful of material and effort and it increased the thrust along the base.

Other, more economical means had to be found to stop the deformation. Arch rings set under the vault or diaphragms over the surface help to strengthen the fabric but they are complex extra elements. A sharp fold along the crown will add little to the weight but will immediately stiffen the structure because the sharply creased inverted v now acts as a longitudinal beam distributing the load over the two canted planes, as in Romanesque pointed barrel vaults.

In turn, the canted planes, whether curved or flat, of this folded plate must be braced into position from the sides if they are not to buckle or deform. Braces along the sides can be used but the simplest answer is to fold both longitudinally and laterally. In such an intersecting roof the folded surfaces interact, bracing each other against buckling.

Thin cylindrical barrel vaults fail when the crown falls, pushing out the sides. Thin stiffening plates can reduce this flexure.

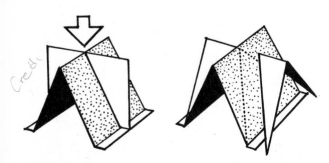

Folding along the crown can replace the longitudinal stiffener. Folded ridges set transversely can brace the sides.

Alternatively a simple pyramid of canted surfaces could be used to cover the space. Folding along the edges would brace each plane into position but such a pyramid would require support around the entire periphery. However, in a crossed roof, created by the intersection of two sharply folded plates, all of the pyramidal surfaces can be cut away. All loads then channel along the folds or groins created in the valley intersections to four isolated points of support, and each support must now absorb merely a diagonal thrust rather than a direct vertical load.

It was this principle of introducing folding at the groin intersection and channeling all loads into this stiff folded plate which was the crucial first step in the change to a specifically Gothic mode of construction. It was no accident that a structural technique dependent upon the use of sharply folded surfaces emerged in a region where builders long had been accustomed to use prismatic roof structures. At the extreme it can be argued that the pointed Gothic vault was no more than the application of the intersecting and folded roof to a masonry fabric. Whatever the source, there is no question that folding or pointing of the ridges stiffened the crown of the vault and groin folding braced the panels of vaulting into position while focussing loads to the pier supports. Though vaulted planes of stone had to be constructed as curved surfaces to wedge into position, as opposed to the flat planes created by wooden rafters, both intersecting roof and cross vault are precisely adapted to point support.

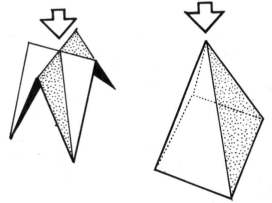

A pyramidal roof is rigid but requires support below the sides. The cross-ridged roof can rest on four isolated supports, channeling loads down the folded groins.

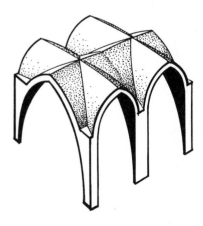

In the pointed Gothic cross vault the panels of vaulting were curved to wedge into position.

In retrospect it is quite easy to see that the logic of the medieval building programme, in which curved shell surfaces were placed on isolated supports, required the eventual use of curved and folded planes. For the medieval mason, during the crucial years of invention from 1050 to 1150, it was by no means so clear. He had to progress step by step, gradually modifying and adapting the continuous curvatures of barrel vault and dome until the pointed cross vault emerged.

The Romans used the cross vault, formed by the intersection of two barrel-vaulted surfaces, for major spans. In minor applications it had been placed over the choir of San de Baños and the aisles of the great pilgrimage churches, but not over the naves of major churches. Romanesque masons used a pointed profile for barrel vaults from the eleventh century in the south of France. They seem to have been aware of the structural advantages inherent in folding at the crown; but it was many years before they applied this to the intersecting cross vaults.

Early cross vaults were invariably created by the intersection of two semicircular barrel vaults. Transverse arch rings of cut stone were used to stiffen the vault at each bay, and along the sides longitudinal arch rings and walling secured the curvatures of the transverse segments. The semicircular cross vault concentrated the loads and thrusts of the vault upon four points by reducing material.

If we diagram the compressive and tensile lines of force on the surface of a barrel vault resting on four supports, it is evident that the tensile stresses are concentrated along the lower edge of the vault. If this area is cut away only material in compression is left. By butting up against this opening a wedge-shaped segment of barrel vaulting, a rigid profile is created in which the thrusts and loads are channelled to the supports by the groin fold. Along the groin individual stones will press outwards and

down against one another to create a new composite pressure and thrust. The weight of the vaulting panels and their thrusting actions fuse to travel down the groin intersection. This concentration of loads along the groin is quite independent of any mortar bond. The mortar will tend to fuse the surfaces into rigid shells, adding extra strength, but it is not essential to the stability of the cross-groined vault. Where the mortar bond is strong enough to resist tensile forces it converts the groin to a rigid arched and folded beam, making the vault safer.

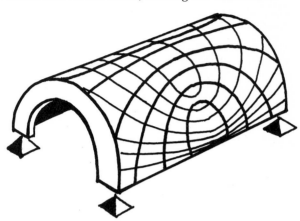

In a barrel vault resting on four supports the sides of the shell between supports are in tension.

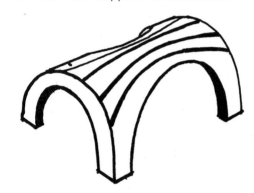

If this material in tension is cut away then the barrel is all in compression, but it is unstable and will collapse at the crown.

In the twelfth-century Cistercian monastery at Silvacane the masons added a cross vault with diagonal ribs at the crossing of the pointed barrel vaults. Because the piers had no springings for these ribs they had to be cut back at the cap.

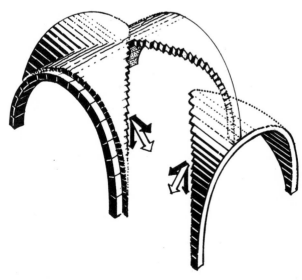

To brace and support the crown place an intersecting barrel butting against the cut-away portion. Compression loads will then be channeled down the groin intersection.

The striking architectural success of the Romans was based on poured concrete, a tenacious material which could resist substantial tensile stresses. But that secret was lost in the Dark Ages. The Romanesque builders had to start anew. Small-stone construction with lime-mortar joints had some strength against tensile stresses but it was quite inferior to the cohesion of hydraulic-cement concrete. Cracking and displacement and eventual failure were frequent and so new forms were developed in the eleventh century.

Although walls and vaulted surfaces were made ponderous and massive in an attempt to restrain the thrusts of vaulting, their superficial air of solidarity was, only too often, but skin deep. The surfacing

stones were cut and shaped to interlock, but the inner massive core was a pudding of fieldstone, gravel, and lime mortar of doubtful structural stability. The early cross vaults used in crypts or over aisles, as at Santiago de Compostela, were devised to carry a floor on pier supports. The spans were short and the rubble shells comparatively thick. The entire vault was locked into position by the weight of rubble and mortar fill laid over it to level the floor. Though they did not have the tenacious strength of Roman cast-cement structures, these vaults were monolithic fabrics. The corbelling action of the poured fill and the minor voussoir wedging action of the vault facings was more than sufficient to ensure stability over the short spans.

In Romanesque structures the masons relied upon heavy masses of rubble stone and lime mortar to stabilize the fabric. St Benoit-sur-Loire, 1005–62

The situation was quite different when cross vaults were built over the main span of the church. The Romanesque builder found that a heavy fill placed over a longer span merely increased the thrust of the vault, endangering the entire fabric. By a process of empirical trial and error, and by judicious adjustment of material to counter evident failures, the mason cut back the mortar and rubble fill to an area just above the haunching. The rest of the vault then became a comparatively thin shell of brick or stone.

The combination of gravity loads and thrusts, the tensile strength of the mortar bond, and the mechanical interlocking of stones at the groin intersection, all worked together in the Romanesque vault to ensure that there was an appreciable stiffening by folded-shell action. If the webs of vaulting are cut away it is clear that the groins acted as curved stiffening arches securing the stability of the entire cross-vaulted surface. John Fitchen, in his study of the erection techniques employed by Gothic masons, points this out when he discusses thin-shell theory.

What has been written on the Gothic structural system in the past two decades or so ignores this modern knowledge and continues to speculate on the nature and characteristics of Gothic vaulting as though its action were solely and exclusively a voussoir action throughout. Viewed from the standpoint of curving shells, however, the crease at the groin where the panels abut each other

above the backs of the ribs is seen to have provided very powerful stiffening – like the folds of accordion pleated paper – which was by no means dependent upon additional support from the ribs.[1]

Fitchen gives credit to Conant for being one of the few art historians aware of this shell action of Romanesque and Gothic vaulting. He goes on to point out that the resistance to deformation or failure in the vaulting webs derives from their single or double curvature, and not alone from the thickness of the vaulting shell.

The folded and arched groins of the Romanesque cross vault can be conceived of as arched bents swinging diagonally across the bay from springing to crown. Their strength is independent of any ribs which may follow the same lines. The point is of some importance because for decades a turgid and acrimonious debate has been waged among art historians on this very topic. Most have emphasized the structural significance of the diagonal rib; a few others have argued from the behaviour of the shell as a structural surface.

Blast damage from bombing and high explosive shells during two world wars has focussed attention on the behaviour of vaulted shells in medieval structures. At times the panels of vaulting fell, leaving only the skeletal frame of the ribs in position. But there were cases where the ribs collapsed, leaving substantial segments of the curved and folded vault still standing. This seemingly contra-

Carefully cut vault springings introduced below an existent cross vault at San Giovanni degli Eremiti, Palermo. Precise cutting of the stones was more effective than a heavy mass of material.

The early diagonal ribs used at St Sauveur, Figeac, provided a true semicircle against which were butted the twisted planes of the vaulting panels.

dictory behaviour in differing instances has emphasized the independence of rib systems and vaulted shells.

Seen in this light, the much disputed primacy of the rib or the panel in the Gothic vault falls into proper perspective. The vaulted shells with their curving surfaces and folded edges can be structurally stable systems in themselves. Arch rings and ribs were added to these shell fabrics by Gothic builders as a constructional convenience. Certainly these added elements stiffened and added supplementary bracing to the curving shells but they were not the primary structural element. It was this indeterminate combination of shell and frame which gave such freedom to the Gothic designer.

NOTE
1 John Fitchen *The Construction of Gothic Cathedrals* (Oxford 1961) 65

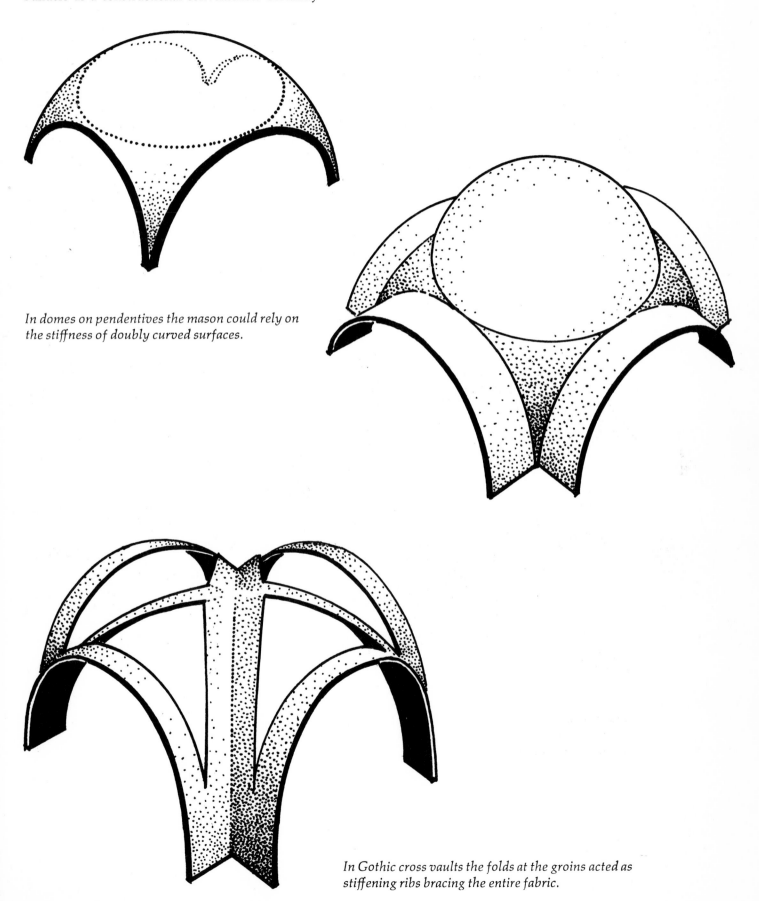

In domes on pendentives the mason could rely on the stiffness of doubly curved surfaces.

In Gothic cross vaults the folds at the groins acted as stiffening ribs bracing the entire fabric.

The semicircular arch and the round barrel vault posed a particular problem for the builder. The relatively flat section at the crown tended to fall as a unit, imposing heavily concentrated overturning moments upon the sides. Although the cross vault introduced valuable resistance to this overturning by sharp folding at the lower portion of the groin, it aggravated the difficulties at the centre. The intersection of two semicircular barrel vaults is elliptical in section, and an ellipse is weaker than a circle, and thus even more likely to fail by collapse. If the cross vault was to be successfully used over major spans, some means had to be found to resolve this weakness.

Lombard brickmasons in the north of Italy solved this problem by building semicircular diagonal groins. In so doing a pseudo-domical vault was created in which the vaulting panels were curved up

to meet the groin, becoming surfaces of double curvature which were more rigid than singly curved panels. The designers were freed from the limitations imposed by the strict geometry of intersecting barrel vaults. Groin curvatures or ribs now could be designed to best take the concentrations of loading. Once this change in approach was made, the builder could vary his vault to suit special conditions, warping the vault panels where necessary to suit the desired groin or rib configuration. When diagonal ribs were introduced into the nave vaults at San Ambrogio, Milan, in the twelfth century, the Lombard masons continued to use concentric coursing – building the vaults as if they were domes.

The domical vault with semicircular diagonals was brought to the south of France by masons schooled in the tradition of shell construction. In the eleventh century churches were built at Angou-

When semicircular diagonal ribs were built across the domical vaults at Sant' Ambrogio, Milan, the pronounced doming broke the nave into quite separate compartments.

In the ribless cross vaults in the narthex of Sant' Ambrogio, Milan, the groins disappeared into the vaulted surface.

Over the nave of St Lazare at Avallon the masons pointed the transverse arch rings, but the shell of the vault was built with radial coursing and only slight folding at the corners.

lême, Perigueux, Cahors, and Souillac, in Aquitaine, with domes supported on corbelled pendantive supports, in imitation of Byzantine models. So strongly rooted was this technique of building with doubly curved shell surfaces that, when cross vaults were built over the naves of churches, the masons relied upon their experience with domes to ensure the stability of the vault.

In the early twelfth century, as far north as Avallon in Burgundy, vaults were built with radial coursing, that is, as domes, although they did have shallow groins. When ribs were introduced into the diagonal groins during the twelfth century, the masons in Aquitaine and the Auvergne turned away from concentric rings of coursing to create panels of vaulting intersecting at the rib, as at St Serge, Angers. Despite this change, domical vaults exert a thrust around their entire periphery and it was necessary to absorb this continuous pressure along the edge of the vault.

Such vaults were ideally suited to the structural demands of the heavy-walled spacious hall churches of the south in which nave and aisles were of equal height. Thrusts were neutralized along the arch rings between each bay, so that each domical vault stayed and buttressed its neighbour. The heavy external wall was more than sufficient to absorb the thrusts above the windows. The domical vault was less than satisfactory when used in the open gridded cages of the north.

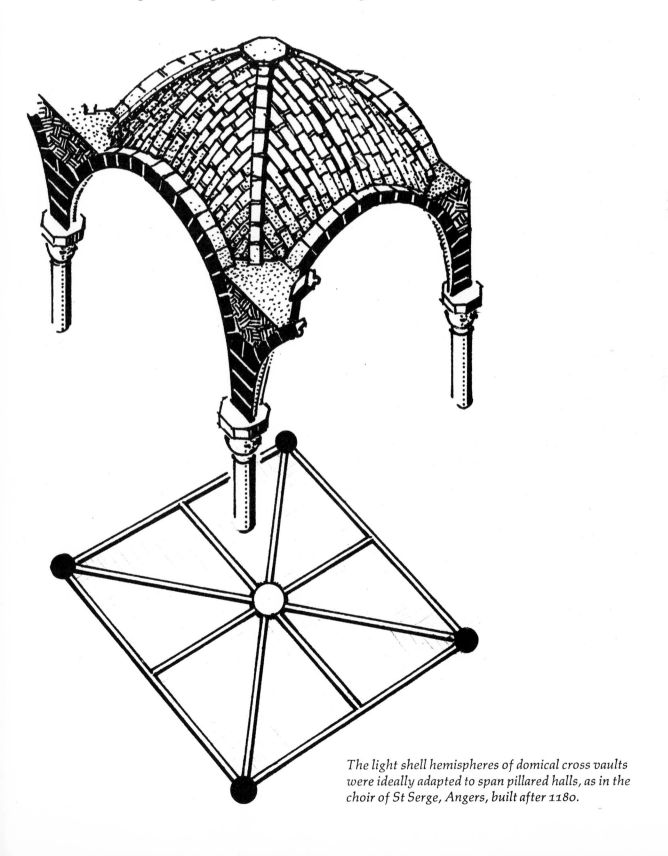

The light shell hemispheres of domical cross vaults were ideally adapted to span pillared halls, as in the choir of St Serge, Angers, built after 1180.

In the absence of documentary sources before the late twelfth century, the intent of the masons must be read from the structural fabrics they conceived. The cursory or distorted accounts of the building operations given by abbots or clerics tend to conceal the decisive role of the amateur mason in shaping the fabric, just as newspaper accounts today give little indication of the disciplined search for order which is the key to scientific, engineering, or architectural creation.

Nonetheless, it is quite evident that, from the middle of the eleventh century, architecture in Europe was beginning to respond to the impact of powerful personalities in the building operations. Masons and carpenters had broken free of the restrictive and provincial bounds of the Dark Ages to travel widely, to compare techniques, and to create new forms. The luxuriant variance of Romanesque design points to a spirit of innovation and a sustained search for novel structural patterns characteristic of trained artificers and widely travelled professionals.

After a fire had destroyed the choir of Canterbury cathedral in 1174, the chronicler Gervase wrote:

Among the architects there was one, William of Sens, a man of great abilities and a most ingenious workman in wood and stone. Dismissing the rest, they chose him for the undertaking. And he, residing many days with the monks and carefully surveying the burnt walls ... went on preparing all things that were necessary, either himself or by the agency of others ... At length they agreed ... to take down the ruined choir. Attention was given to procure stones from abroad. He made the most ingenious machines for loading and unloading ships, and for drawing the mortar and stones. He delivered also to the masons models (cutout wooden templates) for cutting the stones.[1]

The picture emerges of a professional consultant sure of his technical knowledge, skilled in the thrust and parry of meetings with the building committee of monks and possessed by the urge to create a more noble fabric: in short, an architect, not a mere hewer of stone.

The terms, 'architectus,' 'artificum magister,' 'maister of the crafte,' 'deviser of buildyng,' begin to appear in the accounts with ever increasing frequency from the early twelfth century. These masters and architects were described as 'connynge in geometrie ... trassyng and making molds ... devysing and drawynge.' By 1519 William Horman in his English-Latin phrase book *Vulgaria* says: 'He is nat worthy to be called maister of the crafte, that is nat cunnyng in drawynge and purturynge (*non est architecti nomine dignus qui graphidis peritus non est.*)'[2]

About 1235 the notebook or textbook of Villard de Honnecourt from northern France indicates the range and complexity of the Gothic architect's training. Basing his arguments on his experience in Switzerland, Hungary, and France, he drew plans and elevations of choirs and façades, window tracery, ingenious machines for construction, and figures as well as geometric constructions to demonstrate his competence as an architectural teacher.[3]

By the opening of the twelfth century a new rationale began to challenge and invigorate the entire field of building in Europe. Trade specialization under the guild system ensured intense and competitive experimentation in each craft. The architect began to emerge as the master mason co-ordinating the layout and detail of the permanent fabric. The master carpenter brought his special skills to bear upon the design of roof trusses and the erection of scaffolding and centering for the masonry fabric. Glaziers, slateroofers, iron mongers, tile setters, and cabinet makers each now contributed their own special skills within the framework of a co-ordinated team effort.

During this century of intensive experiment and innovation, the new analytic approach to building converted the heavy massive wall of the Romanesque to the pierced screen of the Gothic, while the vault changed from a continuous shell to a fabric of frame and panel.

NOTES
1 R. Willis *Canterbury Cathedral* (1845)
2 M.R. James (ed) *Vulgaria puerorum* (Roxburghe Club 1926) 346
3 H.R. Hahnloser *Villard de Honnecourt* (Vienna 1935)

7

RIBBED VAULTS

By the twelfth century the geometric skill of architects was such that it was quite possible to lay out the groins of a cross vault on a square compartment with reasonable accuracy. The domed form also required only a semicircular template to ensure a reasonably accurate meeting of the vaulting panels. But, where the vault was to be constructed over an oblong compartment, the masons encountered difficulty in achieving a geometrically true line of intersection. The warped and twisted groins evident at la Madeleine, Vézelay, tell the story of a job botched because the masons merely projected the curves of wall arch and transverse arch through to a wavering line of intersection.

Romanesque and early Gothic masons used small split rubble stones for the panels of their vaults. Layout was a rough and ready affair with only a few controlling lines or templates. The masons butted their coursing together at the groins, only occasionally keying together the stones in alternate projections. They relied upon a heavy coat of plaster to make up irregularities. Evidently it was advantageous to first build a masonry rib as a support and as a cover for this erratic line of intersection.

The problem could have been solved by carefully designing each voussoir stone at the groin as a seven-sided wedge keyed to the panels of vaulting to make a hidden rib. Eventually this was to be done during the Renaissance but it did involve a disproportionate outlay of time and energy on complex

Romanesque and early Gothic vaults were built of roughly shaped rubble stones. A diagonal rib helped to conceal the erratic intersections of the courses.

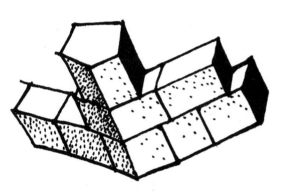

Later Renaissance vaults were constructed of carefully shaped voussoirs. At the groin, seven-sided stones made a rigid hidden rib.

In English vaults the masons usually projected a rib-stem through the webs.

Occasionally the masons keyed or interlocked the vaulting stones at the groins, but this was not possible where the number of courses or the course widths varied from panel to panel.

OVERLEAF *Chapter house, Silvacane*

stereotomy, or stone cutting. The vault had to be planned and laid out in advance, by the use of three-dimensional projective geometry, as a complex of precisely shaped and fitted stones. This was beyond the technical capacity of masons during the early Middle Ages. Roughly shaped fieldstone or rubble, broken along the cleavage planes into elongated cubes only slightly larger than a brick, was the basic constructional material. As far as possible the Romanesque masons restricted their use of cut stone to facings in pier and wall. The builders were local craftsmen turning their vernacular skills to the problem of the church, the abbey, and the hall. Wherever possible they took the customary way to solve an immediate problem in design or construction. Using a rule of thumb based upon a nice feeling for material, the result of a lifetime's experience with building, they made their decisions on the site.

For small structures of short span and single function the technique worked very well. Monk and carpenter, cleric and mason could devise reasonable and economical building responses to the demands of relatively uncomplicated social groupings.

At Avila, the sharp groin line was wedged into a re-entrant corner. At Vézelay, and in the vaults of the crypt of St Eutrope at Saintes, the effort to adapt the cross-groined vault to oblong compartments led to sinuous lines of intersection. Evidently the architects had to establish a true curve for the groin and then warp the panels to suit if they were to arrive at a satisfactory solution. Ready to hand they had the example of the transverse arch ring; it only remained to build ribs diagonally across the bay to create a skeletal frame before laying the shell panels.

It was difficult to achieve a geometrically true line of intersection where the groined cross vault was used over an oblong compartment: nave, la Madeleine, Vezelay, 1120–32.

Over the crypt of St Eutrope at Saintes the masons introduced a corner shaft to take the groin fold, but the surfaces were awkwardly adapted to an oblong bay (1081–96).

The diagonal groins fade awkwardly into a re-entrant corner in the aisle vaults of San Vicente in Avila, Spain.

It had long been customary in building barrel vaults to erect rings of cut stone on separate centerings before completing the rubble shell. In the cross vault the same technique was applied to wall arches, transverse arch rings, and finally to the diagonal rib. On light centering frames, masons built the arches and ribs of cut stone, and then laid over them the panels of vaulting. Reconstructions of the exact techniques employed are, of course, hypothetical, but reasonable approximations can be reached from contemporary manuscript illustrations. These show the erection scaffolding as a light framework of lashed poles.[1] Evidently the builders reserved pit-sawn timbers for permanent construction; poles and bent saplings, wickerwork and lashings were more than satisfactory for temporary props and supports. Here they were able to take full advantage of their long experience with light-framed construction in village and farmstead.

Initially the centerings probably were full semi-circular frames or lagging units, set on wedged supports which could be knocked out (decentered) after the masonry had set. For longer spans it was convenient to use four frames converging on a decentering wedge. This would clear the working platform of the forest of poles necessary earlier. The frames could be reused for the next bay of vaulting.

In the lower two-thirds of each panel of vaulting no centering or support was required between the ribs and arches. The slightly canted coursing could be laid up by corbel action. Only along the ridges of the intersecting panels was support needed. Lightly constructed lagging frames, or small trusses of lashed and bent poles wedged against the ribs and supported by the diagonal bents, sufficed for this closing of the vault.

NOTE
1 John Fitchen *The Construction of Gothic Cathedrals* (Oxford 1961) 118–22

Arch rings and diagonal ribs of masonry were laid on lashed wooden centering frames. Frames could be reused by knocking away the wedged supports. (after Fitchen)

With pointed arches it was more economical to use two small frames wedged together at the crown. The working scaffold was a light construction of lashed poles and wicker mats or hurdles.

The ribs became masonry centering frames guiding and supporting the curved webs of stone, freeing the designer from the need for cumbersome and expensive continuous centering. By breaking the vault into a complex of facets, he and his mason could proceed in a rational step-by-step building operation.

Initially, the panels of vaulting, or severies, were butted together on the top surfaces of the diagonal ribs. This technique continued to be favoured in the north of France well into the Gothic age of the great cathedrals. In England, and in the south of France which, as part of the Plantagenet domain was open to English influence, ribs with stems were used, as in the twelfth-century chapter house at Ripon cathedral or the vaults of St Serge at Angers.

The characteristic dominance of the rib in English design now begins to make its appearance. The diagonal rib was first used consistently at Durham in the choir aisle vaults completed in 1096. It was used again in the high vault of the choir, completed in 1104, but failure of the panels led to replacement in 1235. The nave vault, built from 1128 to 1133, is the earliest extant example of the diagonal rib used over the main span of a church.

In the early years of the twelfth century the manifest advantages of the diagonally ribbed cross vault captured the imagination of builders throughout Europe. Here, at last, they had a structural vocabulary ideally suited to small stone construction. Not only was the rib a constructional convenience but it unified vault and support into a consistent system. Thrusts, seemingly channelled and localized in the rib, were brought down to shafts attached to the mass of the pier. The ponderous weight and solidity of the early Romanesque could now give way to a linear emphasis in design: an emphasis which struck a responsive chord in builders so accustomed to the framed and skeletal tradition of the north.

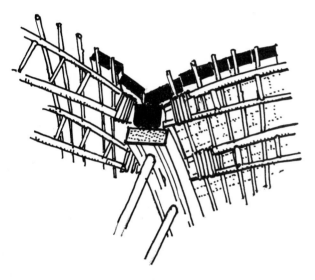

The lower courses of the vaulting panels could be set up without centering. At the crown they used light temporary bents braced against the rib supports.

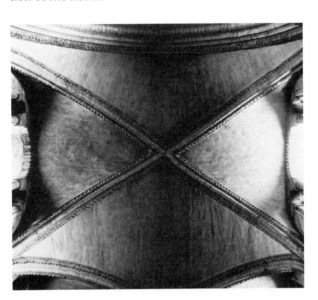

Modelled on the choir of 1104 this structure was the earliest known use of a diagonal rib vault over the main span of a church. Nave vault, Durham, 1128–33

In the chapter house of Senanque abbey the masons used a double mould along the diagonal to lighten its effect.

Semicircular diagonal ribs created a quasi-domical vault. Chapter house, Ripon, 1154–81

During the first quarter of the twelfth century the domical vault with diagonal ribs was adequate to solve the structural problems posed by a square vaulting compartment. Heavy walls and massive fill introduced at the haunching of the vault were more than sufficient to restrain the considerable thrust generated by this comparatively thick structure. With cubiform caps on the heavy piers bracketed out to receive the springing of the ribs the system was structurally stable if heavy and ponderous.

The heavy transverse arch rings, rectilinear in section, clearly developed from the stiffening arch rings of the barrel vault. The diagonals, lighter in section, evidently had a constructional, rather than structural, significance: as a moulding covering the awkward zig-zag intersection of vaulting panels and as built-in centering devices ensuring a true curve at the groin. They evolved from the technique of erection, the modes of building, rather than from a static analysis of the play of forces within the vaulting shell.

The quasi-domical form of the vault with semi-circular ribs and arch rings was structurally stable, but by overemphasizing each bay of vaulting it broke the total design into quite separate elements. To achieve a level crown along the length of the vault, masons began to stilt the arches along the side and transversely across the bay. In stilted arches the semicircle of the arch was swung from a point far above the springing. Thus the diagonal remained semicircular but the sides of the vault were opened up for more effective clerestory lighting. In so doing the vaulting panels had to be warped or twisted to meet the low projection of the diagonal rib.

In the north aisle vaults of St Etienne at Beauvais, pronounced stilting of wall and transverse arches created a relatively level crown. As well, the primitive three-quarter-round diagonals were sprung from angle shafts set into the corner of the pier, so that the shaft picked up the forces generated by the ribs to carry them down the pier surface.

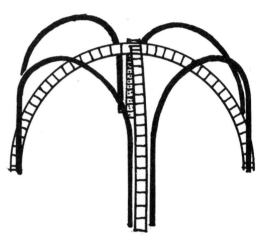

Stilted wall and transverse arches made it possible to level the crowns of the vault.

In the north aisle of St Etienne at Beauvais, 1120–5, this extreme stilting of the arch rings forced the masons to warp the vaulting panels, but this was preferable to the awkwardly twisted groins of the earlier Romanesque. The last bay in shows how pointed arches simplified the whole problem of vaulting.

To reduce the domical shape created by semicircular diagonal ribs the masons stilted the transverse arch rings. Choir aisle, Peterborough, 1117

With the stilted arch and the warped vaulting panel it was now possible to devise ribbed, round-arched, Romanesque vaults which could adjust to oblong compartments and to the wedge-shaped bays surrounding the choir. The heavy rib became the dominant element; vaulting surfaces were distorted to suit it.

But so extreme did this flexing of the panels become, that masons began to search for other ways to adapt the cross vault to oblong compartments. This was a problem of particular concern in the patterning of nave vaults, because each large square bay in the nave often was abutted to two smaller bays in the aisle. Unless some way could be found to break the compartment in the nave into two segments, the intermediate pier determined by the aisle vaulting could contribute little to the stability of the longer span.

The sexpartite vault was one solution. Invented in Normandy, it found universal application in northern France during the twelfth century and its use continued into the thirteenth century (there are examples at Laon, Paris, and Bourges), long after the introduction of pointed Gothic ribbing had made it structurally obsolete. Logically, the vault should dictate the system of support; however, the shape and configuration of the sexpartite vault was an accidental byproduct of the pier system, devised to adjust the nave vaulting to a closely spaced range of piers along the side. Essentially the sexpartite vault was a cross vault in which four side panels of vaulting came to a common focus at the crown. These skewed vaulting compartments reflected the consistent effort of Romanesque designers to reduce shell surfaces to linear patterns.

The reasons for building the first sexpartite vault, over the nave of St Etienne at Caen in Normandy (from 1115), indicate the rationale behind this curious compromise. St Etienne was begun about 1068, with a preliminary consecration in 1073. It was designed for a timber roof, with piers closely spaced along the nave arcade. Later it was decided to cover the nave with masonry vaulting, but the masons apparently doubted the structural stability of ribbed cross vaults over large square compartments and the narrow bays formed by the existing piers which would have emphasized the pronounced warping created by the stilted wall arches. Learning from the example of Durham, where pier and squat column alternated along choir and nave, but adding transverse arches over the squat columns, the masons at Caen joined two vaulting bays in a common focus.

Thus, the Gothic evolved from the vault down, the Romanesque from the pier up to the vault. Not until masons could accept the new primacy of the vault was there to be a full application of Gothic framing.

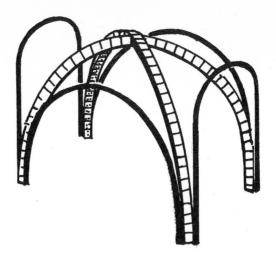

Over oblong bays only the wall arch was stilted.

The sexpartite nave vault at Laon reflected the archaic alternation of supports.

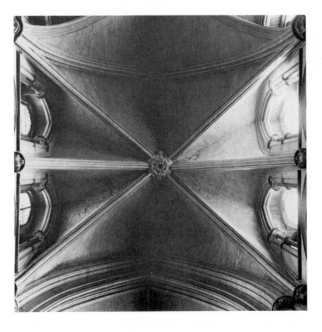

A few sexpartite vaults were used in England as the masons copied the French modes of building. Southeast transept, Lincoln

The sexpartite vault was devised to adapt the large square compartments of the Romanesque nave to the narrow bays of the aisle and gallery.

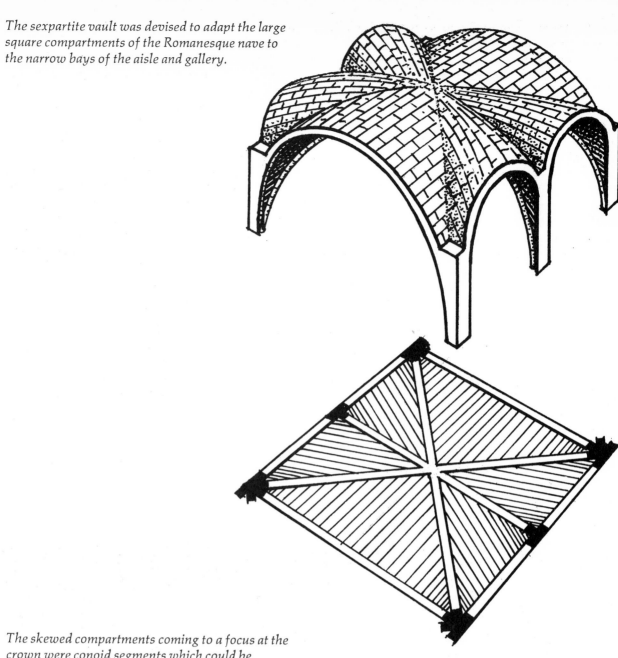

The skewed compartments coming to a focus at the crown were conoid segments which could be adapted to central plans and nave terminations, as is done with modern ferroconcrete shells.

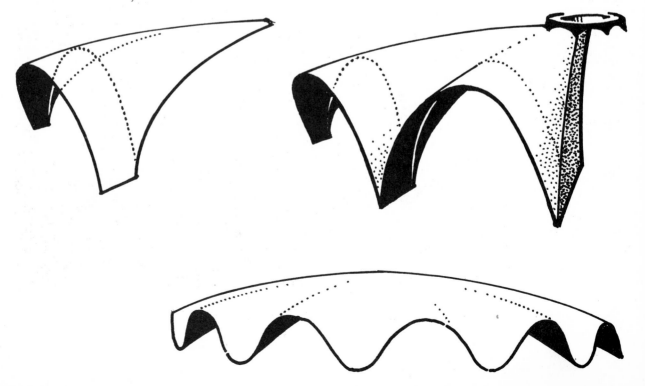

By the twelfth century the monumental solidarity of the round arch, tunnel vault, and heavy pier was proving technically inadequate and could lead only to frustration in the search for more effective lighting. At this point the introduction of the slender rib was the crucial step in a new approach to building. The rib became dominant. The mason now could envisage the vault as a framed apparatus of curved ribs braced into position by panels of thin stone or brick webbing. The parallel with framed systems of construction in timber was too obvious to be missed. Driven to experiment by the insistent need for better lighting, the mason began to define thrusts and concentrate loads in order to pare away the supports. Both mason and carpenter began to converge in their detailing, each learning from the other. The carpenter turned to monumental and permanent fabrics while the mason applied the analytic techniques of the carpenter to the masonry frame. Without a clearly stated and logically developed theory of structure to work from, the mason had to sense intuitively from the evidence of failure and distortion, the lines of pressure in the buttress and vault.

With this new dynamic and open structure the complexities of stilting and skewed panels could be swept aside to make way for a much simpler technique: the pointed arch, with curves swung without change from support to crown. With this pointing of the arch ring the planes of the vault changed from smoothly curved surfaces to acutely folded prisms. The layout of the arch rings and ribs became a simple geometric exercise in the drawing of arcs rather than a wavering and indecisive meeting of planes. Stilting now could be retained as an aesthetic device, as in the adaption of the vault to the tall narrow clerestory window openings in the French Gothic.

Without question, the use of the broken or pointed arch initially was encouraged by contact with Mohammedan builders in the Holy Land and in Spain, who for centuries had used this distinctive motif in their designs. By the middle of the twelfth century masons began to use the pointed arch ring. In Jerusalem, the portal of the Church of the Holy Sepulchre, built from 1140 to 1144, has pointed arches over the doors. Built five years later, the west front of Chartres has recessed and pointed arch rings. This intercultural contact was just the spark needed to kindle the Gothic. Brought to the north by returning crusaders, the pointed arch became the touchstone which freed the Christian church from the dominance of the heavy wall and the classic weight of the round arch. The Christian clerics and apologists of northern Europe gave no credit to the immediate Muslim source for this innovation. Unknowing plagiarism has never been a crime in architecture; in fact it is the lifeblood of design. So useful was the application that in a very few years the pointed arch became *the* motif and signal for Christian fervour.

The severe monumental solidity of the massive arch rings and plain masonry surfaces at Montmajour abbey contrast with the light skeletal linear accents of the diagonal ribs at the crossing.

The future of medieval architecture lay with sparse skeletal frames; the chapter house at Silvacane reflects this new Gothic linear emphasis.

In the fifty years from 1150 the pointed arch became the single most conspicuous element of Gothic architecture. When applied to the arch rings or ribs of vaults, the pointed form, with its intersecting arcs, avoided the tortuous expedients imposed by the round arch. The pointed rib was simpler, more practical, and better suited to the methods of construction and layout. Now arcs could be swung from the supports with varying curvatures to meet at the ridge. On a square compartment with two semicircular diagonals, level crowns were made possible by describing arcs, not from the centre of the span but from separate points on the springing line, usually the third points, creating a 'tierspoint' arch.

The advantages were immediately manifest. Segmental transverse arch rings could not swing up in a smooth curve from the pier springing without the need for stilting. Over the nave the more or less level longitudinal fold powerfully reinforced the linear axis to the altar.

Over the ambulatory, where wedge-shaped trapezoids had proved particularly awkward to vault, the use of pointed profiles for transverse and longitudinal arches avoided the twisted groins created by the intersection of round-arched web profiles. A very early instance of this usage was made at Morienval Abbey, c. 1125. Though the primitive pointed arch vault over the porch at Moissac about 1120 is earlier, the Durham nave vault showed the first consistent application of the pointed form. The transverse arch rings, built 1128, swing up in two segments to meet in a very shallow fold.

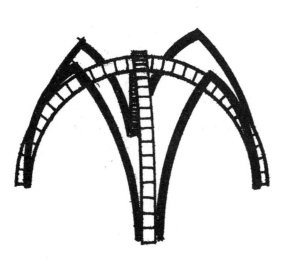

Transverse pointed arch rings could be raised to the height of semicircular diagonals without the need for stilting.

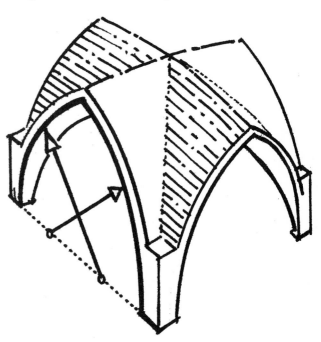

Pointed profiles were swung from centres at varying widths on the springing line. In the 'tierspoint' arch, the third points were centres.

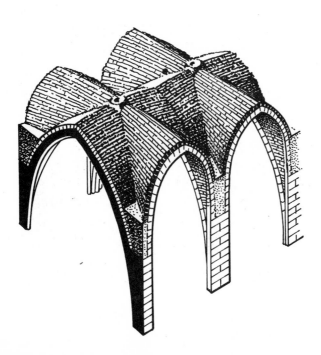

In the pointed vault the arcs intersected to create an entire system of curved and folded plates.

From 1140 to 1180 the architects of St Denis abbey and Sens, Noyon, and Laon cathedrals elaborated upon the themes of rib and panel, shaft and pier, pointing ribs and arches to create a new vocabulary of design, the Gothic.

At Laon, by 1170, the masons began to dissolve the wall to translate its mass into a ribbed and strutted cage. The regular rows of round piers sweeping down the nave accord with the new concept of the building as a modular assemblage of repetitive and framed elements. But the system still was not quite complete. Sexpartite vaulting demanded some recognition of the alternation of supports if the vault was to be properly keyed to the nave arcade. Round piers wtih widely flared stepped caps carried alternating clusters of three or five shafts.

Evidently concerned by the illogicality of this arrangement, the second architect of the building programme after 1178 added shafts to some of the alternate piers which created an awkward link between vault and support but nonetheless pointed the way to the future development of the Gothic in which rib and shaft would interlock to carry the dynamic interplay of structure from the apex of the vault to footing at the floor. The vaults at Laon, again, are typical of this transitional phase. Only the transverse arch rings are pointed. The diagonals remain as semicircular arcs and the wall arches are round.

In a sense, Laon was an engineering achievement in which the masons added new structural components to outworn Romanesque patterns. The complex, horizontal accents of the four-tier nave arcade, composed of aisle with pier and arch, gallery, triforium arcade and, clerestory window, were not yet keyed to the new emphasis upon framed, vertical support. The elements of the Gothic were deployed as a surface decoration over the expanses of walling and the heavy vaulted gallery needed to restrain the thrusts of the vault.

The sober majesty of the eleventh-century Romanesque abbey had been lost. The virile and barbaric sculptural enrichment which had given human scale and emotional impact to the monumental mass of the pilgrimage centre had been rejected. As yet, there were only tantalizing suggestions of the new structural daring which could reinvigorate the main stream of building.

A new freedom and a new flexibility in the handling of structural components had made possible the concentration of loads and thrusts upon isolated pier supports. The logic of framed construction now suggested light and airy open halls suited to the needs of burghers and townsmen in a resurgent Europe. To realize to the full the potentialities of this new structural system demanded a complete rethinking of the problem of the masonry wall.

At the crossing of Laon an ingenious octopartite vault adapted the skewed panels to the rectangular compartment.

Along the nave at Laon cylindrical piers with widely flared caps carried the wall shafts.

*After 1178, the second architect at Laon added
detached shafts to alternate piers.*

*In the internal nave elevation at Laon the four-part
horizontal treatment cuts across the verticality of
the shaft.*

*On the west front of Laon the wheel window of the
Romanesque begins to change to the light tracery
of the Gothic.*

8

BUTTRESSES

The heavy wall of the early Romanesque was ideally suited to absorb the continuous thrusts of barrel vaulting. By the eleventh century masons had found that long semicircular barrels or quarter barrels over the gallery or high aisle were sufficient to carry the thrusts to the external walling. When combined with bracing arches at each bay carrying plate masonry, vault, piers, and wall were locked into a rigid assembly. So successful was this usage in the south of France that in the Auvergne it became a provincial variant which was used well into the Gothic. The severe planar walling, massive simplicity, and tiny windows suited a Mediterranean climate. But when used in Normandy, as at the Abbaye aux Hommes, Caen, about 1075, the quadrant barrel blocked out light needed in the nave.

The Norman masons who built Durham cathedral from 1093 made the earlier Romanesque obsolete by building ribbed cross vaults over the wide spans of the choir.[1] This permitted the use of sizeable clerestory window openings by concentrating the thrusts of the vaulting upon the pier supports. When the upper work of the choir was being carried out from 1099 to 1104 the continuous quadrant barrel was rejected, but the semicircular arches with a diaphragm plate were retained. As it happened, the first vault failed because of inexpert construction of the vaulting webs, built of stones laid on the flat with wide mortar joints, but the arched buttressing over the gallery remained unchanged. Ribbed vaults, pier supports, clerestory lighting, and isolated points of restraint for vault thrusts made Durham a critical point in the history of Gothic.

From what we know of the statics of vault construction it is quite evident that the abutment of these semicircular arch rings just at the springing point of the vault is poorly placed to restrain bursting forces above the haunching. Fortunately, the pier and wall construction in the Durham choir was heavy enough to redistribute the stresses to these gallery arch rings.

Evidently the masons at Durham sensed this problem, because in the work on the nave completed by 1133 they used isolated quadrant arch rings beneath the gallery roof. These were more efficient than the round arches because they abutted on a higher point on the pier. Although they were as yet only tentative responses to the precise articulation and definition of thrust and load, they pointed the way to the continual heightening of buttressing systems to meet the thrusts of the high vaults.

In the change from the Romanesque to the Gothic this posed a particular dilemma to the architect. On the one hand, he was anxious to open the top sides of the nave as much as possible to a flood of light. On the other, as the vaults climbed ever higher on the pier system, some means had to be found to stabilize and restrain the vault thrusts. Quadrant arch rings set under a pitched gallery roof seriously limited the size of the clerestory window openings. About 1175 at St Denis and Vézelay these restraining arch rings were moved up above the gallery roof to become exposed flying buttresses.

NOTE
1 Kenneth John Conant *Carolingian and Romanesque Architecture* (Penguin Books 1959) 290

A quadrant barrel over the gallery was ideally suited to take the continuous thrusts of the barrel vault. (after Viollet-le-Duc)

OVERLEAF *A dramatic technological triumph harnessed to a religious dream. Nave buttresses, Chartres*

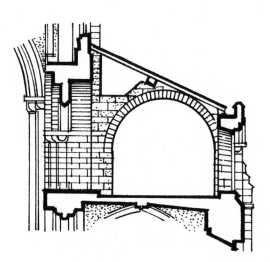

The ribbed cross vaults in the choir at Durham cathedral demanded point buttressing at the piers. About 1104 the masons constructed them as semicircular arch rings. (after Bond)

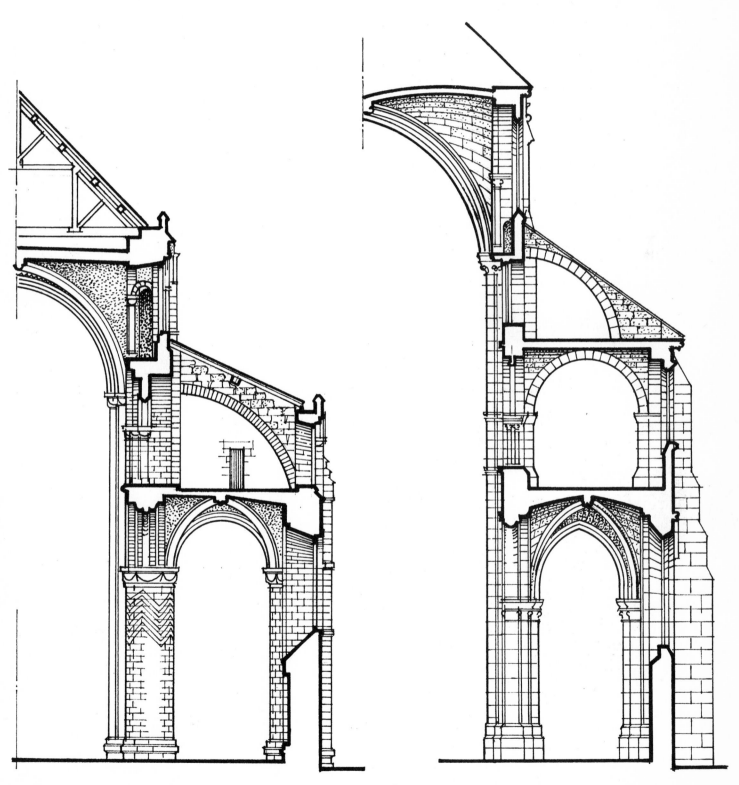

The quadrant arch system of buttressing along the
nave at Durham is better adapted to restrain the
bursting forces above the haunching of the vault.

The quadrant arches carrying the thrusts of the
vaulting across triforium and gallery continued to be
hidden beneath a timber and slate pitched roof in St
Germer abbey, Oise. [see page 92] (after Porter)

The creation of Durham was a brilliant tour de force decades before its time. Not only was the structural system an innovation leading directly into the Gothic, but the three-phase nave elevation with aisle, triforium, and clerestory was a simple and direct solution to the problems of nave lighting, point support, and aisle vaulting.

In northern France in the middle of the twelfth century, designers preferred a more complex nave elevation. At St Germer Abbey near Beauvais, begun after 1132, they placed a substantial gallery over the comparatively low aisle. The triforium then became a blind area on the nave walling, hiding under a pitched roof the arched buttresses necessary to carry the thrusts of the nave vaulting over the gallery to the external buttresses. Finally, in the space above the triforium they punched through the walling with clerestory windows to light the nave.

This aisle, gallery, triforium, and clerestory sequence created tiers of vaulted compartments more than sufficient to brace the nave piers into position against the thrust of the high nave vaults. At the same time the arcades and pierced screens fronting the triforium and the gallery established strong horizontal accents running along the nave. On the other hand, the vaults over the nave, similar to those at Durham, had semicircular diagonal ribs and pointed transverse arch rings. It would have been quite possible to terminate these strongly accented ribs at a bracket corbelled out from the pier without weakening the fabric, but the masons evidently were searching for ways in which the deliberate statement of concentrated thrust and load implied by the skeletal rib could be expressed on the pier. They sprung each rib and arch from a cap carried on a slender vertical shaft attached to the pier. The attached shafts established a strong vertical accent cutting across the horizontal emphasis of gallery and triforium.

When we examine in detail the situation at the springing in this or a typical Burgundian Gothic example it is quite evident that the loads and thrusts generated in the vault ribs are immediately dissipated in the mass of the pier, to travel down to grade via the arched buttresses and vertically through the interlocking stones of the pier core. In a strict interpretation, the ribs, the attached shafts, and vertical pier modellings are structurally not needed. Nonetheless as aesthetic devices they work well, inscribing, as it were, lines of force on the shell of the vault or the mass of the pier to reinforce visually a skeletal emphasis. Here we begin to see the analytic approach of the northern carpenter, who frames an assemblage of narrow linear components into a cage, by changing the heavy mass of Romanesque masonry into carefully articulated skeletal fabrics of stone.

At the clerestory window openings masons emphasized the structure by placing the thin web of stone carrying the glass on the outer surface of the pier. By so doing they divorced the wall and window from the springing of the vault to become thin membranes hung from the supporting piers, a deliberate dissociation of structural frame and sheathing skin.

In construction we build up, but in analysis we must work down from vault to grade, tracing the effects of concentrated lines of thrust upon the supporting piers and buttresses. This is just how the master mason conceived the structure. Starting with the vault form, he designed down the piers carrying the forces through to grade. No longer satisfied with squat and heavy piers which concealed this flow of forces, he modelled his supports to create a coherent unity. More had been achieved than a merely aesthetic incising of lines of support on the pier. The nave was dissolved into a thin tracery of arcaded stone webs. The heavy mass of material in the wall, earlier deemed necessary to accept the thrusts of the vaults, had been moved out to isolated buttresses projecting beyond the aisle at each bay.

The section through the nave at Laon shows the next step in this dissolution of the nave wall. The passageway along the triforium was reduced to a narrow footwalk piercing through the nave piers so that a continuous plate of masonry could guide thrusts to the external pier. The clerestory window-opening began to expand, cramping the triforium arcade. But this brought the buttress restraint to a point well below the haunching of the vault.

The inadequacy of this buttress restraint later forced the architects at Laon to add a new element to each pier: quadrant arches above the triforium roof, based upon the early flying buttresses of Notre Dame at Paris.[1] Swung from a point well above the haunching to the external buttresses, these exposed quadrant arches stabilized the top of the nave pier against bursting forces generated by the nave vaults. The light and tenuous framework of arches and pier buttresses was divorced from wall and roof to become a permanent masonry centering.

NOTE

1 Paul Frankl *Gothic Architecture* (Penguin Books 1962) 44

In the middle of the twelfth century designers began to divorce the screen of glass from the springing of the vault. (after Viollet-le-Duc)

At Laon a continuous passageway, cut through the pier at the triforium level, gave access to the upper construction. The clerestory remained cramped by the pitched roof over the gallery vault, though a flying quadrant buttress between the clerestory windows took the thrusts of the vaults.

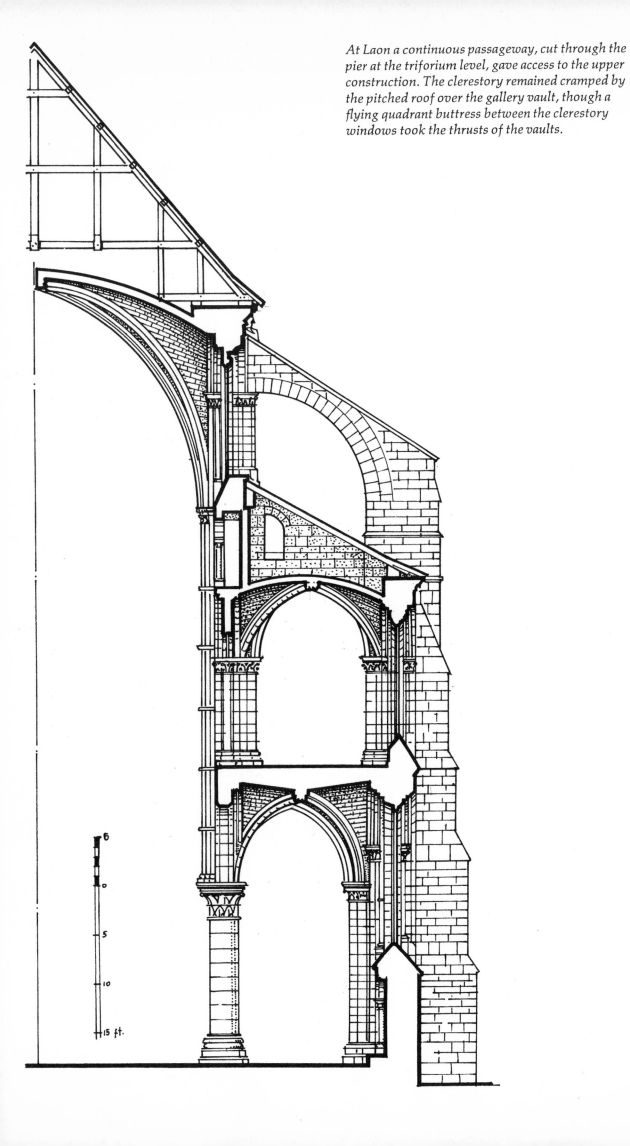

Gothic was above all else an analytic architecture. Too many failures of the towers, vaults, and walls of the early Romanesque had taught the builder that sheer bulk and hulking mass alone could not ensure the stability of the fabric. Indeed, too heavy a vault,

Thirteenth-century Gothic masonry engineering in the nave wall of Notre Dame, Dijon, c 1225. (after Viollet-le-Duc)

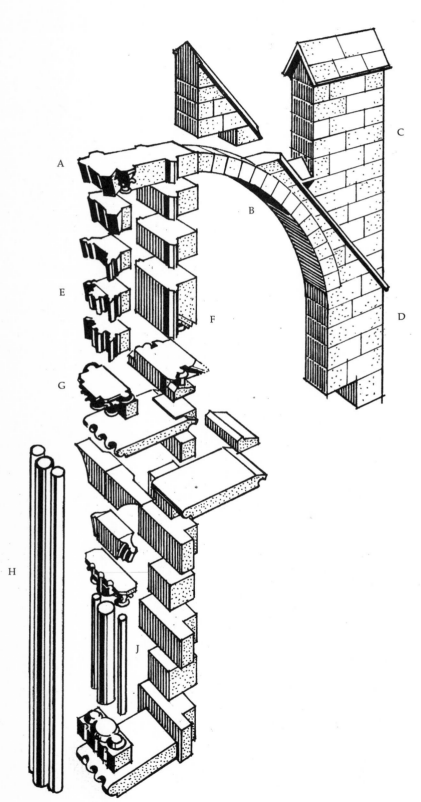

too massive a structure, imperilled rather than strengthened the building. What was needed was a precise and judicious paring away of the design so that there was just enough material to take the load – and no more. The search for greater height in the nave, the effort to open the building to the light of day, meant that the early Romanesque masses of mortar and rubble were replaced by precisely articulated and carefully interlocked cut stone, disposed where it was needed and nowhere else.

By the first quarter of the thirteenth century the stonemason's craft had so improved that architects with refined stereotomy could lock the building elements in continuous restraint against vault thrust, gravity loads, wind loading, and earthquake shock. By interlocking one component with another they could now create an exposed skeletal fabric capable of securing the delicate balance of a vault constructed more than one hundred feet above the floor.

The Gothic masons created static engines of ingenious workmanship which approached the very limits of load-bearing masonry construction. Viollet-le-Duc's study of the wall section of Notre Dame at Dijon, built about 1225, is a good demonstration of this.[1] At the top the thrusts of the vault are received by the 'tas-de-charge' A which pierces through the wall pier to press against the arched ring of the flying buttress B. A canted plane of masonry resting on the arch ring braces the upper portion of the wall pier. Vault thrusts transmitted over the aisle and triforium merge with the vertical loads of the pinnacle C to be deflected down safely through the mass of the external buttress D to resolution at grade outside the main body of the church. The springing of the vaults E sweeps down past the clerestory window openings at F, to be received by the caps G and freestanding shafts H, quite independent of the triforium passage J, which has its own shaft and arcade system. Throughout the structure, ribs and attached shafts dramatically express the linear concentration of load and thrust, though, in actual fact, the loads are for the most part carried by the wall pier F and thrusts are diverted outside to the buttress.

Applied to the fabric of the great French Gothic cathedral churches of the thirteenth century, this analytic separation of traceried screen, pier support, and external buttress spelt the death knell of the heavy wall. So strong was the impact of the vaulting rib that architects extended it down the pier, over to the buttress, across the huge window openings as a stone tracery, and finally over every residual plane of masonry on the interior. The linear accent of the directed thrust became an expressive line concealing every vestige of mass and solidity inside and on the exterior.

NOTE

1 Eugène Viollet-le-Duc *Dictionnaire raisonné de l'architecture française du onzième au seizième siècle* (Paris 1858–68) IV, 'Construction' plate 78

The thirteenth-century cathedral system was dictated by the placement of vaults high above a relatively narrow nave. Thrusts in the vaulting were channelled into the rib and vaulting crease, to be carried across the aisle through exposed flying buttresses to the heavy mass of the external buttress. Gravity loads generated by the weight of vaulting and upper walls were distributed to the nave piers. The designers emphasized this supporting role by attaching vertical shafts to the pier. It was Viollet-le-Duc in the nineteenth century who first grasped that the Gothic cathedral was a carefully articulated frame rather than a box. In his *Discourses on Architecture* he stated: 'The stability of every point of support was regulated by the kind and amount of work it had to perform. Every thrust of an arch found another thrust to cancel it. Walls disappeared, and became only screens, not supports. The whole system became a frame ...'[1] In place of the heavy wall and plastic shell which spread and diffused loads, the Gothic mason concentrated loads and defined supports. In this Cartesian separation of the structure into clear and distinct parts each element had to do more than merely accept its load or transfer a thrust. It had to be so designed that it aggressively proclaimed its role, dramatically evoking in the mind of the viewer the normally hidden play of forces.

With an engineer's bias, Viollet-le-Duc took a deterministic and rational approach to the problems of Gothic structure. He assumed that each element had been shaped to meet a specific structural need. The depth of a rib, the thickness of a vaulting web, the profile of a shaft, all reflected a precise and acute response to structural need. In short, he described the building as a technological artifact in which every part was the end result of a carefully considered logical process, in which the exacting skills of the engineer and the comparative studies of the efficiency expert shaped the whole fabric. Arguing back from the evidence of the completed fabric he showed how each part fulfilled a specific role in the total structure. It was a brilliant summation, a theory which laid the foundations for a century of structural rationalism. In no small way this theory contributed to the growth of a new twentieth-century response to architecture in which structural necessity and functional logic become the catchwords of a new structuralism and a new functionalism.[2]

After one hundred years we have discovered that it is all not quite that simple. The Gothic is not just the creation of an engineer; it is not explicable as merely the result of hardheaded structural analysis and a commonsense response to climate, material, and skill, any more than the imaginative spatial dynamic of design today is the result of businesslike economy. There is an element of theatre in all architecture. At its best it can be seen as an effort to give physical substance at a large scale to the mythic dreams and ideals of a society. At its worst it can be taken as a calculated effort to dress up the image of a power elite. But without the art of the engineer and the imagination of the designer the building is just not built. It remains a phrase on the politician's lips.

NOTES

1 Eugène Viollet-le-Duc *Discourses on Architecture* translated by Henry Van Brunt (Boston 1875) VII, 276–7
2 Donald Hoffman 'Frank Lloyd Wright and Viollet-le-Duc' *Journal of the Society of Architectural Historians* 28, 3 (1969) 173–83

Skeletal wall, arched and framed transverse bents, and folded shell vaults in the nave at Amiens. Triforium and gallery were combined in an arcaded passage. (after Viollet-le-Duc)

By the opening of the thirteenth century, precise cutting of the stones of the vaulting webs and ribs, careful interlocking of the masonry in pier and buttress, and the stiffening action of the warped planes of vaulting, led to a progressive reduction of mass in every element of the Gothic cathedral. Vaulting webs began to thin down from the 12- to 15-inch depths of the twelfth century to the 6- and even 4-inch thicknesses of the later Gothic.[1] With less redundant weight in the vaulting webs, thrusts were proportionately reduced. As a result the wall could be changed to a thin lattice of tracery, ribs, and piers.

At Amiens, about 1220, Robert de Luzarches could confidently embark upon a design in which tall slender piers supported vaults 140 feet above the floor.[2] To counter the thrust of the quadripartite vaults he used two tiers of slender flying buttresses, the lower taking the thrusts of the vault and the upper stabilizing the thin walls and piers against the buffeting of the winds: a considerable force, for walls and roofs projected high above the surrounding buildings.[3]

Though the medieval architects could not analyse loads and thrusts through force-vector diagrams, they evidently had an effective, if empirical, understanding of the capacities of stone. Such mathematical formulae as they used were *ad hoc* generalizations based upon past experience with the material.[4] They brought to the job a refined proprioceptive feeling for the response of material under load, and it is evident that they had no mean skill at qualitative analysis of the elements, even if they could not assign a numerical factor to the precise loading paths.

The thirteenth-century mason effectively substituted for the ponderous massive box of the Romanesque a range of complex portal frames disposed across the main axis of the church. Each portal frame was specifically designed to carry the weight and to resolve the thrusts of the high vaults. Longitudinally, the frames were braced into position by the nave vaulting shells, the clerestory arcade and, at a lower level, by the triforium arcade, the aisle vaults, and the external aisle walls: certainly sufficient to stabilize the main fabric along the nave. But the upper portions of the slender and exposed buttresses were braced in only one plane by the flying buttresses. Under excessive loading conditions – during a storm when winds of up to eighty miles could buffet the tall flank and timber roof of the cathedral – the buttresses would tend to flex or rotate under these loads. The result of these rotational or flexural movements could be cracking of the buttresses above the aisle roofs. Model analysis of bay sections of Amiens and St Ouen at Rouen has disclosed tensile forces in the top outer edge of buttresses and in the outer fibre of the nave piers above the aisle vaults.[5]

The braced portal frames of the thirteenth-century Gothic saved the concept of the tall glass cage for a generation. The combination of buttress, flying arch, rib, pier, and panel ensured that loads could be transmitted from vault to frame and from there to grade without undue cracking of stone or mortar.

Initial model analysis of Gothic structures indicates that the medieval mason managed to avoid extreme concentrations of compressive stresses in his structure.

Stone masonry and lime mortar in combination have some slight tensile strength but the designer who relies upon this bond to hold his fabric together will eventually have trouble, and this is the situation in many Gothic cathedrals today. If the portal frame is braced at A, B, and C the buttress can still deflect in numerous ways. Model analysis shows that there is a measurable tensile stress in the outer surface of the buttress, under gravity loading.[6] The buttress thrusts out and down, compressing the inner surface and extending the outer face. Gothic masons introduced a pinnacle at the outer face of the buttress to counterweight this tendency to crack although it would be normal to assume that the pinnacle would be better placed further in from the face. The Gothic mason evidently knew what he was about.

The thrust of the aisle vaults on the nave pier was small but it was by no means negligible. Over the years, the piers bowed inwards in response to this persistent pressure. In French Gothic cathedrals, built of carefully interlocked masonry with fine mortar joints, this deformation has been so small as to be unnoticeable. But where the cathedrals were built of brick with wide mortar joints, as along the Baltic coast at Lübeck, the plasticity of the mortar has led to a clearly visible deformation. The piers have bent in at the haunching of the aisle vaults and above the aisle this flexure of the pier, in response to the thrusts of the aisle vault and the overturning pressures of the high vaults, has led to some cracking of the outer and exposed surface of the pier above the aisle roofs.[7]

Gothic builders were quite aware of the differing behaviour of materials. They knew that wood was excellent for spans because of its resistance to bending. Metal made a useful cramp or tension tie and stone could never be trusted as a beam. Perhaps they could not explain this in terms of tension or compression but in day by day usage they exhibited an appreciation of the capacities of building materials. Despite highly skeletonized forms the masons proved able to reduce most of the major stresses to compression loadings. But in so doing, they used forms reminiscent of timber framing: the braced portals of stone recall the timber bents of a great hall; the ribs meet at connectors carved as bosses; the tracery reduces mass and plane to a fretwork of line; shafts are physically separated from the piers, so that the support reads as a bundle of linear elements. In a sense, the cathedral is a masonry structure designed *as if* it were of timber or cast metal. Indeed much of the decorative detailing of the thirteenth-century Gothic would appear better suited to cast iron or extruded metal.

*External apparatus of the thirteenth-century Gothic
structural system: shell vaults concentrated loads to
the ribs and then to piers. Vertical loads were carried
down the nave piers and thrusts spread through the
flying arches to the mass of the buttresses, outside
the sheathing wall.*

NOTES

1 John Fitchen *The Contruction of Gothic Cathedrals* (Oxford 1961) appendix E, 256–9
2 Paul Frankl *Gothic Architecture* (Penguin Books 1962) 92–4
3 John Fitchen 'A Comment on the Function of the Upper Flying Buttress in French Gothic Architecture' *Gazette des Beaux Arts* series 6, 45 (February 1955) 69–90
4 George Kubler 'A Late Gothic Computation of Rib Vault Thrusts' *Gazette des Beaux Arts* series 6, 26 (1944) 135–48
5 Robert Mark and Ronald S. Jonash 'Wind Loading on Gothic Structure' *Journal of the Society of Architectural Historians* 29, 3 (1970) 222–30
6 Robert Mark and Richard Alan Prentke 'Model Analysis of Gothic Structure' *Journal of the Society of Architectural Historians* 27, 1 (1968) 44–8
7 Mark and Jonash 'Wind Loading on Gothic Structure' 229

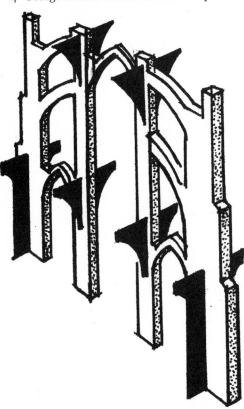

The Gothic substituted transversely braced portal frames for the massive box of the Romanesque, but these delicately poised masonry frames were subject to numerous distortions.

The tall buttresses tended to flex under load in the unsupported outer surface, unless braced longitudinally as at Narbonne, or the entire mass of the buttress rotated under excessive loading.

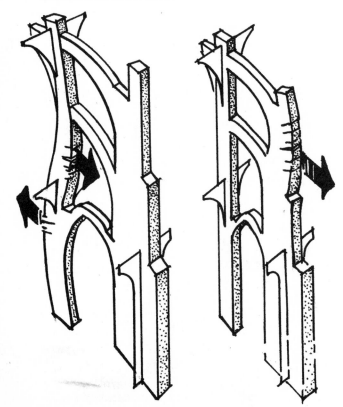

Choir, St Just, Narbonne

Internal piers bowed inwards in response to the pressures of the aisle vaults. Many French Gothic cathedrals show cracks in the outer surface of the buttress piers, the result of flexure.

The thirteenth-century French Gothic cathedral is one of the rare examples in the history of building of an external structural apparatus supporting a much smaller internal space. For the most part, clients want the most building for the least structural expense but in this period abbot and bishop were quite content to pay for a delicate and expensive skeletal frame built around a restricted internal volume. There is a certain grand illogic to this approach. Once having completed the intricate fabric of rib, panel, pier, arch, and buttress the architect placed the sheathing wall of glass, iron, and stone just outside the line of the nave piers, not, as might be expected, along the exterior to protect the whole delicate masonry structure. Opting for a translucent screen wall along the side of the nave, the medieval architect emphasized extreme height, dramatic verticality, and the largest possible window openings to carry the decorative panoply of coloured glass. He designed the building from the inside out, adding flying buttresses, external buttressing piers, and vertical pinnacles to prop the tremulous glass cage into position.

Much of the psychological tension and dynamic effect comes from this decision to emphasize dramatic verticality. The French Gothic cathedral was an abstruse and abstract phenomenon, tensed, lithe, and energetic, but dangerously exposed. As such it is the epitome of the agile and refined scholasticism of medieval Christianity. Harmony and containment, serenity and balance were not the objectives of the enthusiastic European burghers who sponsored its construction. They were searching for daring and exciting romances in stone, in logic, and in religion which could counter the heavy earthbound clay of practical good sense and pragmatic reason.

The designer who rebuilt the nave of Chartres after a fire in 1194 took the critical step which made possible the glass cage of the Gothic.[1] He entirely suppressed the gallery, lowering the side roof to cover the aisle vaults alone. The clerestory window openings could now extend well below the vault springings, flooding the nave with light.

To attain this dissolution of the wall, the master at Chartres devised an external buttressing system with three tiers of arch rings swinging out to a projecting buttress, the two lower arcs braced together by radiating struts to ensure rigidity. Along the nave he shaped these struts as small columns carrying heavy round arches; around the choir they evolved into pierced stone plates, cut with sharp facets and pointed arches.

Because loads and thrusts from the vault were concentrated at isolated points, the architect could design the nave windows with complete freedom. Decorative round windows surmounting tall lancet openings were cut through a plate of stone. In this early 'plate' tracery substantial stone bracing was left to ensure the stability of the sheets of stained glass. Small pieces of chemically tinted glass, with a painted and fired overlay of detail, were set in lead cames or mouldings, and then were braced into position against wind loading by wiring the leaded glass to wrought iron bars. Colour in the interior moved from wall to window, emphasizing the new dominance of the glass screen. The interior of the cathedral turned into a shifting chiaroscuro of colour as the heavy lenses of coloured glass dissolved and refracted the sunlight. Along the nave only a faint echo remains of the earlier Romanesque alternation of pier and column: the shafts change from round to polygonal at each bay.

NOTE

1 Paul Frankl *Gothic Architecture* (Penguin Books 1962) 79

By the opening years of the thirteenth century masons could adapt the ribbed quadripartite vault to narrow bays. The cracking of the webs in the transverse vaults occurred as the wall arches and fill pulled away from the centre of the vault under thrust at the haunching. Chartres, from 1194

At Chartres cathedral after 1194 a three-tiered
buttressing arrangement let the clerestory expand
to carry large windows.

At the opening of the thirteenth century, despite the stunning effect of the structural achievements of the northern French masons, regional diversity in the interpretation of the new Gothic motifs remained as strong a factor as it had been during the Romanesque. In the north a reversed T section with high nave and low aisle favoured the exposed buttress and the immense clerestory window. In the south, where there was less need for large windows and a long tradition of spacious internal volumes, the hall church with nave and aisle of almost equal height remained the dominant form.

Bourges, well to the south of Paris and open to influences from the Auvergne and Burgundy, was the site for a highly original fusion of northern engineering and southern spatial unity. Perhaps because the archbishop of Bourges, Henri de Sully, was a brother of Eude de Sully, archbishop of Paris, it was decided before 1199 at Bourges to build a new cathedral with double aisles on the model of Paris.[1] As at Chartres the architect rejected galleries, but he added the space so gained to the inner aisle. The high vaults of the inner aisles, the two ranges of triforium arcading in the nave and aisle, and the stepped fenestration, compose a generous internal volume, a broadly based triangle quite different from the narrow verticality of Chartres.

The experimental nature of Bourges is revealed in the twisted ribs used over the skew-shaped bays of the ambulatory. In this regression back to a form which had perplexed the Romanesque masons, the first architect of Bourges failed to follow the logical expedient which had been devised for Notre Dame in Paris where interlocking triangular segments of vaulting simply solved the continuing problem of the irregular compartments over the ambulatory. As well, the sexpartite vaults over the nave at Bourges look back to the Romanesque rather than forward to the Gothic. On the exterior, the wall plates are pierced by simple geometric figures and the buttressing sweeps up in doubled tiers over the stepped aisles to meet the thrust of the high vaults. The aedicular 'temples,' which make Chartres so reminiscent of the early Gothic of Laon, do not disfigure Bourges'. In plan, the suppression of the transept unifies the internal axis so that there is no impediment to the focus upon the altar.

Bourges is marked by straightforward, if conservative, engineering, a surety of touch in the details and a spacious simplicity of treatment. There is an inventive freshness and an architectonic imagination evident in the over-all concept which stands in direct contrast to the hard codification of the vocabulary of the Gothic emerging in the Paris basin. The broad straddling strength of the design, evolving from the logic of structure, is not dissimilar to the pyramidal volumes and braced structures of the great timbered halls of the Middle Ages. In each the structural module dictates the solution; it is not added as an afterthought to brace or stay a preconceived volume. Had the designers of northern France followed the trail blazed by Bourges the folly of Beauvais would have been avoided.

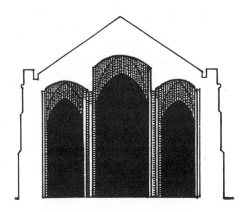

In the south of France the hall church with one or two rows of piers emphasized a cool, spacious interior.

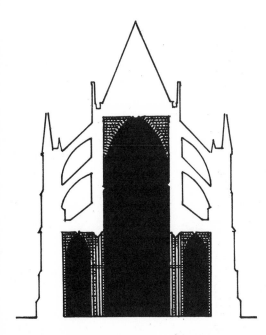

Northern Gothic architects preferred a reversed T section with high nave and low aisle. Reims

At Bourges the stepped aisles allowed soaring height in the nave and a spatial continuity in the triangular volume.

*The stepped aisles at Bourges were logically adjusted
to the sweep of the buttressing. (after Branner and
Viollet-le-Duc)*

NOTE

1 Robert Branner *La cathédrale de Bourges et sa place
dans l'architecture gothique* (Paris/Bourges 1962)
153–4

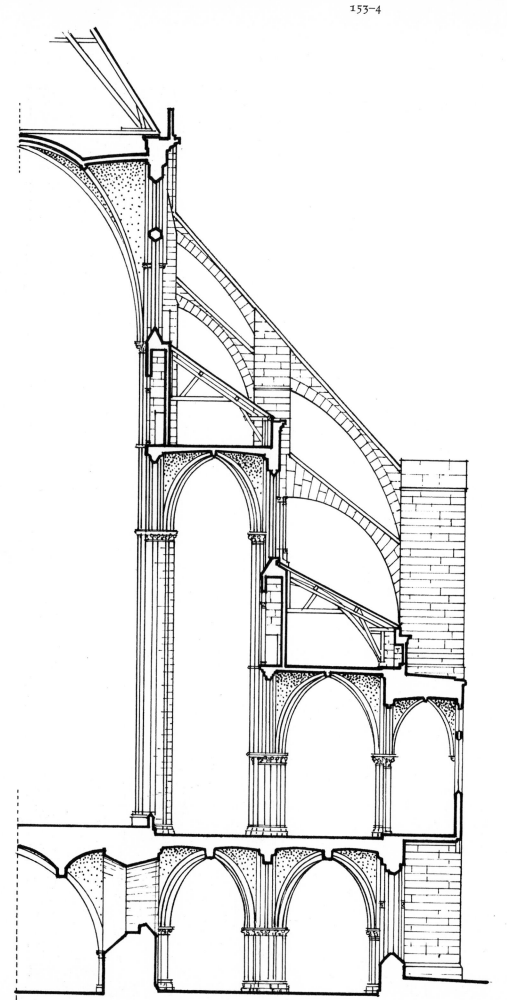

*Twisted ribs in the trapezoidal compartments of the
ambulatory at Bourges. 1199–1218*

Perhaps the neatest solution to the vaulting problem of wedged compartments was devised over the ambulatory at Notre Dame, Paris. Suppressing one diagonal converted the vault to interlocking triangular segments.

The high inner aisle at Bourges gave prominence to the soaring accent of the tall piers. The large square sexpartite compartments of the nave vaulting were conservatively designed with slender rib profiles.

Buttresses at Bourges were designed with a spare, engineered simplicity. The clerestory windows were cut through a plate of stone to give the greatest emphasis to the glass pattern.

Building in the Middle Ages was a versatile discipline, peculiarly responsive to local needs, and masons were singularly adept at contriving diverse and novel responses to the ever-changing demands of a rapidly evolving society. The cathedral was but one facet of the energetic technology of a reawakened Europe, but it brought to a narrow focus the aspirations of the local community. The High Gothic cathedrals of northern France were 'engines' of the faith and testaments to civic pride.

The northern interpretation of the Gothic was confined to the elaboration of the tall, narrow cage of glass for political reasons. Jean d'Orbais, the architect of Reims, elected in 1210 to follow the conservative basilican section of Chartres rather than the pyramidal volume of Bourges, rejecting the influence of the south.[1] To have modelled Reims, the coronation church of the kings of France, upon Bourges would have been a clear admission of the supremacy of the Angevin south in matters of design. For so important a structure local patriotism outweighed the purely architectural factors.

At Reims, the tentative experiments of Chartres were formed into a consistent system. D'Orbais kept the aisle comparatively low, giving greatest emphasis to the curtain wall of glass. Flying buttresses were simplified to two arcs swinging up from the pier. Adding a pinnacle to each buttress counterweighted the thrust of the high flying buttresses and directed the pressures into the heavy mass. He carved and modelled the pinnacles with arcade, shafts, and crockets, minimizing their apparent bulk and lightening their apparent importance.

The special concern of the architects at Reims with problems of structural stability is evident in the membrane walls of masonry introduced above the vaults at each bay to take the thrust of the upper tiers of flying buttresses. As well, flying arches were constructed above the vaulting at the crossing to stabilize the corner piers.

At Chartres and Bourges the clerestory windows had been pierced through plates of stone. At Reims the architect applied the principle of the rib to brace the immense sheets of leaded glass against the wind. A structural expedient, bar tracery in stone, contributed to the over-all unity of the final design. The ribbing of vaults, the tracery of the windows, the rippling modulation of the shafts cutting down the piers, were linear motifs scribing lines of force over the structure, and pulling the design into an integrated whole.

One problem remained for solution in this unified

At Reims the thin shells of the vaulting webs and the delicate ribs were braced by fill and by membrane walls at each haunching.

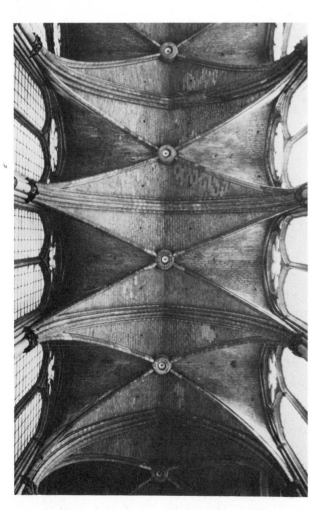

Jean d'Orbais at Reims turned back to the basilican section, keeping the aisle low. He braced the large glass area of the clerestories with bars of stone. The ribs of the quadripartite vaults over the nave dictated a pier system shaped to receive each rib.

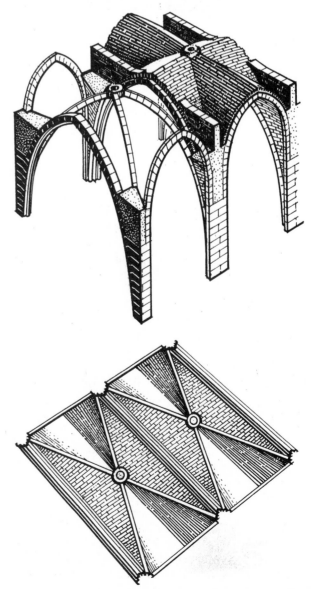

programme. The triforium arcade was blind, blacked out by the pitched roof over the aisle. In the nave of Amiens, from 1220, Robert de Luzarches retained a blind triforium but treated the arcading with tracery to key it to the clerestory windows above. The decisive step was taken by the succeeding architect after 1258 who glazed the triforium arcade in the choir. With this innovation all opaque walling, other than the spandrels above the aisle arcade, was swept away. In the interior, the choir became a vessel of glass, ribbed with stone and covered by a convoluted masonry shell.

NOTE
1 Paul Frankl *Gothic Architecture* (Penguin Books 1962) 86

The system of Reims was copied throughout Europe. At Strasbourg the triforium was pierced for light by surmounting the aisle with a gabled roof. Deep buttressing arches gave a broad support to the vault haunchings.

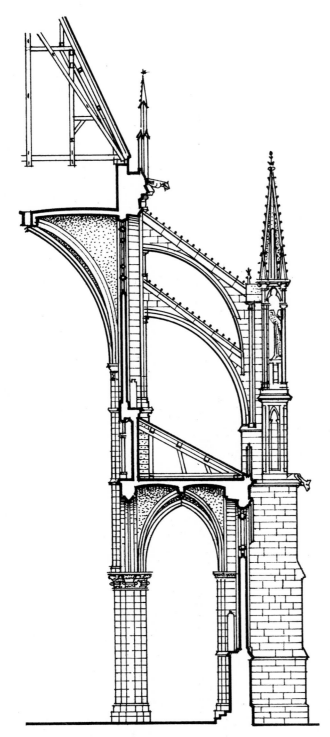

In the cathedral at Reims, Jean d'Orbais reduced mass and surface to line and frame, converted the wall to a braced sheet of glass and the structure to a permanent prop of masonry. (after de Baudot)

The delicate bar tracery at Strasbourg was braced by a grid of wrought iron bars. In turn, the panels of leaded glass were wired to these armatures.

After 1258 the choir arcade at Amiens was glazed, opening the entire wall surface to light. The thin plates of the flying buttresses were pierced with tracery.

109

HIGH GOTHIC:
REIMS
AND AMIENS

The first architect of Beauvais cathedral designed a choir between 1230 and 1240 with vaults higher than any other Gothic church. He introduced a glazed triforium before its use at Amiens, pushed the crown of the vault to over 157 feet above the floor, and spaced the piers widely. In this first use of the glazed triforium, all wall surfaces were cut away, to be replaced by translucent and traceried panels. But he had failed to provide adequate foundations for the crushing loads so generated. The piers settled, and in 1284 the choir vaults fell. Extreme height coupled with attenuation of the supports surpassed the capacities of compression masonry.

Guillaume de Roye and his assistant Aubert d'Aubigny rebuilt the choir with intermediate piers and cross-braced tracery built into the older fabric.[1] To ensure stability in the narrow compartments, they turned back to sexpartite vaulting over the choir and transepts, and keyed the new piers to the existing aisle vaults with a rib and membrane wall.

In the aisles of Beauvais ingenious new membrane stiffeners braced the vaults.

So slender are the buttresses around the choir at Beauvais that they have to be tied together by a lacework of wrought iron bars.

At Beauvais the architects so exaggerated the height that the vaults fell. 1272-

The stone patchwork below the triforium shows where intermediate piers were added to spread the load of the new sexpartite vaults at Beauvais.

The dramatic buttressing of the choir is today held together by a lacework of wrought-iron tie bars, introduced after the collapse of the vaults. Not content with this extreme solution, in 1569 the burghers and clergy of Beauvais, driven by an intemperate and competitive greed for ever greater height, perched a lead-sheathed wood spire 502 feet in height on the crossing piers. Within four years it had fallen, and this last and most desperate venture in the upward striving urge of the Gothic came to an ignominious end.

NOTE

1 Paul Frankl *Gothic Architecture* (Penguin Books 1962) 100

*Elaborate decoration on the south transept,
Beauvais.*

Beauvais was a convincing demonstration that the combination of extreme height with an external skeletal fabric of masonry over the aisles could be carried just so far and no further. Evidently the aim or programme of the Gothic church needed rephrasing. Tense, frenetic, and busy on the exterior, the Gothic cathedral of northern France represented the triumph of a dynamic rationale over cool reason. The exaggerated emphasis upon height, when combined with transparency, dissolved the orderly bounds of building. Dramatic to the extreme, but illogical in its fundamental shape, the classic Gothic substituted a bewildering interplay of structural props and supports for the comprehensible geometry of simple building forms.

One obvious response was to raise the aisle vaults to the nave height, obviating the need for the busy complexity of flying buttressing. In the hall churches of southern France, Catalonia, and central Europe

this approach ensured two more centuries of creative Gothic experiment and will be analysed in later chapters.

In another reaction against the exaggerated engineering of the basilican Gothic the aisle was suppressed, to be replaced by internal or external pier buttresses carrying the glass. Very often small chapels were set between each buttress. In this drastic revision of the customary cathedral plan, French architects again showed the way, in the Sainte Chapelle begun in 1243 at Paris and in the fourteenth-century cathedral at Albi.

The Sainte Chapelle in Paris was a royal chapel dedicated to the display of relics of the crucifixion brought to France by Louis IX from Syria and Constantinople. It had no need for aisles. Freed from functional and structural difficulties imposed by the programmes for the great civic cathedrals, the architect could very simply state the theme of the translucent and delicate glass cage. Quite simple stepped buttresses absorbed the thrusts of the quadripartite ribbed vaults and freed the walls for the introduction of traceried windows. Gables were introduced above each opening, cutting across the heavy horizontal line of the balustrade. These gables add a characteristic rhythmic play to the façade and at the same time stabilize the outer courses of the vaulting webs by adding needed weight above the longitudinal arch ring. The example of this imaginative structure was to challenge the English to comparable feats during the fourteenth and fifteenth centuries.

With no aisles, the royal chapel, la Sainte Chapelle, in Paris, was constructed as a self-contained, framed box.

Sainte Chapelle: pier buttresses and traceried windows reduced the wall to a translucent screen braced between rigid supports.

Across the Pyrenees and along the Mediterranean medieval architects continued to build heavy-walled churches with pointed barrel vaults long after the Normans and the Parisians had turned to Gothic frame structures, for it made good practical sense to turn the building inwards, away from the glaring sun of the southern summer. Certainly this emphasis upon a containing wall simplified the structural problems because loads and thrusts could be dissipated by distribution throughout a heavy mass of walling and buttressing. When Henry II of England and his queen, Eleanor of Anjou, commissioned the choir of Poitiers cathedral about 1162 no attempt was made to copy the emergent glass cage of the north. Instead aisles were built almost to the same

height as the nave so that the effect is that of a vaulted hall. Each vault was built with a very pronounced domical profile. The mason introduced slender diagonal ribs contrasting with the heavy transverse arch ring, but there is little folding in the vault.

When, a century later, the Dominicans built the church, still known as Les Jacobins, at Toulouse, they adapted the concept of the open hall to the new requirements of an order of preaching friars. They used a double nave in which a row of slender central pillars completely destroyed the axis to the altar. Instead the emphasis shifted to the pulpit as the critical element in the church. Not surprisingly, since the area was still under English domination,

In les Jacobins at Toulouse, the double nave with a central row of cylindrical piers was designed for preaching rather than ceremony.

the masons used the complex ribbed vaulting, typical of English Gothic structures, at the terminus of the two naves.

The cathedral at Albi was begun in 1282 by the Dominican inquisitor, Bishop Bernard de Castanct, to celebrate his suppression of the Albigensian heresy. Fittingly, the external aspect of the building is that of a fortress rather than a church, set upon a hilltop with rounded pier buttresses and a tower with archery slits. The architect who completed the original design of the nave in 1390 projected the pier buttresses into the interior, protecting them by the flanking screen walls. He set lateral chapels between the pier buttresses and linked them by openings cut through the buttress base. The vault, a narrow quad-ripartite structure of folded planes, was modelled upon northern techniques, but in every other respect the building looks to the south and the contained simplicity of heavy masonry.

The single great nave of Albi was to influence the design of the nave at Gerona cathedral in Catalonia. In 1416 Guillermo Bofill argued that it was possible to add to the existing choir a nave of single span of 73 feet. His arguments are of some technical interest because they indicate the reliance upon a body of traditional rules for the proportioning of buttresses in relation to vaulting span.[1] He asserted that 'since [the buttresses] have a third more breadth than is required,' the foundations could be used for the striking novelty of dispensing entirely with

Albi cathedral was a brilliant adaptation of the Gothic to the south. The spacious nave was con- *tained by internal buttress masses, expressed on the exterior by cylindrical projections.*

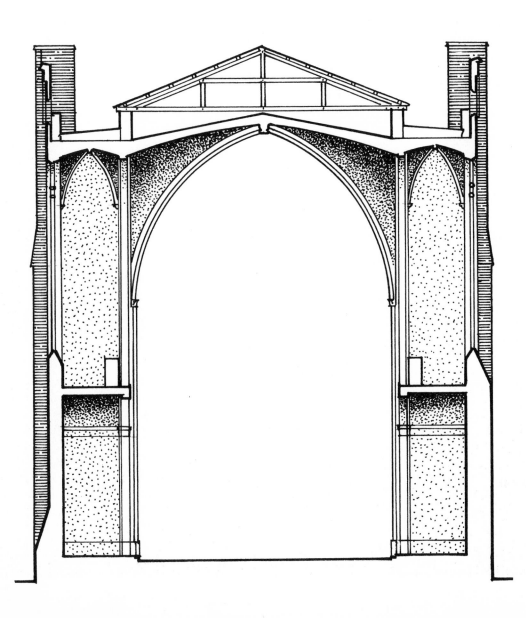

aisles to create a single span. The result is the longest clear span in a Gothic cathedral. It is a splendid piece of engineering but curiously unsatisfying as a design. Spanish designers were to turn back to the pillared hall for the last phase of medieval architecture.

At Barcelona and at Palma de Mallorca the soaring height and slenderness of the piers open up the interiors so that the inside reads as a monumental and dramatic box of space, quite different than the narrow glass nave of the French Gothic. From 1368 to 1406 Jaime Mates used plain octagonal piers at Palma to carry the sharply folded quadripartite vaults. These vaults are higher than Amiens and yet the stepped section effectively pulls the whole construct into a unified space. In these Catalan halls structural gymnastics are less obtrusive than in the northern cathedrals. Where the architects used a flying buttress it was conceived of as a purely utilitarian device largely hidden above the aisle roof. At Seville in the Andaluzian south the largest Gothic cathedral in Europe has braced complexes of flying buttresses quite hidden above the double aisle roofs. In the south, where the vaults are not endangered by the heaving action of frost in the winter, there is no need for a heavy and expensive timber roof. The upper surfaces of the vaults are sealed with a layer of tiles and mortar.

The Gothic continued to be the customary mode of church building in conservative Castile throughout the first half of the sixteenth century. In the great university cathedral at Salamanca, Juan Gil de Hontañon used the stepped section of Bourges to unify the internal volumes; from side chapels to aisle and thence to the rich vaulting of the nave, the interior steps up in graded sequence. In Andaluzia, Malaga, Granada, Guadix, and Jaén cathedrals were built from 1520 as hall churches of this Gothic type. But, in response to the currents of Renaissance taste sweeping in from Italy, the architects cased piers and shafts, arches and ribs, tracery and walling with Italianate motifs. The result is grotesque; the Roman order, devised to be used with mass concrete and brick structures, wars with the essentially linear accent of the Gothic.

NOTE
1 John Harvey *The Cathedrals of Spain* (London 1957) 149

Guillermo Boffiy placed quadripartite vaults spanning 73 feet over the external pier buttresses at Gerona cathedral.

At Palma cathedral Jaime Mates and Guillermo Oliveras devised a stepped section with high aisles and nave vaults higher than Amiens.

In Andaluzia, Spain, where frost damage was a negligible factor the vaults were left open to the weather. Vaulting, Seville cathedral, 1467–98

At Seville the high aisles left room for only a small clerestory. Purely utilitarian bracing arches stiffened the piers above the aisle roofs.

Hall churches continued to be built in Spain during the sixteenth century. They were cased with decorative Renaissance detail clashing with the Gothic structural order. Granada cathedral, by Enrique Egas, from 1521-

Juan Gil de Hontañon designed the sixteenth-century Castillian Gothic cathedral at Salamanca with a stepped section.

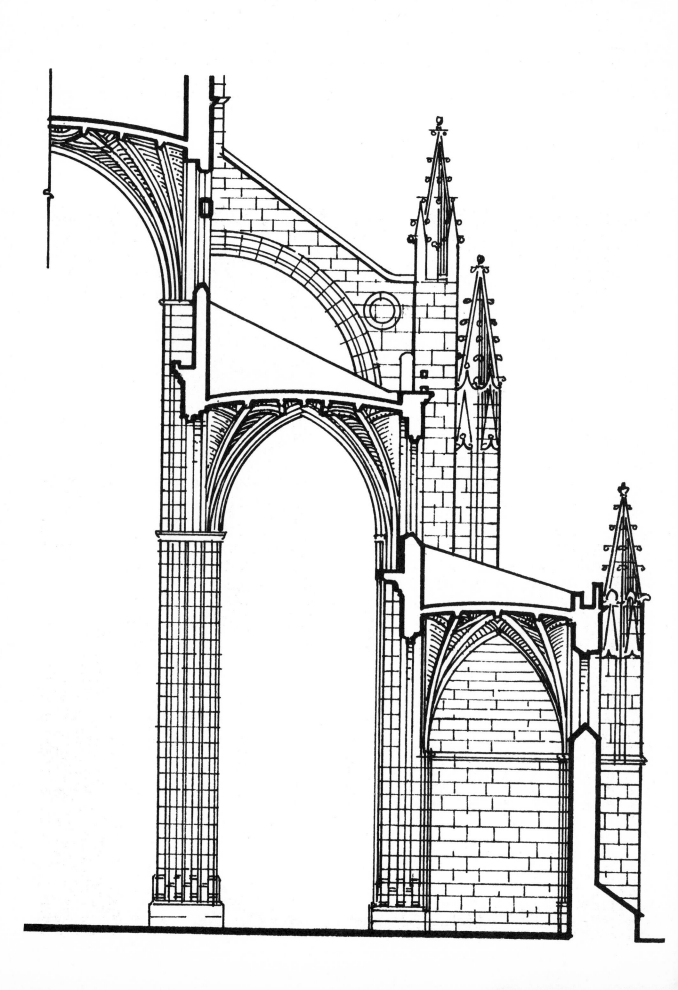

For clarity the argument has focussed upon problems of church building during the twelfth and thirteenth centuries. The major building effort of the time was directed to these competitive urban symbols, and the cutting edge of experiment and innovation was to be found in the shops and work places of the new and specialized guild craftsmen who overnight devised new job organizations and techniques to meet this unprecedented demand. But this novel, predictable, and controlled mode of building could be and was applied to other problems in architecture.

In medieval fortifications the contrast between heavy massive wall and Gothic delicacy of structure in the internal arrangements is particularly striking. On the exterior, the crenellated walls and sloping glacis of the castles of the crusading knights and feudal barons in the Holy Land and in Europe appear to be solid mountains of masonry. In the interior, we find vaulted storerooms, halls, and water catchment basins using every device of the engineering skill of the time to create fireproof complexes of masonry. The skills of the mason were pressed into service to devise tortuous entries with portcullis slots and firing positions. Corbels, arches, and brackets overhung the narrow defiles, and inside

Square keep with machicolations, round towers, and flanking crenellated walls in Gothic military architecture. Fenis, Italy

the wall a multitude of interlocking chambers and narrow corridors confused the attacker.

The keep at Coucy, built during the second quarter of the thirteenth century, was a complete defensive residence, with a well, fireplaces, latrines, halls, and storerooms. External walls with vaulted passageways and fire steps surrounded rib-vaulted internal rooms.[1] Eyes in the vaults allowed light to penetrate through the three levels and were useful for hoisting supplies and projectiles from level to level. Here the vault proved to be a thoroughly utilitarian fireproof structure.

The relatively thin-skinned medieval fortified wall proved to be inadequate to withstand the impact of stone or iron shot fired from guns. By the sixteenth century military engineers began to use heavy masonry walls cramped together with wrought iron bonding and resilient layers of earth or rubble stone to absorb the shock of gunfire. The vault, with its counterposed pressure, was found to be most useful in defensive design, for under shock impact it could flex and spring back into position when hit.

From the seventeenth to the nineteenth century vaulted chambers, relieving arches, and transverse barrels were an integral part of the design of the gun bastions and casemates girdling European and North American towns. Medieval engineering skill in the design of shell constructions proved to be easily adapted to the problems and needs of a new age.

NOTE
1 Sidney Toy *A History of Fortification* (London 1955) 137

At Agde the church was fortified as a strong point by royal decree.

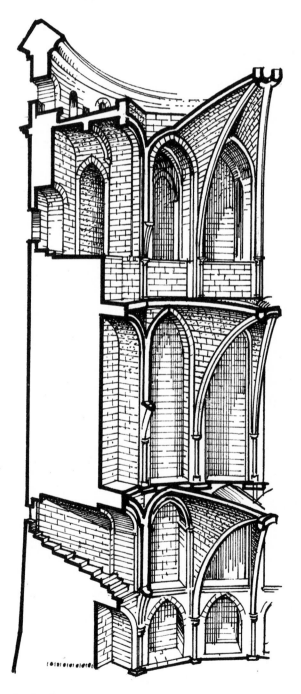

In the keep at Coucy each floor was supported by ribbed and pointed vault segments radiating from an opening ring. (after Viollet-le-Duc)

The vault proved equally useful in civil and military architecture during the Middle Ages. Rhodes

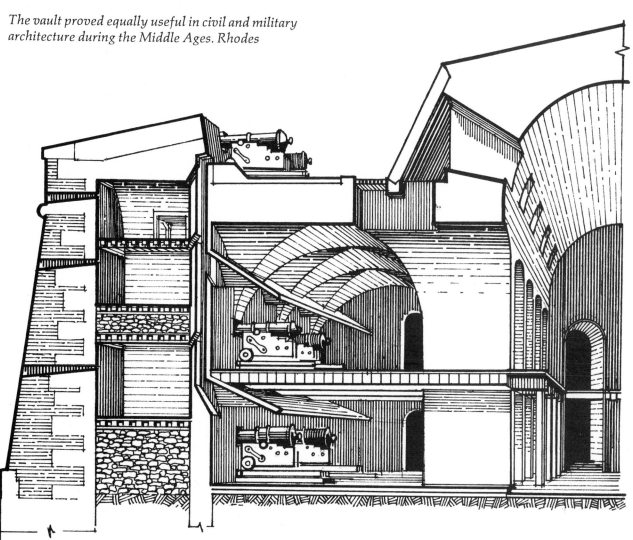

Proposal by de Montalembert, 1776, for a double-deck casemate gallery reinforced by cross and barrel vaulting.

The construction of a Gothic cathedral demanded complex methods of financing, the skills of specialists in many trades, and a substantial commitment of building apparatus. It was big business, and it must have been extraordinarily good fun for those involved. Far removed from the rough and ready makeshifts of early Romanesque building, the great Gothic cathedrals bear the imprint of powerful personalities, men whose sure touch and imperious command shaped the processes of design and erection. This was the context within which the architect, the mason, and the carpenter worked, not the shadowy and insubstantial realm of aesthetic theory or the subtle and devious area of regional or national policy. A certain earthy common sense, a new capacity to envisage physical form, and the means of attaining it amidst the masonry chips, spilled mortar, and confusing timber and cordage of the building site, have always been the architect's special province. The layman may envisage the architect as a lone genius working late over the drawing board, but the master builder knows that the essential decisions in building are made at the site and only later transferred to the drawing board to be refined and given coherence.

On the site the work had to proceed in an orderly step-by-step progression. Top soil was removed from the area of building operations and the markings for footings to carry piers and walls were set out on the cleared site with pegs and cordage. Right angles were simply achieved by means of a triangle with sides in proportion 3, 4, and 5. Footings were dug to rock or hard-packed gravel, and on marshy sites squared piles with ends shod with iron were driven in to make a level platform. Footings were usually somewhat inadequate, nothing more than a trench filled with rubble, flints, and chips rammed hard; occasionally, however, a mix of rubble and mortar created a firmer base. Not until well along in the Gothic, as the result of numerous settlement failures, did architects use cut-stone footings to spread the loads over the soil.

As the walls progressed, putlog holes were left for the carpenters to put the logs or struts of the scaffolding and working platforms into the wall. The scaffolds were light and economical temporary workspaces, made of lashed poles and woven wicker platforms. Through most of this period planks were rare and expensive items used only for finished work: each one had to be hand-sawn laboriously from the log. By the fifteenth century wind- and water-powered mills operating gang saws finally made cut planks readily available.

Improvements in the smelting and forging of iron made wrought iron a useful metal tie to resist hidden strains. As the piers and buttresses were raised, window bars of wrought iron to hold the glass were grouted across the window openings. In some particularly delicate structures, iron reinforcing was used in the fabric: a chain was embedded in the walls of the Sainte Chapelle and the vaulting ribs were stiffened with iron bars. Iron cramps and dowels were commonly used to clamp together the delicate fabric of spires. Iron was boiled in linseed oil, tallow, resins, and fats to retard its rusting. By the fifteenth century it was quite customary to use tension bars of wrought iron to take the thrust of vaults and arch rings.

To judge from the evidence of contemporary manuscript illustrations, the site was a scene of diverse activity. Around the base of the structure clustered the mason's lodges and the bankers for finished stonework and the sheds and workshops where carpenters roughed up centerings, scaffolds, and trusses. Smiths hammered at tie bars and dowels. Plumbers cast and rolled lead for waterproofing at gutters, copings, and parapets. Tilers and slaters cut and shaped the roofing slates and fixed them on the roof with wrought-iron nails forged by the smiths.

As early as possible the great timber roof with its slate, tile, or lead cover was constructed to shelter the interior. In our example the cathedral church has been roofed in and consecrated after what might have been a six-year initial building programme. Flooring is complete as is much of the lower sculptural enrichment. Walls, piers, and buttresses are structurally finished. Around the piers of a new bay, working platforms step up to follow the construction.

On the inside the floor is clear and usable for daily services. As yet the glass is not complete and the openings are screened by canvas or wicker shields. The principal working platform at the line of the vault has been perched on bracketed props hung from the piers. On this platform the line of the ribs is traced out and projected up to the rib line by plumb bobs. Four braced construction bents made of bent and lashed poles spring from seatings pegged into the masonry and are ready to receive the carefully cut stones of the ribs. Hoisting machinery, drums, and windlasses hung in the heavy timber work of the roof raise the masonry blocks into position.

Once the permanent centering of the ribs has set, the masons can proceed with the vaulting webs, constructing them without centering in the lower two-thirds of the rise and with light centerings braced into the main bents for the upper portions.

The scale of this operation and the logistics involved point to a command structure of some complexity. From the twelfth century the master mason becomes more and more the architect – more concerned with layout and design, responsible for the general timing of the operations and continually co-ordinating the work of the differing crafts. Indeed contemporary passages indicate only too clearly the growing importance and independence of architects. The sermons of the Dominican Nicolas de Biard show a characteristic distrust of this new technical role. 'Masters of masons, holding a [measuring] rod and gloves in their hands, say to others: Cut it for me this way, and do no labour, and yet they receive a higher fee, as do many modern prelates.' and 'Some work by word alone. Note: that in these great buildings, there is wont to be one chief master who only ordains by word, and rarely or never sets hand [to the work]; and yet he takes higher pay than the rest.'[1]

Architects today can take heart from the tone of

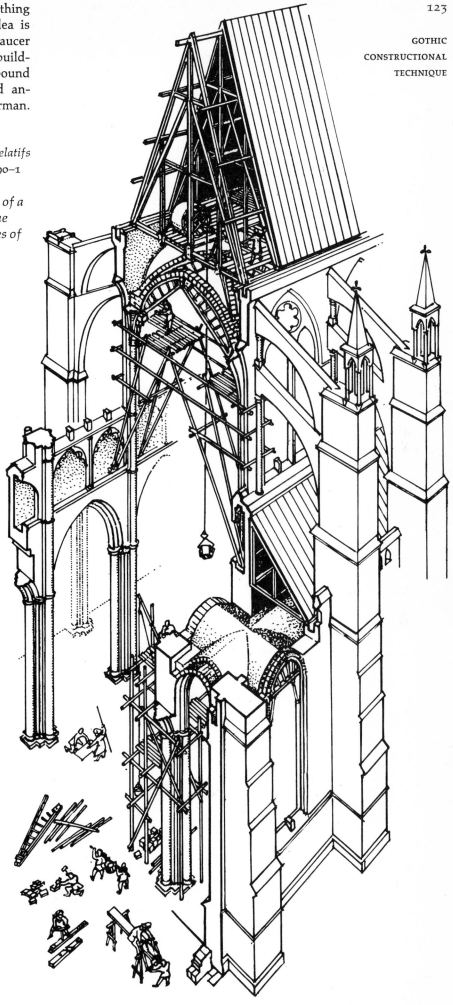

these diatribes. The architect's problem is nothing new. Indeed over the centuries a moving plea is transmitted from the Somnour's tale in Chaucer when he complains regarding the cost of the building operations, 'By God, we owen fourty pound for stones.' There speaks the authentic and anguished voice of the building committee's chairman.

NOTE

1 V. Mortet and P. Deschamps *Recueil de textes relatifs à l'histoire de l'architecture* (Paris 1911–29) II, 290–1

The architect, in co-ordinating the construction of a medieval cathedral church, had to draw upon the skills of many trades and the technical capacities of specialist artisans.

By the twelfth century the architect's responsibility shifted from the execution of the work to the conception and control of the job. Directed design and controlled supervision implied a clearly understood model or diagram for the operation.[1] The drawing office for 'trassyng and makyn molds' became the nerve centre for decision and control, though much final revision and adjustment might be carried out on the scaffolds by judicious compromise and last minute ingenuity. The notebooks of Villard de Honnecourt from the first half of the thirteenth century show a precision and technique in the manipulation of freehand and scaled drawing which argue for a long tradition of drawing skill on the part of the mason. Undoubtedly, while the curiously linear quality of the Gothic ultimately derived from the northern tradition of frame design, its development was encouraged by the change to two-dimensional linear and diagrammatic working drawings.

The Gothic architect did not make complete and repetitious elevation drawings. Rather, he set the number of bays required and then detailed one example, leaving to the masons on the site or in the shop the exact configuration of, say, the foliage in a capital. The firm co-ordinating lines of structure and form were set, however, by his directing personality. Presumably wooden models were used to show the general massing of the work to the chapter or guild, and then precise linear working drawings were used on the job. There are parchments existing for the façade of major churches, as at Strasbourg in the middle of the thirteenth century.[2]

These elaborate and careful drawings were made on 'tracing tables,' the large wooden tables on trestles referred to in many expense accounts. For the striking of exact curves at full scale for the accurate layout of centering and masonry, the mason drew on plastered flooring in the trassing house or on plastered wall surfaces, slate, or granite slabs on the site. Interesting examples of these can still be seen with the scratched lines made by the mason's metal stylus. Compasses, set squares, and some kind of ruling pen were used for ink drawing on the parchment. Graphite pencils were not yet known, and temporary lines were traced with chalk or red oxides of iron.

In retrospect it can be seen that the special genius of these European architects from 1100 to 1250 lay in the rapid conversion of heavy-walled mass structures to light and open skeletal fabrics. This flowering of a new mode of building in masonry was the direct result of the meeting of two traditions, the one from the south emphasizing the wall and the shell roof, the other from the north based upon framed supports with a sheathing skin.

Each step in the process was the result of logical and workmanlike design decisions made by practical builders coping with the problems raised by their predecessors' choices. The masonry wall of the early Romanesque abbey was a monumental structure suited to a great church, but the exposed timber roof could still burn, destroying the entire fabric. A heavy barrel vault of masonry retarded fire damage, and unified the interior into a monumental whole, but excluded light. The folded and ribbed vault made it possible to pierce the wall for lighting but in turn involved the architect in a struggle to bring the point loads safely to earth. At each stage the response represented a new fusion correcting the weaknesses and amplifying the potential of the previous solution, until with the thirteenth-century French Gothic cathedral a classic, if tenuous, balance was achieved. Beyond this classic archetype the linear progression failed and architects were forced to turn to new programmes and new solutions.

The impact of these Gothic cathedrals comes from the subtle opposition of contrasting tendencies – the search for volume in the interior denied by the forest of permanent props on the exterior, the illogic of the static machine of the vault perched high on seemingly insubstantial supports, the conflict of length and height, and the constant interplay between the containment of space and its dispersal by effects of transparency. Little wonder that the clergy of the new towns embraced this dramatic evocation of the Christian faith. The cathedral summed up in visual terms the unresolved psychological tensions implicit in the Christian faith. The imposition of a subtle and demanding ethical philosophy over the crude certitudes of common experience, the divisive split between theology and the new empiricism, were echoed by the soaring spires, glassy walls, and tensed vaults of these fragile monuments.

NOTE
1 John Harvey *The Gothic World 1100–1600* (London 1950) 25

ENGLAND

9

TIERCERON VAULTS

The late medieval architect was in a peculiarly favoured position. He had emerged from the relative obscurity of the mason's role. His clientele was varied. Abbots and prelates, councillors and tradesmen, barons and kings vied for his services. Not trapped in the endless personal trivia of the palace and an equal to the powerful clerics and townsmen of the time, he could speak with authority of a profession of which he was the master. As yet he had not sunk to the role of a theatrical producer concerned only with the over-all massing and florid detailing of public works. To use the parlance of film, he was still a director intimately involved in the production of the art and not an administrative producer. Nonetheless there were signs that the co-operative team effort, which was the particular strength of medieval social organization, was beginning to break down. The real wages of craftsmen and artisans, which were relatively higher in the fifteenth century than they were to be again until our own century, were beginning that comparative decline which marked the Renaissance and Baroque, when power was concentrated in royal households and dynastic families. But, leavened by the new efficiency introduced by specialized effort, the medieval craftsmen, designers, and architects were still capable of building within the firm tradition of democratic effort.

OVERLEAF *In the Angel choir at Lincoln (from 1256), the stellar vaults with tierceron and ridge ribs herald the complexity of late Gothic vaults.*

In the tenth-century Anglo Saxon tower at Earls Barton, England, masonry was treated as if it were wood with stones laid vertically in a grid with a diagonal interlace. Though there are arches cut from a single stone and relieving arches built of two curved stone flakes, the entire facing strongly suggests a timber prototype.

Medieval builders showed remarkable skill in adapting the light skeletal frame of timber to permanent masonry construction. In so doing, they retraced a path typical of technological evolution. Starting with a monolithic mass – crude and oversized vaults perched on heavy walls – they broke it into separate and calculable parts. By the thirteenth century they had evolved a predictable assemblage of elements braced into position by masses of masonry sited outside the framed grid. A design in an unfamiliar material is apt to be coarse, clumsy, and redundant; unsure of just how the material will behave, the builder 'plays it safe' by adding a bit here and a touch there. The inevitable result is too heavy a structure which by its very weight can overload the supports. Casting about for some solution to this clumsy excess the designer will tend to argue from similar or parallel techniques in other materials or other trades. And this is just what the medieval mason did. He turned to the framing of the carpenter as a useful analogy, rejecting the diffused loads and equivocal reactions of planes of masonry.

Concentrating upon the nodes at which linear components were joined, the Gothic mason broke the heavy box into repetitive bays. Each bay now could be designed in isolation by applying an intuitive sense of the behaviour of material against the evidence of failures. Design thus became an affair of stitching together calculable components. In the vault, the meeting line of the groin demanded a rib to canalize the concentrated loads and each bay a transverse arch-ring to tie together the piers. In turn, the concentration of loads upon the haunching and the pier necessitated a rigid support for the vault: a difficult problem where the pier was not stiffened and braced by supporting walls. It was just this nodal concentration of gravity loads and thrusting forces which suggested the flying-buttress arc and the external mass of the buttress to stabilize the fabric.

By the fourteenth century the designer began to use fabrics which did not channel and bring together loads to isolated supports. He did not turn back to the excessive mass of the eleventh century but rather diffused and spread the loads and pressures into an interlacing meshed grid of small linear elements. Accepting a certain degree of indeterminacy in the design, he created an interlocking assemblage of elastic elements, none of which was emphasized or stressed above the others. The total structure became much lighter than the heavy mass of the Romanesque and avoided the concentrated buttress masses of the early Gothic.

These later Gothic vaults became thin rigid shells stiffened and braced by a complex armature of ribs. Sharp folds and creases disappeared to be replaced by warped and twisted surfaces of double curvature. Vaulting panels were reduced to thicknesses of four inches as opposed to the twelve to sixteen inches of earlier vaults. This lessening of the weight of the vault minimized the thrusts. The lessened thrusts were spread over a wider surface of walling. The upshot was that the vault became a thin, warped, and gridded shell wedged into a relatively thin boxy system of supports. Rejecting the heavy bay articulation of the early Gothic based upon the heavy timber frame, later Gothic designers devised lattice shells whose shape ensured stability without the need for heavy buttressing restraint.

The rib became the ideal medium to effect the transition between the point support of the pier and the curving shell of the vault. So that the point upthrust of the pier would not punch through the thin shell of the vault, architects multiplied the ribs fanning out from the support to effect a smooth transition between pier and rib. Many and various expedients were devised but in the end they all came down to the simple resolution of a loading problem: how to pick up and concentrate the diffuse weights and thrusts of a shell so that they could be safely channelled down a slender support. Simple barrel vaults and shallow domes could now be used with ease. Their light thrusts could be restrained by quite simple pier buttresses on the exterior or by internal buttressing set between bay chapels.

Essentially, the late Gothic designer took the lattice weave of the primitive hut, translated it into a delicate grid of curved masonry ribs, braced the ribs with a superposed shell, and then perched this delicately poised static contrivance up to one hundred feet above the floor on slender piers. It is little wonder that a rigidly braced transition between rib and pier became the special preoccupation of the medieval engineer.

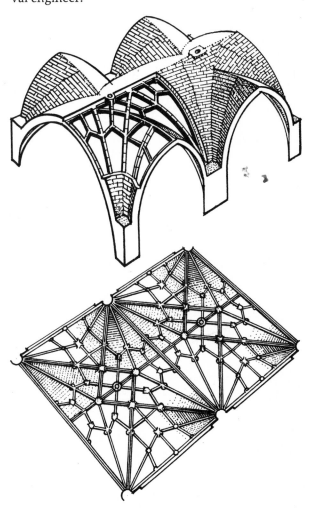

In late Gothic vaults thin shells were braced by a complex rib interlace: nave vault, Winchester, by William Wynford, c 1450.

Gothic changed as it spread. Despite the stunning impact of the thirteenth-century French skeletal cage, masons who travelled – and many worked and visited throughout the length and breadth of Europe so that they were familiar with the work of lodges in France, Hungary, and Spain – tended only to adapt and modify the details of what they saw for use in their own local traditions of building. Occasionally, as at Westminster or Avila, at Prague or Cologne, typically French cathedrals were built in direct imitation of the 'opus francigenum' of Paris and Amiens. But these remained isolated monuments. A European Gothic may have been the ideal of a unified church, but it fragmented and splintered into national schools of design in the face of local prejudice and well-founded traditional modes.

This flexibility was a strength. The Gothic as a style could flex and change over the decades in a continuously evolving process, without becoming trapped in a rigid formula. In adapting to varied structural materials and contrasting climatic needs, the architects very sensibly devised new shapes and new plans.

By the opening of the thirteenth century, the French had evolved a very simple plan even though they required an intricate structure to contain it. The transept was suppressed and isolated towers were minimized. The external structure became a repetitive framework, carrying, bracing, and supporting the high and narrow glass cage of the nave. The reduction of the gallery and the comparatively low aisles were the inevitable result of this emphasis upon internal unity.

In the south of France and Catalonia, structural support for the vaulting was built as part of the shell of the building. In response to the climate windows were narrower and smaller than in the north. More concerned with the sculptural plasticity of the whole concept than with the modular grid of structure, masons in the south kept true to the Mediterranean tradition of massive wall and shell surface.

In central Europe and around the Baltic the predominant use of brick encouraged architects to turn to simple planar walls. The hall church with two rows of slender piers carrying the vaulting over a simple boxy hall became well-nigh universal in this region during the fifteenth and sixteenth centuries.

In England, prior to the Conquest, the carpenter was the builder. Germanic and Scandinavian tribesmen pouring into England after the Roman collapse brought with them the traditions of timber building in frame. Only the Irish monks continued to build with masonry and such few Anglo-Saxon masonry buildings as remain show the pronounced impact of frame techniques.

Although, after the Conquest, French and particularly Norman influence was strong in England, this linear and modular emphasis encouraged the continuing use of conservative plans little changed from the Romanesque abbey. Often two transepts cut across the length of the building, and the English continued to favour crossing towers as well as those at the façade. The square east end, initially the result of Cistercian rigour in design, was ideally suited to this rectilinear concept of building.

Interiors were never as high nor as structurally daring as in France, the English preferring attenuated length to soaring height. Instead of exaggerated verticality, the English masons held to strong horizontal accents, such as the continuing use of the gallery which emphasized the parade of repetitive bays. Without the extreme structural problems posed by vaulting over high and narrow naves, flying buttresses on the exterior were kept low and remained unobtrusive elements. The English architects turned their structural ingenuity to the design of new forms of ribbed vaulting.

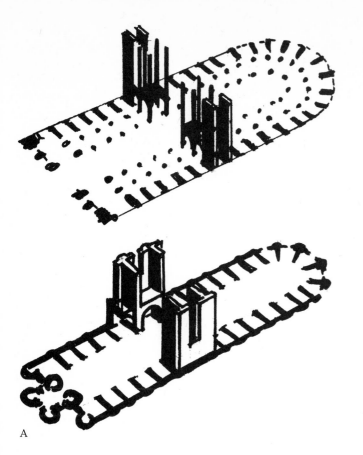

A

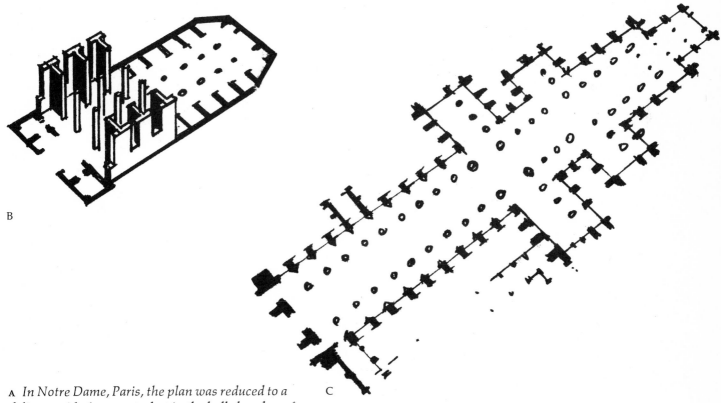

B

C

A *In Notre Dame, Paris, the plan was reduced to a delicate grid of supports, but in the hall churches of the south at Albi or les Jacobins at Toulouse, the supports become part of the shell wall.* B *The plasticity of brick and mortar encouraged the use of simple planar walls in central Europe.* C *The complex additive plans of English cathedrals reflected a conservative tendency in design and suited the English liking for repetitive framing techniques.*

The mason naturally thinks first in terms of mass and shell surfacing, but so strong was the influence of the linear skeleton in England that her masons denied massing and the expression of planar shell to concentrate upon the manipulation of line. The frame composed of repetitive grids became the dominant element in the structure and found full expression in decorative enrichment of vault and wall. As early as 1093 in the fortress church of Durham at the very frontier of the Norman domain, built at a scale which dwarfed any of the contemporary achievements on the mainland of France, Norman craftsmen turned the cutting edge of English experiment to the vault rather than to the pier and buttress. The diagonal ribs of the choir vault were the first expression of this new approach.

For the next seventy-five years, after the initial wave of building which accompanied the consolidation of the newly conquered island, it was left to French masons to realize the implications of the masonry rib. But twelfth-century barons and abbots made good use of the native Anglo-Saxon skill at carpentry: at Winchester, Canterbury, Peterborough, and Ely the Norman buildings were roofed with timber ceilings. Fire in the nave of Canterbury in 1174 brought French detailing once again to England for William of Sens was called in to rebuild and he used sexpartite vaults in the choir. These dictated

a system of alternate round and octagonal piers. The choir of the cathedral was well in advance of French models; the octagonal piers were the model for those at Chartres and the attached shafts preceded the work at Laon. He used detached shafts of dark Purbeck marble contrasting sharply with the light-coloured stone of the piers, a device which was to be used with great effect in thirteenth-century English designs and one which emphasized line over mass.

At Wells cathedral an English master mason created the first fully Gothic interior in all Europe.[1] The nave, begun between 1186 and 1190, has no traces of Romanesque heaviness and mass: the wall is dissolved into a sheet or membrane of masonry carried on sharply pointed arcades. Where the French cut away the wall to isolated pier supports, the English minimized the effect of mass by bounding the walls within a sharply accented framework of horizontal and vertical lines. The twenty-four shafts undulating and rippling about the pier, the deeply cut and modelled arcading, and the sharply pointed multiple ribbing of the vaults combined to create a rich surface texture of lines.

NOTE
1 Paul Frankl *Gothic Architecture* (Penguin Books 1962) 50

English designers, working within the tradition of Anglo Saxon and Danish timberwork, evolved compartmented and framed facades. West front, Wells, c 1220–39

The designer of the west front at Wells, 1220–39, used slender shafts and projecting arcades as a structural cage for the sculpture.

The severe and simple nave treatment at Wells, built from 1192 to 1206, is the first to emphasize. fully the typically Gothic play with repetitive line and multiple mouldings. Because the transverse rings spring from corbelled brackets, the wall spandrels still emphasize the continuous surfaces of the Romanesque.

With the refinement of the ribbed vault to a quadripartite form the curtain appeared to have been rung down on further technical modification of the vault. The codification of the northern French Gothic into a grand but limited formula tended to stifle the continuous adjustment of building to new demands and changing circumstance. With pointed ribs and arch rings, with bosses emphasizing the intersection of ribs, with stilting easing the transition to the expanse of clerestory, and with the rib extended down the pier and over the window openings, the vault required no further adjustment or change. And yet, as it proved, the ribbed and pointed quadripartite vault was only the starting point for almost three full centuries of technical experiment and aesthetic elaboration. The independent originality of English masons opened new possibilities for the continued growth of medieval architecture.

The astonishing irregularity of the choir vaults of Lincoln cathedral, designed in 1192 by Geoffrey de Noyer and carried out in 1208, signalled the opening of this new phase.[1] First he introduced a ridge rib running along the apex of the vaults. Dispensing with the slightly domed profile customary in France, he made this rib a straight linear element, emphasizing the cage of ribs rather than the curved surfaces of the vault. Then, rejecting the strict regularity of intersecting diagonals, he introduced a third rib, the 'tierceron,' springing from the haunching to third points on the ridge. This created diagonal cells opening to the clerestory windows. No erratic aberration, this new form was a deliberate effort to break free of the rigid bay system which was limiting the evolution of the vault.

NOTE

1 Paul Frankl 'The Crazy vaults of Lincoln Cathedral' *Art Bulletin* 35 (1953) 95

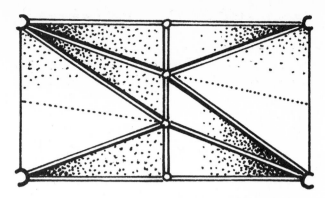

In this 1192 choir vault at Lincoln, the tierceron, springing from haunching to crown independently of the vault folding, makes its first appearance.

The sexpartite vaults of the southeast transept at Lincoln seem to have been used as a model for the skew compartments of the choir vault.

In the 'crazy vault' over the choir at Lincoln, Geoffrey de Noyer in 1192 introduced a ridge rib and an eccentric disposition of the segments.

English designers rapidly exploited the potential in this combination of tierceron rib and ridge ribs. Master Alexander, the successor of Geoffrey de Noyer at Lincoln, devised the first tierceron star vaults over the nave in the building programme between 1225 and 1235.[1] Instead of the skewed placement of the choir segments he reverted to crossed diagonals, adding short transverse ridge ribs with tiercerons springing up to both transverse and longitudinal ridges. The basic form of the vault was still quadripartite, but, in marked contrast to the curved surfaces of French vaulting, the closely spaced splay of ribs overpowered the shell surfaces, substituting a stellar configuration.

In the lower stages of the central crossing tower at Lincoln he applied the ridge and tierceron rib combination to the difficult problem of designing a large square vault, which would key in scale and pattern to the work in the nave. He solved it by setting a faceted and ribbed cloister vault on the diagonal, and supported it on vaulting segments sprung from eight points in the tower.

The multiplication of ribs on the surface of the vaults diffused stresses throughout the ribbed pattern. The west country masons carried this to the extreme in the vaulting over the nave at Wells and in the nave vault at Exeter completed by 1309. Transverse ridge ribs now were carried through to the window openings and a closely spaced splay of ribs was sprung from the support to carry the ridge ribs. What had started as a shell masonry form had become translated into a ribbed cage.

NOTE
1 John Harvey *The Gothic World 1100–1600* (London 1950) 75

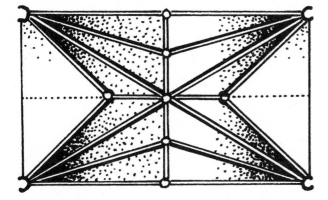

In the Lincoln nave the ribs evolve into decorative stars independent of the vault folding.

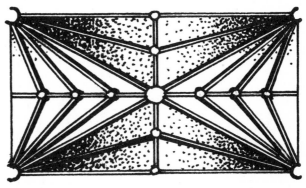

In the nave vault at Exeter this multiplication of ridge ribs and tiercerons obscured the folded and curved plates of the vaulted shell. The vault became a framed grid.

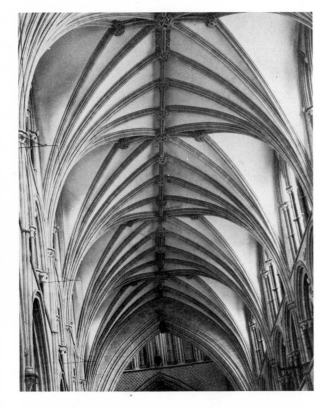

In the nave vault at Lincoln, mid-thirteenth century, a transverse ridge rib was added, with tiercerons coming to a focus in decorative bosses.

These new devices, the ridge rib and the tierceron rib, liberated the vault designers so that they could effectively adapt the vault to square crossings: Lincoln crossing, 1238.

The introduction of the tierceron has always been a difficult problem for the historian of the Gothic. Evidently the French masons had solved all the static and mechanical problems of the vault, and yet here were English designers deliberately breaking the rules and disregarding the formulae which had created the great Gothic cathedrals of the Paris basin. Why?

Francis Bond, following Viollet-le-Duc, argued that the English introduced the ridge rib and the subsidiary tiercerons because they were less technically adept at vault construction.[1] The argument is ingenious and well documented. The pronounced twisting of the large vaulting panels of thirteenth-century French Gothic, dictated by the use of stilted clerestory window openings, forced the mason to build his vaulting webs of carefully cut stones. He adjusted his coursing to the transverse and diagonal ribs so that at the crown it paralleled the ridge. In addition it was customary in France to curve each panel doubly so that the vault was slightly domed and therefore more rigid.

But English masons used roughly squared rubble coursing for their vaults with no attempt to adjust or wedge the coursing panels. The result was an awkward zigzag intersection at the ridge. There are many examples, among them the side panels of the vaults over the transept and in the chapter house at Westminster. Bond argues that the rib was introduced to cover this awkward joint.

The tierceron, he further argues, followed automatically from the change to a continuous flat ridge for the vault. Once the slight doming of each bay was dropped, the vaulting panels were constructed as singly curved shells so that it became necessary to introduce an intermediary rib which would both brace the ridge rib into position and stiffen the relatively weaker panels.

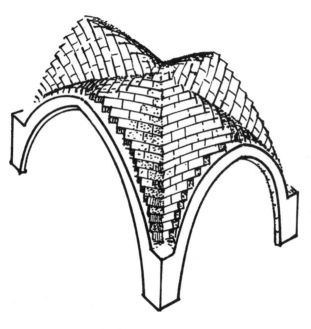

English masons, using roughly squared rubble coursing, laid up their vault webs with parallel courses. The panels interlocked in an awkward zigzag at the crown.

The steep pitches and sharply folded surfaces of the vault over the Lady Chapel at Salisbury, 1220–5, are supported on delicate attenuated piers.

The wall of the Merveille at Mont St Michel, Normandy, 1203–28, has chamfered cuts sloping in to the narrow lancet windows, converting the wall to a range of buttresses.

The thesis is ingenious, precise, and seemingly logical. Within a narrow context it is quite correct. Certainly, the existence of these troublesome and erratic panel intersections and the weaker profile of singly curved web surfaces encouraged the mason to use subsidiary ribs which could strengthen and clarify the vaulted form. But the theory is just a trifle too linear and mechanistic in its reasoning. It is hardly likely that a minor constructional difficulty was the generating source for two centuries of vault evolution in England.

By the opening of the thirteenth century English masons shaped their vaults with steep pitches and sharply folded crowns, as in the Lady Chapel of Salisbury cathedral. There, Nicholas of Ely used a folding of the vaulted shell to create level crowns and singly curved panel surfaces, not through technical incompetence but because he was searching for a structural shape based on his own experience. The steeply pitched profile reflected proportions modelled upon the prismatic timber roofs of a northern climate. The angular, staccato, repetitive forms of the emergent Gothic were indigenous to, and derivative from the northern tradition of timber building.

Both in England and in northern France the birth of the Gothic reflected a renewed interest in the framed tradition of building. The responses differed, with the French emphasizing monumental height and clear articulation of bays, while the English turned to impressive length and an interlacing grid of elements. The differing interpretations ultimately stemmed from climatic and geographic factors but there can be little question that these differences were encouraged by the growing national awareness of the designers and their patrons. A distinctive regional flavour in design powerfully reinforced the emergent identity of each country.

NOTE
1 Francis Bond *Gothic Architecture in England* (London 1906) 323–35

On the exterior of the Lady Chapel at Salisbury, chamfered pier buttresses and lancet windows cut sharply into the masonry wall.

*The vault over the north transept at Westminster
abbey, completed in 1269, shows this erratic intersection in the transverse ridges.*

The chapter house of the monastic abbey was the room or hall in which the monks conducted their corporate affairs. Decisions regarding policy, building programmes, disciplinary problems, and the operation of farm and workshop were settled there. In Cistercian abbeys in the south of France and in Spain, as at Poblet or Santas Creus, the chapter house was a comparatively modest vaulted rectangular hall sited below the dormitory off the cloisters. But by the twelfth century the affluence of the monasteries led to a demand for more spacious and dignified assembly places. In keeping with the rigour of the order, English architects designed large rectangular halls for the Cistercian abbeys of the north, but elsewhere tended to build polygonal chapter houses.[1]

A circular or polygonal plan had psychological advantage for a council in which all members had ostensibly equal status. Moreover, the new forms of vaulting which had been devised by English masons were admirably suited to solve the technical problems posed by a plan in which the vault radiated from a central pier. In the cathedral churches such as Wells, Salisbury, or Lincoln the canons were not bound to the rigorous restraint of the monks, and they enthusiastically adopted the dramatic polygonal form for their chapter houses.

When the chapter house was erected outside the bounds of the cloisters architects could exploit to the full its potential as an important element in the cathedral complex. At Wells an undercroft for an octagonal chapter house was built adjacent to the choir as early as 1220. By 1300 work was begun on the upper stage and completed by 1319.[2] So closely spaced are the ribs springing from the slender central pier that the distinction between panel and its bounding rib is lost. The flaring conoid of ribs energetically expresses the thrust and counterthrust of forces within the vault. Polygonal plans and intersecting tiercerons conferred a new flexibility upon the designers of vaults. At Durham between 1366 and 1371 John Lewyn vaulted the Prior's Kitchen with a stellar polygon in which eight tiercerons were interlaced to leave an opening in the centre to vent the smoke.[3]

NOTES
1 Geoffrey Webb *Architecture in Britain in the Middle Ages* (Penguin Books 1956) 59ff
2 Paul Frankl *Gothic Architecture* (Penguin Books 1962) 146
3 John Harvey and Herbert Felton *The English Cathedrals* (London 1950) 64

Rectangular chapter house, Cistercian monastery, Santas Creus, Spain.

The designer of the chapter house at Wells used a central conoid and abutting vaulted segments over the canons' meeting hall.

By the opening of the fourteenth century the broad patterns and firm limits of the early Gothic had begun to dissolve into a shifting chiaroscuro of linear pattern. Yet, as the designers combined and recombined the elements of the Gothic into ever more subtle grids and meshes of structure, the basic geometry of internal space became relatively more simple. Freed from the dictates of repetitive structures evolving from a rigid bay system, the architects could now use structure as a complex frame for capacious halls and handsomely proportioned meeting spaces. An advanced structural technology led, not to erratic or highly sophisticated large shapes, but to buildings more easily adapted to human use. The new skill at handling small-scale structural elements in interlocking stability was ideally suited to the more complex functional demands made by the emergent middleclasses of the new cities.

The church remained the dominant structure in the town – the urban clergy saw to that – but no longer was it the undisputed centre of all urban activity. As hospitals and inns began to separate from the monastic abbey, they required new plans and new structural dispositions. Town halls and market halls increased in size and importance, overshadowing, if copying, the motifs of the castle and baronial hall. In this new, more complex, and lively society, medieval design motifs which had been painstakingly clarified in church design began to be used with a new versatility and a new freedom.

In the undercroft of the conversi used for buttery and cellars at Fountains abbey the vaults became repetitive elements easily adapted to utilitarian applications. The rigorous Cistercian rejection of unneeded decoration led to remarkably handsome fabrics.

10

STELLAR VAULTS AND LIERNE RIBS

A splay of tierceron ribs effectively concealed the planar folding of the vault, but the concentration of all ribs to a focus at the pier too strongly emphasized the support rather than the crown of the vault. To remedy this aesthetic fault, architects in the early fourteenth century introduced a new structural element – short secondary ribs which tied together the tiercerons into a meshed pattern and further diffused the load. These tieing or 'lierne' ribs let the tiercerons branch out and interweave to create a lattice or grid in the structural crown of the vault.

John Wysbeck used lierne ribs in the Lady Chapel at Ely, built from 1321 to 1349 (at the same time as the Sacrist, Alan of Walsingham, was working out the crossing tower and chancel). The mesh remained indeterminate in pattern. As yet he was not certain of his design: whether it was to emphasize the radial splay of the tiercerons or the tightly knit grid of the liernes. Though the design remains equivocal and indeterminate there is an evident effort here to reduce the clear and distinct bay system of the earlier Gothic to a dramatic interlace of small components.

In short, Wysbeck and his fellow masons in the fourteenth century were not concerned only with a purely decorative pattern-making. They were searching for a light and inexpensive fireproof structure, easy to lay out and build, and yet dramatic in its impact. If the construction of the vault could be eased without recourse to heavy centering, this was a distinct advantage. Building a mesh of ribs first gave permanent masonry centerings for the final construction of the shell. By breaking down the smooth expanse of the curving shell into distinct and manageable components of rib and panel, they could envisage each unit in isolation and thus cut it away, in the design, to the lightest possible configuration.

From this concern with structure, certain decorative patterns followed. The mason was anxious to so dispose the elements of design that they would tell the observer of the building something of the inner forces operating in its fabric. For this the rib was a most useful device. It could be used to 'draw' apparent lines of force on the surface of the vault. Usually these reinforced the contrast between the vertical cage of masonry supports and the complex interplay of pressures in the masonry shell. That too acute and too sensitive an emphasis upon this descriptive play of forces led the designers of the fourteenth century into almost neurasthenic excesses of structural sensibility does not invalidate their basic objective – the evocative, dramatic display of structural principle.

The involved engineering of these late Gothic vaults has much in common with the tense and strained visual art of the north. Schöngauer, Dürer, Grünewald, and Cranach each in their way attempted to 'freeze' an instantaneous play of human emotions in a carefully detailed descriptive 'snapshot.' It is this quality of powerful forces and tensions caught and held in an instant of time in painting or architecture which is the peculiarly northern European contribution to the arts and sciences.

OVERLEAF *The lierne rib created an intricate gridded pattern. Choir, Wells, c 1329*

In the elaborate lierne vault built over the Lady Chapel at Ely, 1321–49, folding in the vaulted shell was concealed by a radial splay of tiercerons interlacing at the crown. Subsidiary lierne members cut across the tiercerons to create an equivocal decorative grid.

By the fifteenth century architects could design light rigidly braced grids carrying a thin shell of stone to be built into existing older fabrics without the need for new buttressing. Nave vault, Norwich, c 1463–72

The freedom from the bay system granted by the lierne rib led to new vaulting patterns. The sharp folds at the groin and crown were softened, and the vault reverted to a thin barrel shell with panels to the windows cutting into the sides. In the new type, the mesh vault, diagonals cut across two bays. The prototype for this new use of the lierne rib was built over the rood screen at Exeter cathedral, during the furnishing and fitting of the choir in 1317.[1]

The new pattern was carried over a major space in the vaults of Tewkesbury abbey, which were built about 1330 over the existing Romanesque nave. Although diagonal ribs also cut across each bay, the significant diagonals were those spanning two bays. The segments opening to the windows now were cut into the sides of a barrel vault, decorated with and stiffened by a mesh-ribbed pattern on its lower surface.

At Gloucester, the south transept was rebuilt between 1331 and 1337 with a highly decorative net vault. Diagonals were strongly emphasized, but parallel liernes intersected to create a rectilinear grid of rhomboids. Over the choir the extraordinary complexity of these fourteenth-century vaults reached its peak. The double bay diagonal reappeared as a device linking bay to bay. Three ridge ribs cut through a complex interlace of lierne ribs. Elaborately carved bosses at the rib intersections, together with the profuse interlocking of lines of force, cancelled out every suggestion of mass and weight. The light skeletal diagrid took complete precedence over the solidity of masonry building.

While the Gloucester masons were concentrating upon ever more complexity, William Joy devised a simple and direct mesh vault for the choir at Wells, built between 1329 and 1350.[2] The sharp fold at the crown had long since disappeared and this was reflected in the suppression of the ridge rib. The vault had become a shallow barrel of masonry rather than a prismatic shell. The last lingering echo of the heavy transverse arch rings which had once divided bay from bay remained in the slender ribs swung between supports. But the pattern of the liernes is independent of these vestiges. Joy created a dominant pattern in which interlacing diagonal ribs swing across two bays to meet at squares of liernes. The effect is of a light and lacy carpentered mesh suppressing all suggestion of mass. The equivocal and dematerialized mesh of the vault exactly echoes the pierced and fretted skeleton of the wall. The entire choir reflects a subtle engineering and a sophisticated aesthetic which could integrate all elements of the design into a unified, consistent whole.

NOTES

1 Henning Bock 'Exeter Rood Screen' *Architectural Review* (London 1961) 313–17

2 Paul Frankl *Gothic Architecture* (Penguin Books 1962) 148

By the opening of the fourteenth century English masons began to design the vault as a thin barrel-shell with openings cutting into the sides. Vault over the passage of the rood screen, Exeter cathedral, c 1317

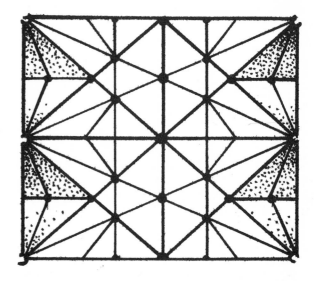

The equivocal interlocking of diagonals across two bays in the nave vault built at Tewkesbury after 1321 created a thin decorative barrel vault with severies cut into the side.

By 1337 Gloucester masons had devised a diagonal net pattern which freed the vault from strict bay articulation. South transept, Gloucester

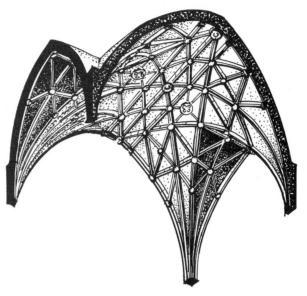

At Wells cathedral, William Joy in 1329 devised a mesh vault in which the diagonals cut across two bays.

A light skeletal grid of ribs disposed in a complex geometry carried the thin shell of the vault over the choir at Gloucester.

The walls of the choir in Gloucester cathedral were cut and shaped to carry a complex interlace of ribs (1337–50).

As architects rebuilt the Norman abbeys and cathedrals the new concepts explored in the vault spread downwards to the walls. At Exeter, Wells, and Gloucester, west country masons evolved their own characteristically English interpretation of the diaphanous cage of glass formulated at the Sainte Chapelle: they converted every surface to a traceried screen of ribs. At Gloucester, this occurred when the masons rebuilt the choir about 1345, raising a tall clerestory over the existing walls while keeping the aisle and galleries intact. Over the massive Romanesque walls of the choir they extended an open-work web of stone, a rectilinear tracery based on the French bar motif. With this expedient they unified the interior. It was a deliberate attempt to deny the mass of a homogeneous wall. In it the English preference for framing and a close articulation of linear elements found its peculiar statement and became the source for the Perpendicular work of the fifteenth century.

When the crossing tower at Gloucester was rebuilt between 1450 and 1460 the crushing weight of the spire made it necessary to distribute the loads beyond the four crossing piers. Diagonal compression struts were devised to spread the loads over adjacent bays. The masons left these struts exposed in the interior, interlacing and cutting through the tracery of the south transept. Everywhere, the designer replaced mass by an ingenious construct of framed members precisely adjusted to meet the load. Rather than attempting to conceal the new thrusts introduced into the fabric by the building of the tower, he openly avowed their existence and celebrated the drama of force and thrust. It was the same evolution which had seen the planar vaulted shell disappear to be replaced by a continuous grid of ribs. In the walls, the ponderous and apparent stability of coursed masonry was concealed by an intricate filigree of stone mullions and bars, precisely echoing the scale and suggesting the sharp cutting of timber construction.

The English masons showed remarkable versatility in recutting and shaping Norman heavy piers to carry new vaulted structures. Nave pier, Glastonbury

Diagonal compression struts introduced into the existing fabric of the crossing at Gloucester distributed the heavy loads of the crossing tower over several bays.

Elaborate tracery, crockets, and finials denied every suggestion of mass in the crossing tower at Gloucester, 1450–60. The sheathing wall dissolved into a delicate, curved and equivocal plane, which echoed the complexity of the vaulted shell.

Where the local designers in the west of England broke the dominance of the bay to create intricate meshes of stone, in the east and south the court school of masons continued to follow a strict division into separate structural compartments. They used the lierne rib to emphasize the stellar pattern of the tierceron vault, the liernes forming an octagonal centrepiece in each bay.

The masons working in London and Canterbury were open to continental influence. They brought geometrical tracery to England and tended to follow French precedent in matters of design. The choir at Canterbury and the choir and transept at Westminster both were modelled on French achievements.[1] This conservative tendency to respect existing traditions is most evident in the design for the nave of Westminster abbey. Henry Yvele, despite what must have been an almost overwhelming temptation to exploit the new structural dynamics of the west country masons, created a nave from 1362 which is in complete harmony with the choir and transept. Only minor details – the introduction of tierceron and transverse ridge ribs in the vault, and the rejection of detached shafts in the piers – distinguish this new work of the fourteenth century from the thirteenth-century choir.

At Canterbury cathedral Yvele had the opportunity to display the profound originality of which he was capable. At his death in 1400 the work on the aisles and the basic design for the nave were complete. Undoubtedly influenced by the high aisles at Westminster, he unified the internal effect at Canterbury by raising the aisle vault to almost two-thirds the height of the nave. The result is a stepped progression of space reminiscent of Bourges, held within a disciplined and orderly frame by the use of soaring vertical shafts. In the vault a four-petalled rosette of liernes at each bay was designed to give a rhythmic progression of accents sweeping to the crossing. The nave at Canterbury has an effect of cool and ordered logic. And yet Yvele was quite capable of turning his hand to richly textured and structurally ingenious vaults. In the cloisters at Canterbury, begun under his direction in 1397 and completed by 1414, the sweeping fans of tierceron ribs culminate in a rich interplay of heraldic bosses and crocketed liernes.

NOTE
1 Geoffrey Webb *Architecture in Britain in the Middle Ages* (Penguin Books 1956) 136

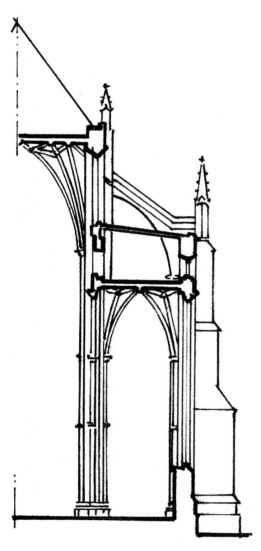

At Canterbury, the nave designed by Henry Yvele from 1377 is flanked by high aisles and surmounted by a rhythmically patterned lierne vault.

When Henry Yvele designed the new nave of Westminster abbey from 1362 he made it a faithful copy of the existing choir, only adding tierceron ribs to the vault.

In the vaults over the cloisters at Canterbury, built from 1397 to 1414, the elaborate interlace of ribs carries thin shell stone planking in the webs. The bearded head is claimed to be a portrait of Yvele.

The Canterbury cloister vaults, with armourial bearings, flowered bosses, figured heads, and crocketed projections are an expression of the chivalric fantasy of the late Middle Ages.

By the end of the fourteenth century English masons had evolved a distinctive variant of the Gothic. In every aspect framed principles of construction had triumphed. Plan and spatial organization reflected a design based upon a light skeletal fabric. Plane surfaces and heavy masses were everywhere subordinated to frame and panel articulation. Mouldings, the profiles of shafts, and the modelling of tracery had changed from rounded sections to sharp-cut angular facets directly derivative of the carpenter's art. The result was a flexible medium of design for monumental civic and ecclesiastical structures which accorded in spirit and scale with the surrounding vernacular buildings.

The flexibility of lierne vaulting and perpendicular panelling became evident in the complete remodelling of the Romanesque nave at Winchester. William of Wynford, an architect who had been strongly influenced by the demands of the court while in charge of the work at Windsor castle, was brought to the job by William of Wykeham from 1394 to 1403.[1] He elected to keep the piers of the existing structure, paring them away and recasing them in the new mode. Rather than simply covering the older work with a thin traceried screen, as at Gloucester, he reshaped and remodelled the entire fabric.

The ribs of the vault, completed by 1450, are in a stellar pattern, the vault itself being pitched more steeply than was customary in late Gothic vaults so that it has a pronounced fold at the crown. Wynford needed to raise the vault sufficiently to accept high lunettes breaking in from the window openings, which were cramped by the height of the aisle roofs over the flying buttresses. Nonetheless, the structural diagram exhibits the characteristic form of the late Gothic vault in England: a thin-shell barrel over a branching and interlacing grid of ribs.

The sharp edges, rectilinear profiles, and concave cutting of mouldings which we associate with fine carpentry and cabinet work were substituted for the swelling arcs and tubular profiles of the earlier Gothic. This uncompromising rectilinearity suggests a fibrous material such as wood which can be split, planed, or cut rather than a granular substance such as stone which can be more readily ground or abraded to rounded profiles. Not only does the detail of the cutting suggest wood, the scale of framing and the reduction of all large surfaces to a rib and panel pattern derives from the linear artistry of the carpenter. At St Mary Redcliffe, Bristol, built from 1375 to 1400, the panelling on the nave walls, the interlaced mesh of the lierne vault and the rectilinear tracery of the windows compose a close-knit unity. The wall was treated as a light curtain, the window as a fretted silhouette, and the vault as a cage of small compression elements. The architect followed the cage and the curtain wall to its logical conclusion, denying all weight, all mass, and all opacity in the fabric. He did this by rigorously applying the local and vernacular modes of building to a monumental structure.

NOTE
1 Geoffrey Webb *Architecture in Britain in the Middle Ages* (Penguin Books 1956) 146

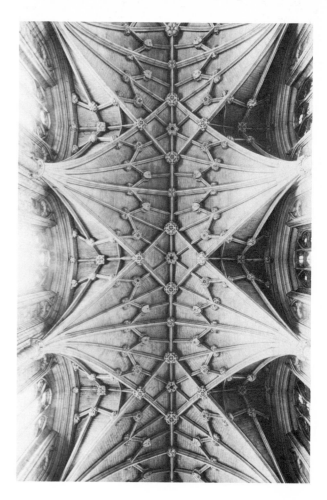

Thin shell vaults braced by a decorative armature of ribs could be built into the existing fabric of heavy-walled Norman churches. Nave vault, Winchester, by William Wynford, 1394–1450

In the nave of St Mary Redcliffe, Bristol, the rectilinear tracery of the clerestory window was projected over the wall surface and the vault was designed as a delicate filigree of compression struts.

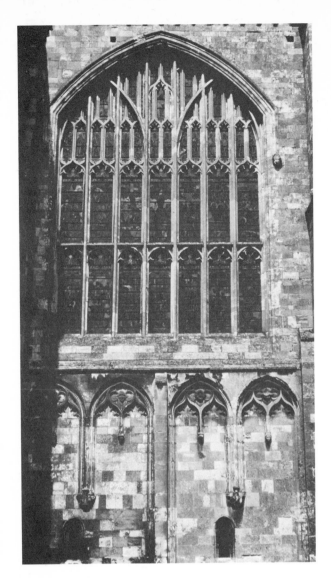

At Winchester, Wynford cut and pared away the older heavy walls, covered them with a new sheathing and introduced large stone mullioned windows.

The south porch added to the Angel choir at Lincoln is designed as a translucent lacework of masonry and glass.

Rectilinear panelling, which treated stone as if it were wood, replaced the heavy mouldings and planar surfaces of the thirteenth century. Bell tower, Evesham abbey, 1538–9

Late in the fourteenth century English masons began to convert every element in the church fabric to a sharply cut panelling of stone. St Mary Redcliffe, Bristol, 1375–1400

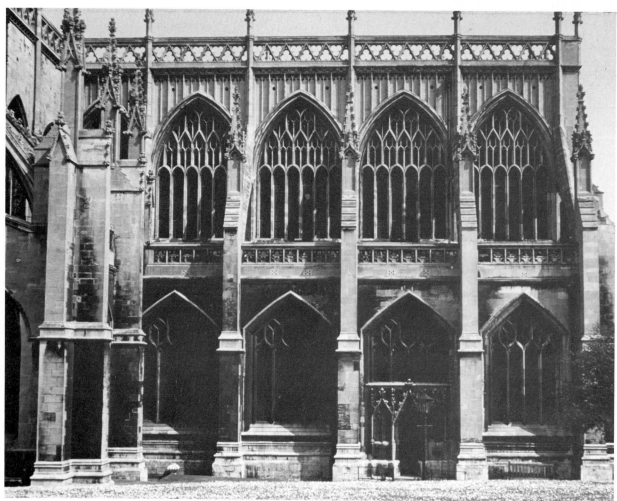

11

FLYING RIBS AND FAN VAULTS

If there is any kernel of truth in the much-misused term 'organic' as applied to architecture, it is to be found in its application to structure. Stripped of its romantic connotations, the term is a perfectly valid measure of the fitness of structure, referring to an ecological balance of processes or forces which mutually act and adjust. The architect's skill then can be measured by the 'organic' interlocking of components in a resiliant construct which can flex, adapt, and readjust to physical forces and pressures.

Were we able to 'grow' our buildings, to use a crystalline material which would set up into space lattices and geometric frames, or if we had a quasi-living plastic foam in which the bubbles would interlock and harden to create a large honeycomb of usable space, our problem would be simple. In the place of abstruse calculation and the tiresome joining of unit to unit which is the architect's lot, we could sit back and let the geometry of nature take its course. At a microscopic scale this is exactly what occurs in the crystalline or colloid setting of plastics or cements. Composite materials in which steel or glass fibres are disposed in a resilient matrix have a grain or texture which can adjust and flex under loading. Wood itself in its cellular structure, in which plastic boxes grow together in a binding medium, exhibits just this process.

But, as yet, architects at the macroscopic scale of the five- to six-foot module of man must laboriously cut, cast, or shape units of structure and then fasten them together into constructs suitable for man. Seen in this light, the lattices and shells of the medieval builder were no mean attainment. Progressively paring away waste material in their designs and refining their basic concepts, they were able to create economical and resilient structural frames in timber and masonry which challenge our own achievements in steel or ferroconcrete. As we have seen, they achieved this by dissolving the wall to a skeletal armature carrying panels of masonry or glass, and in the vault closely spaced ribs carried 'planks' of stone. So extreme was this mimicry of the framed tradition during the fourteenth century that the rib finally broke free of the bounding plane of the shell vault to become a buttress arch, stone tracery in the window, or a free-flying arch ring below the vault. As shall be seen, an inevitable reaction set in by the fifteenth century. At the end of the Gothic the masons turned back to the firm limits of shell surfacing, re-established the continuity of the planar wall, and once again embraced the geometric order and simple closure of the box.

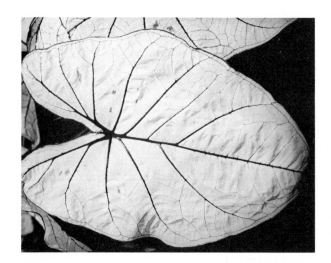

The branching interlace of structure in the leaf which carries a thin membrane is analogous to the elaborate ribbed fabric of the masonry vault.

The designers of medieval vaults became fascinated by effects of structural ingenuity and elaborate virtuosity, in their effort to devise ever more daring shells. Crossing, Peterborough

OVERLEAF *Flying ribs, choir, St Mary, Warwick*

West country masons did not restrict their originality in the use of structural components to new patterns of ribbing and panelling. They went on to radical recompositions of the nave-to-aisle complex which was at the root of the general design problem of the medieval church. The choir of Bristol cathedral was rebuilt from 1311 to 1340 with aisles as high as the nave. In this hall-church design, clerestory and flying buttress, the elements which caused such trouble in the design of the medieval church, were done away with in favour of the much simpler answer of lighting the church directly from the high aisles.[1] Rather than employ the heavy internal buttressing of Aquitaine, the English designers turned to an ingenious structure in which narrow transverse cross-vaults were sprung from flying arches set across the aisles. The hall church had been used earlier in England – notably in the choir of the Temple church, London, and in many parish churches where nave and aisle were of equal height – but this design is typical of the west of England in its exposure of skeletal structure within the building. Essentially, it was an advanced and delicate variant of the old eleventh-century transverse barrel vault used at St Philibert, Tournus, or the aisles of Fountains abbey; but in the fourteenth century this was transmuted into an apparatus of struts and props cutting through the interior.

Typical of English structural ingenuity during the fourteenth century is this transverse aisle vaulting carried on a free arch ring in the choir at Bristol.

Transversely vaulted aisles as high as the nave, and a low-pitched lead sheathed roof made the choir at Bristol cathedral a complex rectangular box. 1311–40

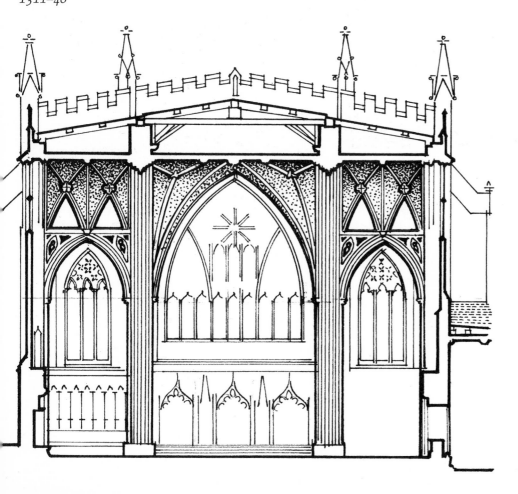

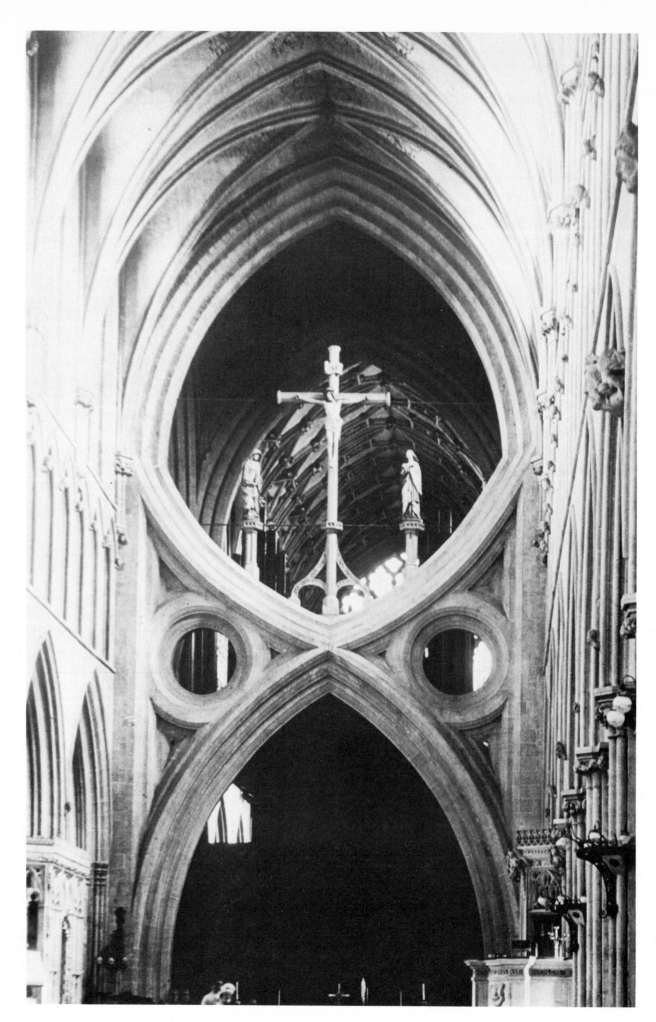

*Faced with the progressive deformation of the
crossing piers at Wells, William Joy built interlocking strainer arches in 1338 to stabilize the piers.*

Again in the west country, strainer arches were built between the crossing at Wells about 1338. We have noted the later difficulties encountered by the builders at Gloucester in their effort to distribute the loads of a crossing tower over the central piers. Rather than carry a stone beam or flat arch across the nave and prop it into position with an arch as at Salisbury, the architect at Wells introduced a pointed flying arch cutting between the piers.[2] Continuing the curves of these arches upwards, he created a reverse arch ring which effectively braced the upper portion of the pier. Into the spandrels created by the intersection of these arches he introduced traceried circles to spread the haunching or bracing over the whole surface of the pier. It is an engineer's solution, using arched bracing frames to solve a dangerous concentration of loads.

In the choir vault of St Mary, Warwick, constructed from 1381 to 1391, the influence of the carpenter is everywhere dominant. Flying ribs spring up from the piers to brace the longitudinal ridge rib. Above these slender braces, tiercerons with sharp facetings and concave mouldings swing from the pier to carry a remarkably flat vaulting surface. The webs of the vault are constructed of planks of stone spanning from rib to rib. Although there is sufficient curvature in the severies to ensure that these masonry planks will wedge into a shell surface, the architect introduced flying arches to make doubly sure of the stability of the vault apex. So slender are the ribs and so accurately cut are the profiles and mouldings that this vault is more elegant, more sparing of material, than the comparatively heavy hammer-beam trusses then finding favour with the master carpenters.

NOTES
1 Francis Bond *The Cathedrals of England and Wales* (London 1912) 14–17
2 Paul Frankl *Gothic Architecture* (Penguin Books 1962) 152

English Gothic rectilinearity in the choir of St Mary, Warwick: completed by 1391, the vault was designed as a braced cage and stone plank construction. In place of the smoothly modelled curved surfaces developed in small stone webbing, the masons treated stone as if it were wood. The flying braces may be of dubious structural value but they dramatically signal the change away from shell surfaces and massive piers.

At Salisbury the repetitive bay system of the Gothic nave did not give adequate bearing for the heavy loads of crossing towers. Here, as at Wells, the strainer arches arrested the deformation of the crossing piers. 1417–23

Although lierne vaults and flying ribs continued to be built well into the sixteenth century, the cutting edge of English experiment was turned, during the fifteenth century, to the fan vault. Rejecting the customary elaborate apparatus of interlaced rib and diagonal pattern, English architects now built vaults in which the ribbed pattern became secondary to the shell surface. Again the west country proved to be a source for a major innovation in architecture. At Gloucester, before 1377, the southeastern bays of the cloister were built with fully developed fan vaults. Though small in scale, the cloister being but twelve feet wide, these vaults have the basic elements of the fan: a flaring conoid giving a repetitive constant curvature to every rib on the surface, and a system of ribs and horizontal hoops which allow the rib pattern to double as it moves up the vaulted shell.

The designers of fan vaults dropped all folding in the vault, substituting reversed curvatures, constant in profile. The flaring conoids of shell masonry were sprung from the supports to meet tangentially at the crown of the vault. The surfaces left between the fans were constructed as flat arched plates wedged in against the conoids. No sharp angles or acute folding disrupt the effect of continuously stressed smoothly curved surfaces flowing from support to support. Ribs were modelled in the stones of the basic shell, not built as separate structural units. To lighten the vault the undersurface was cut away in coffers bounded by a pattern of integral ribs. This denial of the separate structural significance of the rib had distinct advantages. The system of the fan vault was simple to lay out and comparatively straightforward to build. In place of

the complex patterning imposed by the mesh of ribs in a lierne vault it provided a predictable and economical shell span. The reverse curvatures in the flaring conoid ensured a rigid, simple shell ideally suited to span the large boxy churches of the fifteenth century.

Structurally the one point of weakness was the flat panel of vaulting between the conoids, which would have made the vault unsound if applied to wider spans. The answer to the problem was also found at Gloucester: one bay in the cloister was oblong rather than square, and the architect intersected the conoids to reduce the flat spandrel.

Rather than being separate elements, ribs in the fan vault were cut from the shell of stone. Vaults over cloister, Gloucester, by Robert Leysingham, 1381–1412

In the fan vault English masons turned away from two centuries of experiment with folding and ribbing to experiment once again with curved shell surfaces.
Intersecting reversed curvatures in the flaring conoids of the fans ensured rigid shells. Conoids were butted together to reduce the flat spandrels.

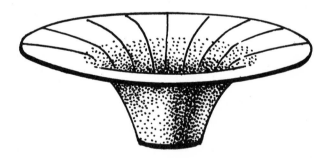

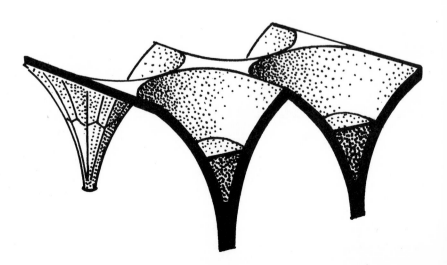

6

a) Detailed Soil investigation is an essential aspect of the development of Contaminated land' Discuss the validity of this statement.

b) Review the various investigation strategies for Contaminated land, and comment on their advantages and disadvantages.

How did the fan vault evolve? The most obvious source was the flaring bundle of tierceron ribs which was so distinctive a feature of the polygonal chapter house. Panelled ribbing appears in the central conoid of the lost chapter house at Hereford, in a drawing by Stukely from 1721. This Hereford fan vault, built from 1360 to 1370, was contemporary with the Gloucester cloister.[1] Even earlier, a tomb canopy over the memorial to Sir Hugh le Despenser, dating from 1350, had regular conoids without ribs to support a flat ceiling. Later the fan vault proved a form ideally suited to decorative canopies over tomb effigies, as in the Cardinal Beaufort chantry at Winchester built in 1447.

Despite the fourteenth-century applications,

English architects were hesitant to apply the fan to major spans. During the first half of the fifteenth century the fan was used at Milton Abbas and Sherbourne abbey in Dorset, but in a secondary role, as a support for richly patterned lierne vaults. In both cases the radiating ribs of the fans were still structural elements carrying the panel infills. The structural diagram of the vault built over the choir at Sherbourne after 1446 clearly indicates the ingenious techniques used. Ribs were pierced through to the upper surface of the fan to carry the small infill stones on narrow haunchings. But where the ribs interlocked in a delicate tracery of cusps the architect introduced a ring of large stones, with the ribs and cusping carved on the lower surface. In the

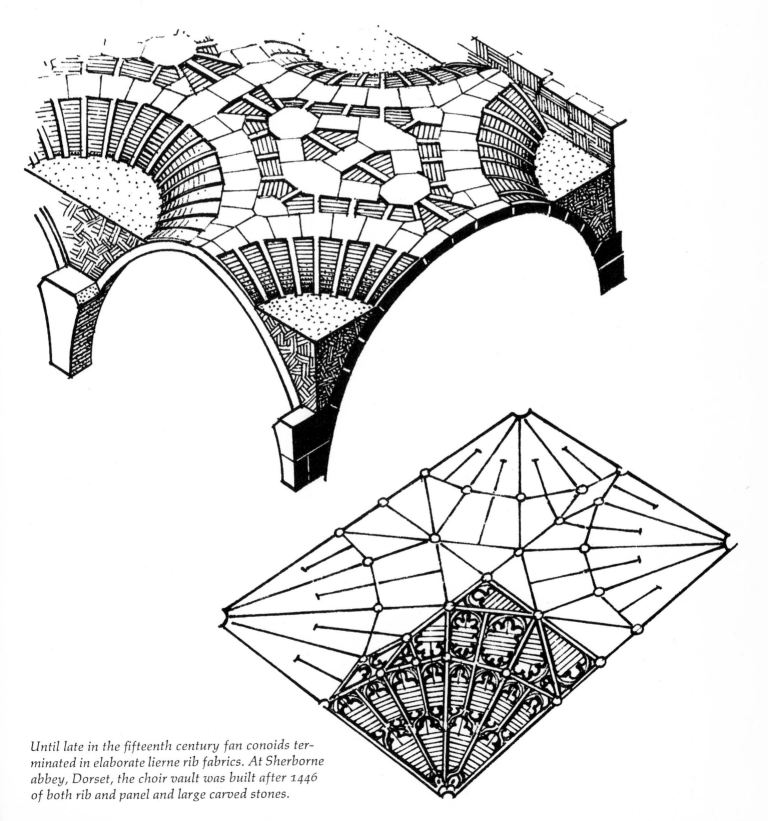

Until late in the fifteenth century fan conoids terminated in elaborate lierne rib fabrics. At Sherborne abbey, Dorset, the choir vault was built after 1446 of both rib and panel and large carved stones.

comparatively flat centre of the vault, rib and panel and large-stone construction were mixed. Evidently, the linear pattern of the lierne vault, with its multiplication of lierne ribs and interlacing of tiercerons, had become so complex that it was no longer logical to build it as a lattice carrying a thin shell; as a sheer matter of structural economy it was simpler to build a shell and then carve a decorative interlace, in effect a system of coffers, to lighten the fabric.

No doctrinaire rule forced the designer to choose between lierne or fan construction. This is evident in the vault of St George's chapel at Windsor, built by William Vertue from 1506 to 1511 after he had completed the strictly regular fans of Bath abbey. Here he turned back to the mixed construction of Sherbourne to create a vault in which the crown is of shell and the supporting fans are of rib and panel. Strictly speaking the vaulting conoids are not even fans, their independent ribs spring in differing curvatures to meet transverse and longitudinal ridge ribs. Vertue built the vault with an extremely flat curvature, relying upon the lightness of the shell, and the precise and careful interlocking of the stones in the central barrel, the bracing ribs and the severies to minimize thrust. He dropped cusping and carved detail to re-emphasize the ribbed pattern. The chapel at Windsor in its spare architectonic detailing represents the supreme triumph of the mason engineer over the sculptor artist.

NOTE

1 Geoffrey Webb *Architecture in Britain in the Middle Ages* (Penguin Books 1956) 143

Early fan vaults evolved as decorative canopies over tomb effigies. Beaufort chantry chapel, Winchester, 1404–47

With this mixed fan and lierne construction the mason had complete freedom to vary the design to suit any need. The handsome structural shell could be enriched by any desired texture or pattern of ribs. Nave vault, Sherborne abbey, 1475–90

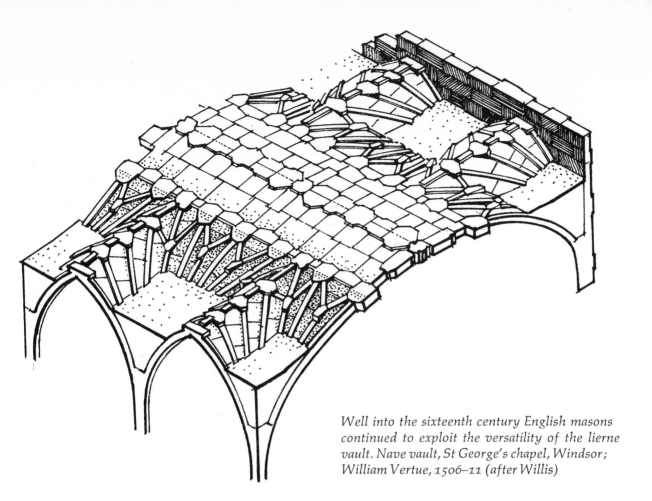

Well into the sixteenth century English masons continued to exploit the versatility of the lierne vault. Nave vault, St George's chapel, Windsor; William Vertue, 1506–11 (after Willis)

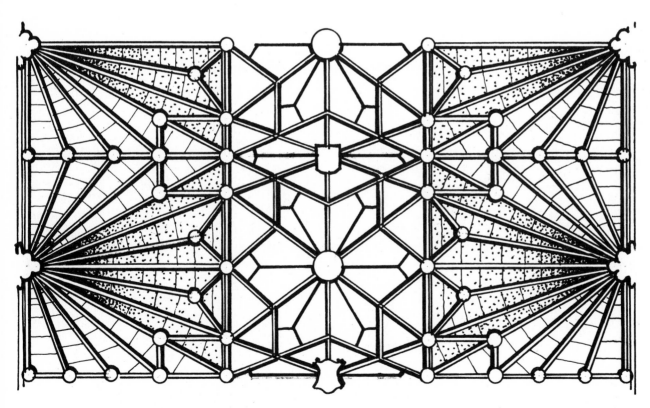

Strictly speaking the Windsor vault was not a fan: the ribs did not develop from a conoid surface. William Vertue cut the elaborate interlace of liernes from a thin masonry barrel constructed of carefully interlocked large stones.

The continuing vitality of medieval traditions of building, which gave a special savour and splendid magnificence to Tudor building during the sixteenth century, was based upon the firm bedrock of skilled and articulate engineering. Perhaps never before or since has the architect been in as favourable a position to create monuments which could sum up the special glory of a local building tradition. The growing professionalism and specialization of the building trades had progressed to the point where major commissions could be carried out with dispatch and efficiency. Contract work let out to subsidiary craftsmen freed the architect to concentrate upon the administrative and design aspects of building. But the architect still participated actively in the detailed execution of the work, ensuring that the building would retain the stamp of his personality.

The new retrochoir built by John Wastell from 1496 to 1508 at Peterborough reflects this healthy balance between technical competence, design skill,

and aesthetic insight. The total composition was so devised that all decorative elements were to evolve from and remain subordinate to the wide sweeping fans of the vaulting conoids.[1] He reduced the ribs to slender, rectilinear projections on the shell. Where earlier fans had an interlocking splay of panels, in this vault he swung the ribs straight through from springing to crown. In the three closely spaced, horizontal rings at the top of the conoid he emphasized the regular curvature of the shell. By intersecting the shells the vaults were adapted to oblong bays, leaving only a small wedge of space between the fans. Instead of treating this space with a mesh pattern of lierne ribs, Wastell projected the fan ribs to meet at a slender ridge rib, accenting the centre of each bay with a pendant boss. In this vault the tierceron rib and ridge rib reappear as the essential linear elements in English design.

Examination of the stereotomy of the vault shows, however, just how far these late Gothic

In the retrochoir at Peterborough from 1496–1508, John Wastell used wide sweeping fans with a de- *liberately spare use of decoration. The fans were interlocked to reduce the spandrel to the minimum.*

masons had moved in the direction of shell structures. Although the decorative soffit still celebrated the typical English fascination with effects of line, the upper surface discloses a quite different approach to structure. The vault was built of carefully shaped, large, stone voussoirs locked into a rigid shell. Only the lower range of the fans is built in a rib and panel construction. The decorative patterning of the soffit becomes a device by which excess material can be cut away to lighten the large flat stones of the shell. Gothic had come to full term; the original motivating principle of a framed skeleton with web or panel infills was being replaced by a continuous web of masonry or structural shell complete in itself. The structure of this vault discloses a static engine of great refinement in which the voussoirs lock in complex play of thrust and counterthrust into a three-dimensionally curved continuum of masonry.

This was no isolated achievement: in 1501 Robert and William Vertue designed shell fans to an even larger scale for the choir of Bath abbey.[2] Completed by 1539, these sweeping shells are economical, sparse, and simply detailed.[3] The interlocking reversed curvatures, and the construction with thin, flat stones, reduced thrust and minimized buttressing. The effect at Bath is quite startling because the fans are perched above wide clerestory windows. The diffracted light pouring through the glass walls quite literally makes these shells appear to 'float' without support.

Perhaps the most famed of these late medieval buildings is the chapel at King's college, Cambridge, where Reginald Ely had designed and started a great glass hall in 1446. John Wastell completed it with a fan vault immediately after his work at Peterborough.[4] He introduced transverse arch rings separating each bay, but in other respects it is identical to the vaults at Peterborough. However rich the interior decoration, the total effect is superbly unified: a vast and noble barn, the epitome of English building.

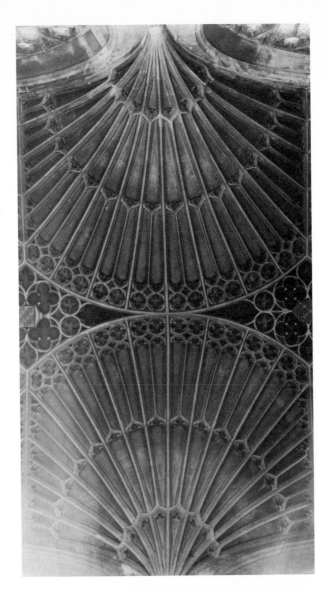

Over the choir at Bath abbey, Robert and William Vertue built fan vaults, in 1501, applying these shell techniques to a major span. The delicately incised ribs serve to accent the curvatures of the shell surfaces.

NOTES
1 Geoffrey Webb *Architecture in Britain in the Middle Ages* (Penguin Books 1956) 197
2 Ibid 198
3 John Harvey *Gothic England* (London 1947) 129–30
4 F. Mackenzie *Observations on the Construction of the Roof of King's College Chapel, Cambridge* (London 1840). In this a drawing gives a measurement of 4⅞″ for the thickness of the vaulting panels. 'It is remarkable that the panels are found to vary from 2 to 6 inches in thickness. – The late Mr. Wilkins, measuring them in two or three places, found them from 4 to 6 inches. And the measurement taken for these plates gave 4½ inches. And all this difference must occur in the three upper tiers of panels, within a span of about 11 feet.' page 16.

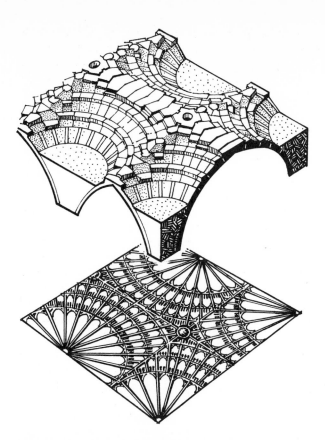

John Wastell created an elegantly adjusted and counterpoised static engine in the structural fabric of the vault over the retrochoir at Peterborough, built from 1496–1508. (after Willis).

In 1515 John Wastell introduced transverse arch rings below the fans of the vault at King's College chapel, Cambridge.

Perhaps it was inevitable that the fan vault and the flying rib would be combined in one structural complex during this phase of highly experimental engineering. The new centralization of power in the Tudor court at Westminster, the need for effective and impressive images of the new prosperity under the monarch, and the turn away from the rather prosy and practical affairs of town councils and local abbots, encouraged a pageant architecture of exotic display. The new religion of statecraft and national interest needed compelling and dramatic symbols. The versatile masons, carpenters, and architects, schooled in the long apprenticeship of medieval building, hastened to create a sumptuous architecture of frothy extravagance.

The fan vault by itself was a workmanlike simple shell surface, economical to build and severe in outline. But when combined with an arch ring, so that it was sprung not from the wall pier but from an intermediate point on the arch as at Christ Church cathedral, Oxford, it could recapture the spatial imagination and ingenious construction technique of the fourteenth century. Evidently English architects were loath to sacrifice the variety of the lierne, as was evident when William Vertue turned back to the complex lierne at St George's, Windsor. Turning away from the puritanical rigour of Bath or Peterborough, sixteenth-century royal architecture rejected the boxy outline, planar surfaces, and disciplined linearity of the characteristic local mode to create a last, blazing triumph of structural imagination.

Late in the fifteenth century experiments had been made with vaults in which shells of stone were sprung from transverse arch rings set across a nave, notably at Oxford in the Divinity School built by William Orchard in 1479. With this device the fans could radiate in a full 360° arc.

William Vertue made use of this in the vault of the Henry VII chapel built during the first quarter of the sixteenth century. Here, fans were sprung from the voussoirs of a transverse arch ring. Seen from above, the structural apparatus of the vault is clear and precise. The arch rings pierce through the vaulting shell to swing across the chapel as transverse bents carrying the smoothly modelled undulating curvatures of the vaulted shell.

But below in the theatrical interior, this severe structural rigour dissolves into an equivocal display of conceits. Vertue projected elaborate crockets from the arch ring, hung pendants to carry the springing of the fans, and introduced pierced screens into the space between flying arch and wall in a deliberate effort to conceal the engineered fabric with a breath-taking display of decoration. Pierced vaults, closely spaced mullions, and finely modelled panelling dissolve every surface into a mannered display of the mason's artistry. Gilded and carved wood in the rich stalls, painted heraldic panels on the walls, and a striking display of armourial bearings make this the supreme instance of Gothic 'rococo,' fully equalling in its sumptuous extravagance the Bavarian rococo of the eighteenth century.

On the exterior Robert and William Vertue sculptured the aisle wall with octagonal buttresses and

Robert and William Vertue, from 1503–19, built the elaborate vaults over the Henry VII chapel at Westminster abbey as shells springing from points on the transverse arch rings.

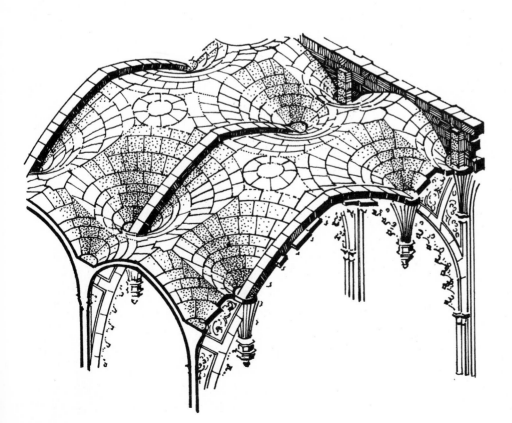

projecting oriel windows. The projecting oriel was a device which was to find increasing favour in the sixteenth century, when it was used to give textural interest and rich variety to the walls of the new palaces of the aristocracy and to an occasional church addition, as at Cirencester.

In the Henry VII chapel, not content with fretted skyline created by pinnacles and sham crenelation, the Vertues topped the buttresses with pierced cupolas. Originally these were crowned by heraldic sculptures of the king's beasts, each carrying a gilded vane which rotated and twinkled in the wind. The elaborate theatricality can only be paralleled by the gorgeous and temporary display of masques and pavilions erected on the Field of the Cloth of Gold as Henry VIII and Francis I vied in international prestige. The decorations for those celebrations also were designed by William Vertue, setting the pattern for the future role of the architect as designer of masques, extravaganzas, and follies.

Eventually fan and lierne constructions were sprung from intermediate points on an arch ring. The technique is similar to that used in hammer beam trusses. Vault, presbytery, Oxford cathedral, 1480–1500

In the Henry VII chapel, Westminster abbey, elaborate pendants and crockets were hung from the masonry shell in seeming defiance of gravity.

On the exterior of the Henry VII chapel, Westminster, Robert and William Vertue broke the wall
into projecting bays and polygonal buttresses,
decoratively sheathed with rectilinear panelling.

GOTHIC
AND RENAISSANCE

A splendid public-relations job for the Tudor dynasts, a brilliant aesthetic mirage, the Henry VII chapel signalled the end of medieval harmony and balance. As architecture became the plaything of the new national powers, virtuosity replaced vigour and fantasy thrust aside logic. Patronage by the crown, and commissions executed for the new condottieri and adventurers of an expansive and turbulent time, divorced the architect from the roots of building, at the same time that they freed him from the niggling squabbles of town councils. No longer need the architect struggle to convince recalcitrant churchmen and tight-fisted tradesmen; he had only to gain the ear of the prince and the commission was made fact. In place of schools, universities, hospitals, housing, and churches, the architect turned to sumptuary palaces and royal residences. Made independent of his roots in the craft of building by the heady excitement of acceptance in court circles, he began that long slow decline marked by loss of technical competence to the engineer and of social responsibility to the planner.

Fashion and the new literacy collaborated to divorce the architect from his primary role as a geometer skilled in the shaping of man's physical environment. The onslaught of a classical antique taste, the Italianate fashion which became the favoured weapon of the new aristocracy, was a double-edged sword. The architect escaped the constrictive detail of the Gothic, but his reliance upon engravings in books and crude wood-cut sketches of Roman detail substituted a melange of motifs for a consistent system. The hasty improvisations and façade frontispieces purporting to follow the new southern taste were intrusive and often discordant theatre sets plastered without logic and without restraint on what remained of the medieval tradition of sound building. All too often, temporary patchwork and stylistic improvisation replaced the fundamental logic of building. This was particularly the case in the architecture of the courts and the nobility. Building became splendid rather than solid, theatrical rather than logical, and an imported affair of taste rather than an indigenous local matter of

Under the crossing tower at Winchester, in 1634, wooden trusswork and casing simulated the pattern of fifteenth-century fan vaulting.

The parishioners of St Mary Aldermary, London, in 1682 obliged Christopher Wren to recall medieval detail in the plaster fan vaults over the nave.

168

balance and economy. For the architect of northern countries the Renaissance was an unmitigated disaster, forcing him to substitute style and fashion for the fundamental verities of structure and function.

And yet, as an architect it is difficult not to feel some sympathy for the protagonists of the new style. The final florid outburst of decorative enrichment in the sixteenth century, though the direct result of royal demand, was too heated, too enriched to be lasting. The severe plastered wall of the south-ern Renaissance was a welcome relief after the fantastic enrichment of every surface in the later Gothic. The Renaissance forms, however clumsily adapted, evolved from a sparse vocabulary of geometric forms. The new shapes were plastic and sculptural. They owed nothing to the complex and subtle demands of structure.

But it was almost one hundred years before Inigo Jones in England was to make a first successful statement of this formal geometry in the Queen's

As late as 1640 fan vaults with a four-centered arch profile and sparse ribbing were built over the stair at Christ Church college, Oxford.

House. These years are not part of the present story but it is of some interest to see how remarkably resistant the forms of the Gothic proved to be. In the provinces, in out-of-the-way parishes, in the conservative universities, so much creatures of the Middle Ages, builders continued to use unselfconscious adaptations of the late Gothic right up until the last quarter of the eighteenth century, when the Gothic Revival turned the Palladians to a Romantic interest in the 'Gothik' past. In England, the Gothic never quite died out. The Englishness of English art, to use Pevsner's phrase, is basically medieval.

Heavy incised ribs over the Bishop West chantry chapel in Ely cathedral, in 1534, suggest a new prismatic folding of surface.

Eventually medieval detail was to be reborn in the early Gothic Revival as in this plaster fan in the chantry at St Mary, Warwick.

CENTRAL EUROPE

12

HALL CHURCH AND MESH VAULT

The accidents of history and the profound conservatism of abbots and clerics had restricted early Gothic designers in the north and west of Europe to the limiting formula of the basilican church. The high nave and low aisle configuration remained a compromise, needing complex external scaffolding to support a disproportionately high and narrow interior. The limited spans attainable with compression masonry vaults dictated internal pier supports to carry the vault. Aisles widened the effective floor area of the church but, because they were low in height, did not relate directly to the high volume of the nave.

But quite another approach was possible: in the south of France and in Catalonia, builders solved the problem with the box. A heavy wall – built outside the delicate fabric of buttress, vault, or dome – surrounded the structural machine and protected its elements from the weather. By raising the aisle vaults to the full height of the nave, an external masonry or brick shell could be made to tie the entire fabric together in a simple envelope.

In so doing the builders sacrificed the dramatic effect of wide expanses of translucent glass supported at the clerestory by a delicate cage or frame. But in the south, around the Mediterranean shores, this was a positive advantage. There was no need here for the prismatic interplay of sunlight streaming into a bright and cheerful interior; rather, the aim was to achieve a cool and shaded interior free of the blinding glare and oppressive heat of the street.

In central Europe, along the shores of the Baltic, in Germany and Poland, and in the Bohemian and Austrian heart of the land mass, architects during the Middle Ages could choose between a light glass cage or a massive sheltering box. During the thirteenth and the early fourteenth centuries they

copied the French mode. The profound impact of the 'opus francigenum' was such that it swept away traditional modes of building. From Prague to Danzig, by the end of the thirteenth century, the towering glass cage was triumphant. Yet, was this a logical and reasoned response to the environmental conditions, functional needs, and construction techniques of these regions? Evidently not, for by the middle of the fourteenth century architects from the Baltic to the Tatra highlands were devising new and quite different responses which looked back to their native building techniques.

Along the coasts of northern Europe, warmed by the Gulf Stream, winters were wet and cloudy not bitterly cold. The Bretons, Normans, and English sought a type of construction which would let light and air into the fabric to brighten the damp and dreary interior.[1] Skeletal structures with large window areas were a reasoned response to these conditions.

But in central Europe hot summers and sunny but cold winters encouraged the use of a wall which could both retain heat in the winter and exclude glare and heat in the summer. The loghouse, which used wood as an insulator, was a valuable ally in the winter-long fight against heat loss. The heavy masonry wall built in fireproof brick or stone fulfilled the same function, keeping heat in during the winter, and excluding it during the summer.

There were other reasons why the spacious sheltering box was better suited to conditions in central Europe. It was, first, dangerous to expose to the action of frost and snow a complex external lacework of arches and buttresses. Rain may gradually erode and dissolve masonry but frost, with its heaving action, is the immediate enemy of all intricate external detail.[2] Cold frosty climates have always encouraged simple boxy forms which offer no re-

OVERLEAF *Sixteenth-century aisled hall church with decorated mesh vault. Marienkirche, Halle, Saxony*

Though many of the structures have been rebuilt in the seventeenth and eighteenth centuries, the scale of the dense medieval town keyed to pack animal traffic remains little changed. Regensburg, Germany

entrant angles in which water can freeze and pry apart the components of the building.

Another factor was the kind of building material available. The Jurassic limestones bordering the Paris and London basins were ideally adapted to fine cutting and complex stereotomy. Easy to quarry and model and hardening upon exposure to the air, these strong and enduring stones made the Gothic possible.[3] Without them masons would have encountered great difficulty in translating the timber frame into permanent masonry. In the north, sandstones with similar characteristics were used at Durham and Fountains while along the Rhine the buff and red sandstones extended the range of the French Gothic to Cologne, Strasbourg, and Freiburg.

Along the Baltic coast there was little or no good building stone. Masons had to use fired-clay bricks for fireproof construction. Yet the use of brick with wide mortar joints was ill-suited to the light structural framework and concentrated loads of the French Gothic pattern. At Lübeck and other cities the plastic flow of the lime mortar over the centuries has left the buildings with pronounced and clearly noticeable distortions. To be used to good effect structurally, brick and mortar require continuous surfaces which can interlock to distribute the loads uniformly. The simple planar box of brick solved this problem.

But neither climatic logic nor structural economy can determine alone the shape or configuration of a building. The structure must adapt to specific social needs or it will not be built. With the collapse of the Ottonian empire Germany regressed to a loose confederation of free towns and small principalities. Building programmes were no longer set by dictat from a central ecclesiastical authority or royal courts; they evolved from the practical exigencies and needs of local communities. Also, during the fourteenth century the emphasis of the Christian faith began to change from a strictly hieratic organization to a highly personal emphasis upon individual salvation. The stunning impact of the Black Death, the devastations of dynastic war, and the rigid cruelties of religious persecution set a term to the optimistic pan-European hopes of the twelfth century. Rejecting the appeal to a united Christendom, men turned inwards to their own town and their own province. The expansive mood which had sparked the crusades and encouraged the settlement of new towns along the Baltic and in Spain was replaced by a conservative consolidation of the existing urban fabric.

As the townsfolk of the prosperous trading communities began to participate ever more strongly in the ceremony of the church, and as the burghers paid the bills to advertise the worth of their town, they demanded a more active part in the church. The friars were quick to seize upon the implications to their advantage. They created wide preaching halls rather than linear ceremonial spaces. Long before the Reformation became established fact, the physical structure of the church began to reflect a new concept of design – one which converted the graded magic space of the Romanesque and early Gothic to a simple, whitewashed, crowd container. Both Re-

formation rigour and Renaissance formalism cast long shadows before they became accepted fact.

The problem was to adapt the Gothic to a severe northern climate, in a region lacking good building stone, and to create an impressive preaching hall. The solution was the hall church.

NOTES
1 William C. Wachs 'Historical Geography of Medieval Church Architecture' (unpublished PH D thesis, University of Cincinnati 1961) 76
2 Ibid 73–5
3 Ibid 290

Where wood was in short supply, the builders used fire-proof brick laid up in heavy planar walls, but the decoration continued to echo the detail of frame. St Mathias, Nowe, Poland

Two traditions met along the Alpine ridge. The wide sheltering pitched roof of the north was perched over the sheltering masonry box of the south. South Tirol, Italy

The German Romanesque was an architecture of
severe planar surfaces and massive supports. Nave,
Speyer cathedral

German Romanesque buildings were massive structures. Speyer cathedral on the Rhine, for example, was built with small clerestory windows and severely planar masses of walling. The change from a timber ceiling to groined masonry vaulting only enhanced the effect of containment: the predominant statement is of a heavy insulating box. This German version of the Romanesque continued long after the wholesale adoption of French techniques along the Rhine at Strasbourg and Cologne; elsewhere there was a marked resistance to the opening of the wall.

At Bamberg, Ulm, and the Sebalduskirche at Nürnberg the absence of a gallery, the low aisles, and the small clerestory windows combined to leave large expanses of walling enclosing the nave. The late thirteenth-century nave of the Lorenzkirche at Nürnberg still shows this regional preference for closure. There is no penetration through the wall, no prismatic cage of glass, no attempt to focus and accent concentrations of loads from the vault. Though Gothic in detail of ribs, shafts, and tracery, the nave remains a box of planar masonry, more akin to the architecture of the Mediterranean than to the experimental masonry frames of France and England. As in the coastal lands of the Mediterranean, the wall was a heavy structural plane designed to carry the structure and insulate the interior. It only remained to move this containing wall to the outside of a high aisle to create the unified interior of the hall church.

Long after French and English masons had converted their churches to translucent glass cages German designers emphasized the containing wall. Nave, Ulm

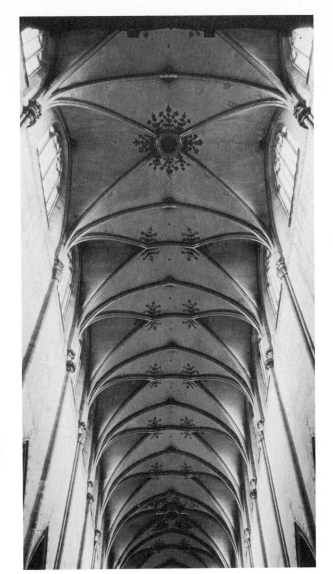

In this change from the bishops' cathedral to the friar's preaching hall the interior became a spacious box in which two ranges of piers carried the folded apparatus of the vault. Simple planar walls of brick, plastered and lime-washed on the interior, were pierced only by narrow lancet windows. Stepped buttressing on the exterior of the wall betrayed the continuing influence of the western European bay articulation. The trussed timber roofs were built high in a steep pitch and it became customary to erect a decorative brick gable over the façade to express the roof. Turning away from the balanced frontal towers of the Romanesque or the early Gothic, the architects went back to the local mode of residential building, faithfully echoing the gabled roof line of the medieval street, for example in the gable of St Mattias, Nowe, in Poland or the soaring roof line of the Martinikirche at Landshut, Bavaria, built from 1392 to 1432.

Just after 1300 the nave of the cathedral at Meissen in Saxony was built with aisle and nave vaults at the same height. Though still adhering to the ac-

centuated framing and quadripartite vaults of the French Gothic, this hall church section set a pattern for the later Gothic of central Europe. By 1320 the Heiligkreuzkirche at Schwäbisch-Gmünd had been built as a hall and the Weissenkirche at Soest was completed by 1331 as a hall with simple quadripartite vaulting.[1] From 1340 the type was carried to Silesia in the east. The Sandkirche and the Dorotheenkirche in Breslau (Wrocław) have the characteristic brick envelope, brick vaults, and spacious hall interiors which were to revolutionize the Gothic of eastern Europe.[2]

By the late fifteenth century, the last vestiges of external buttressing disappeared. The wall was pressed out to the extreme outer face of the structure, as at the Marienkirche, Toruń (Thorn) or in the rebuilt aisles of the Marienkirche at Danzig. Buttresses remained but they were placed inside as solid membranes of masonry or brick bracing the external wall against vaulting pressures. To doubly ensure stability of the fabric, masons began to introduce wrought-iron tie-bars cutting through to the

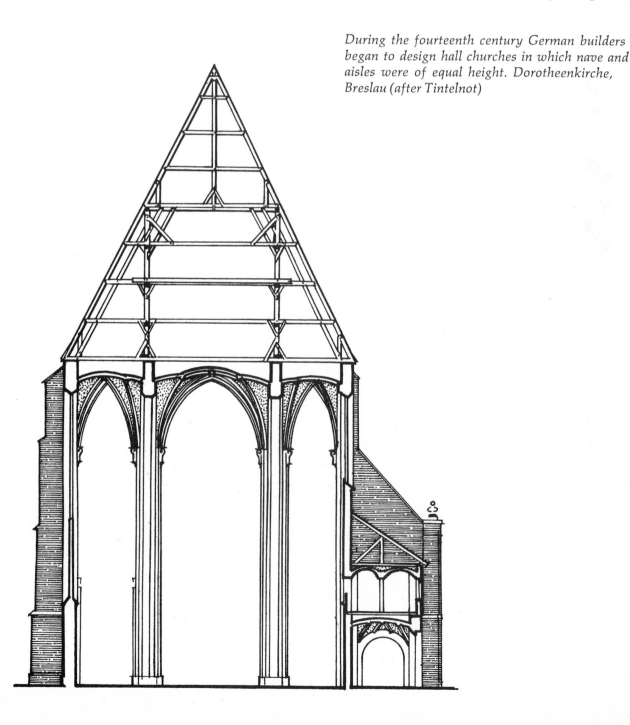

During the fourteenth century German builders began to design hall churches in which nave and aisles were of equal height. Dorotheenkirche, Breslau (after Tintelnot)

outer surfaces of the walls well above the vault haunchings. It was an architecture of planar surfaces. Light membrane walls of brick were braced and propped one against the other to ensure a continuous restraint to the diffuse loadings and thrusts of thin-shell brick vaults. Where the English and French masons denied mass by changing to a skeletal frame, the German masons reduced the mass and weight of the fabric by taking full advantage of continuous interlocking surfaces of brick and mortar.

NOTES
1 Paul Frankl *Gothic Architecture* (Penguin Books 1962) 157
2 Hans Tintelnot *Die mittelalterliche Baukunst schliesens* (Kitzingen 1951)

The characteristic fourteenth-century German hall church had external stepped pier buttresses, brick walls, tall narrow windows, and a high pitched timber roof over the folded vaults.

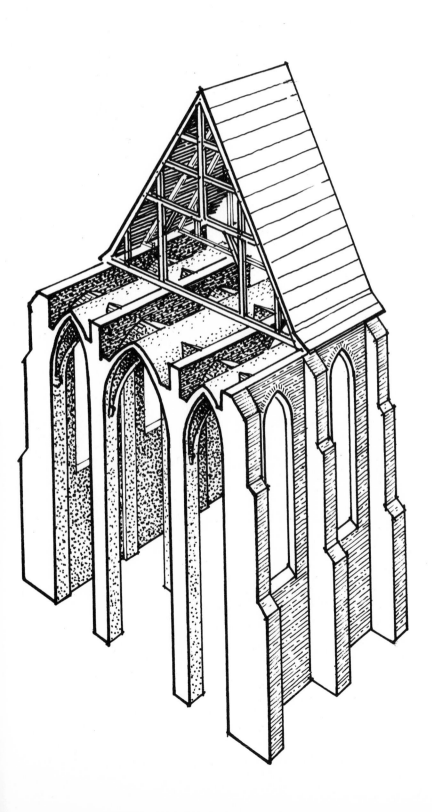

Just after 1300 the cathedral nave at Meissen,
Saxony, was built as a hall with simple quadripartite
vaults.

In the nave of the Martinikirche, Landshut, the
slender polygonal piers carry a simple chevron
vault.

By the late fifteenth century the sheathing wall was
outside the buttressing; wrought iron ties held the
vaulting fabric together. St Mary, Toruń

The hall church, c 1500, was designed as a box of brick with narrow windows and internal buttresses. The high-pitched gable front was decorated with framed and stepped elements.

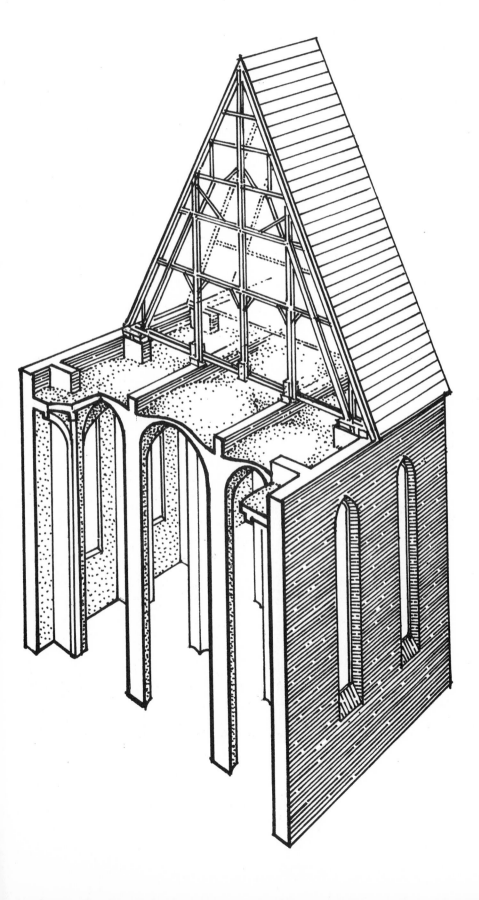

The simple planar walls of the hall church and the slender piers disposed along the internal volume freed the vault designer from the dominance of the bay. No longer was it necessary to conceive of the vault as a repetitive series of folded quadripartite shells, each sharply distinguished from its neighbour by a heavy transverse arch ring. Now the mason or the architect could create gridded patterns or meshs of ribs. In this undulating surface of shell masonry, curved to counter the forces of gravity, ribs became a stiffening lattice breaking the continuous shell into manageable and comprehensible components. More and more the rib began to assume the function of a brace or tie which could collect the diffuse pressures and thrusts of the vault to carry them to the pier. Nodes, clusters, or fans of ribs gathered together the static forces of the shell to effect a smooth transition between vault and pier. Without this intermediary the upthrust piers could have punched through the thin shell of the vault.

The vaults built by Nicolaus Eseler, the elder, in the church of St Georg at Dinkelsbühl are a good example: the exact disposition of the ribs at the crown was evidently only of minor concern because

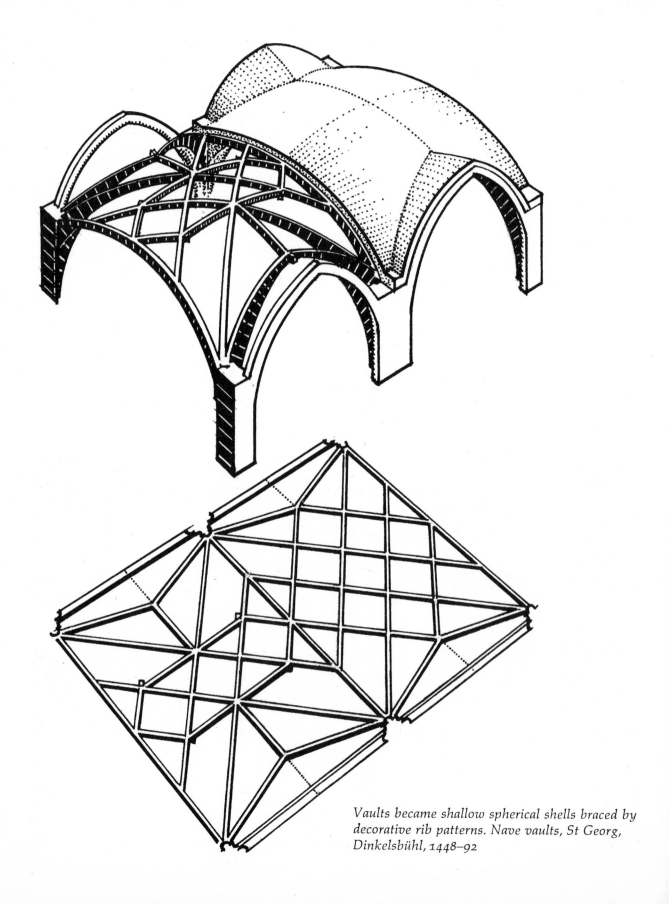

Vaults became shallow spherical shells braced by decorative rib patterns. Nave vaults, St Georg, Dinkelsbühl, 1448–92

he did not hesitate to vary the pattern from bay to bay. But when it came to the transition between pier and rib he completely rejected the column cap, doing away with the last vestigial remnant of Romanesque horizontality to permit a total integration of vertical support and curving shell. To brace the shell, he introduced a thin, deep tierceron, more a curved plate of stone than a rib, springing from the pier face. Here the flying rib was used in purely structural and utilitarian manner by interposing a plate of masonry between it and the surface of the vault.

It now became possible to create vaults with a variety of stellar or mesh patterns in which there was no impediment to the visual or conceptual flow of thrust and load to the pier. The pier with its channeled facets gave rise to a branching and interlaced flight of ribs. The rib could now grow from the pier in accord with the logic of structure, and not be constrained by the tight horizontal girdle of the pier cap. The exact point at which it began its rise to vaulted surface was dictated by considerations of structural convenience and not by an arbitrary aesthetic division between rib and pier. Certainly the advantages this conferred becomes clear in those cases where a later vault was added to an existent pier structure, as in the choir of the Lorenzkirche at Nürnberg.

This technique entailed no change in the layout and execution of the vault. The masons still were able to scribe comparatively simple geometric patterns on the working platform and then project them up to the predetermined curve of the vaulted shell, but the ensuing structural form operated on a new principle. It became a curving space-frame or lattice mesh of ribs quite in contrast to the folded shells of an earlier time. The contrast is precisely analagous to the modern distinction between gridded space frames composed of steel or aluminum members and planar shells of ferroconcrete.

Mouldings pierced one through the other in the choir of Freiburg cathedral.

Nicolaus Eseler devised thin diaphragm plates of stone projecting from the pier to brace the thin shell. Aisle, St Georg, Dinkelsbühl

During the thirteenth century English masons had embarked upon that series of experiments with tierceron ribs which was to culminate in the mesh and stellar patterns of the fourteenth century. Strongly influenced by the carpentered frame, they had hit upon a vocabulary of design which could free the mason from the classic formulae of the French Gothic. The distinctive vernacular idiom of the English craftsmen was exported to southern France, Spain, Portugal, and to central Europe, to create a base for a new flowering of the Gothic: one which could adjust to local climate, available materials, and special needs in flexible adaptations quite independent of the severe restrictions of the classic French culmination.

Masons in each region of the medieval world evolved their own particular variant. The Spaniards turned inwards and away from the sun to create luminescent halls with more than a trace of Moorish influence. In the Germanic centre of Europe, Westphalian, Bavarian, and Austrian architects devised halls with a particular emphasis upon mesh vaulting; the brick masons of the Baltic states and the towns of the Hanseatic league created gabled boxes with rich stellar vaults; in Slavic Bohemia, designers tended to look to England for their sources and they made a great play with ingenious ribbed constructions. Architects in Silesia and in Poland looked to the north for inspiration from Baltic prototypes.

In Franconia and Bavaria, hall churches with mesh vaults ideally stated this new concept of dispersed loading. In these, a curving lattice of small ribs substituted for the sharp folding of earlier vaults. The nave of the Heiligkreuzkirche at Schwäbisch-Gmünd, built about 1320, was one of the earliest hall churches erected in central Europe.[6] With his son Peter, Heinrich Parler designed a choir

Once the transverse arch ring was suppressed, the gridded rib pattern could be swung across two or more bays to create any desired pattern. Choir, Freiburg cathedral, 1354–60, and vault, 1510–13

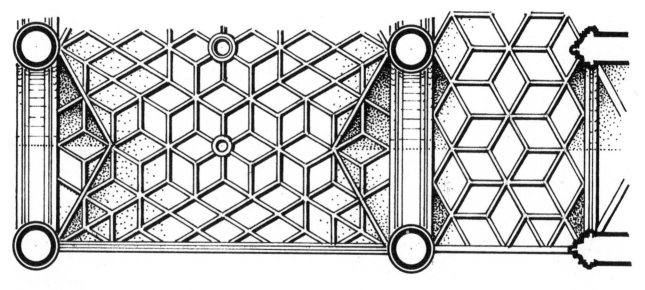

The ribbing pattern was laid out as a regular geometric grid on the working platform and projected up to the curving vaulted surface. Heiligkreuzkirche, Schwäbisch-Gmünd

extension in 1351 in which the vaulting mesh-pattern of Gloucester was regularized and simplified. Rejecting the ridge ribs and residual diagonals which had complicated the English design, Parler broke quite free of a division of the vault into bays. Instead he emphasized a regular pattern of rhomboids over the entire surface of the vault. Round piers in both nave and choir were conservatively topped by sculptured ring caps.

With this new and flexible geometry, problems which had bedevilled masons for centuries could now be solved with relative ease. In the choir vaults of the cathedral at Freiburg-im-Breisgau, Johannes Parler (another of this influential family of architects) used a reticulated lattice of ribs. He was able to avoid warped surfaces and twisted groins in the skew compartments of the ambulatory by freely disposing the ribs and folds to suit the irregular compartment. The suppression of the pier cap, unifying vault and support, let ribs grow in easy transition from the pier to a branching interlace perfectly suited to the structural thrust of the shell, no matter how complex the compartment shape.

NOTE

1 Paul Frankl *Gothic Architecture* (Penguin Books 1962) 157

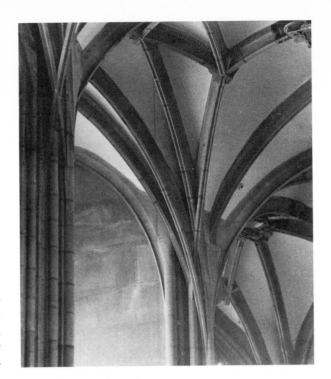

In the aisle vaults of the choir of Freiburg cathedral ribs were pierced through one another to terminate in abrupt truncations. The vault dramatically emphasized the energetic flow of forces.

Vaults became thin barrel shells carried on slender piers. A mesh pattern of ribs suppressed the earlier division into bays. Choir, Heiligkreuzkirche, Schwäbisch-Gmünd

In a Slavic peninsula surrounded and threatened by Germanic principalities and dukedoms, the Bohemians and Moravians of Czechoslovakia tried to look beyond the immediate horizon of German building to French or to English sources for their designs. Charles IV made Prague a centre for Bohemian nationalism and brought Mathieu d'Arras from Avignon in 1344 to design the new cathedral choir of St. Viet. But after Crécy, French influence in politics and in the arts was on the wane, and when Mathieu died in 1352 Peter Parler was appointed to complete the work. The glazed triforium and the subtly modulated string course which sweeps out to embrace the pier in its horizontal grasp clearly derive from France. But Peter Parler's vault with a chevron interlace breaking free of the strict division into bays looks north to Germany and beyond to England for its inspiration.

As Peter Parler completed the chapels surrounding the choir at St Viet, he took full advantage of the new spatial and structural dynamics which had been explored at Gloucester. Between 1355 and 1360, in the sacristy, he set the vaults at a 45° angle to the compartment (a device which had been used to great effect in the crossing vaults of English cathedrals) and then from the boss at the centre hung a support for flying ribs. In the south porch and in the chapel of St Catherine he again used the flying rib in a deliberate effort to break free of the boundary plane of the shell vault. The use of interlacing diagonals to create a grid independent of the bay, the deliberate cutting away of the rib from its panel in the flying rib, and the use of heavy bosses ornately carved are all characteristic of English fourteenth-century design. Certainly, if Parler did not visit England, he must have been quite conversant with west country English design from drawings or descriptions.

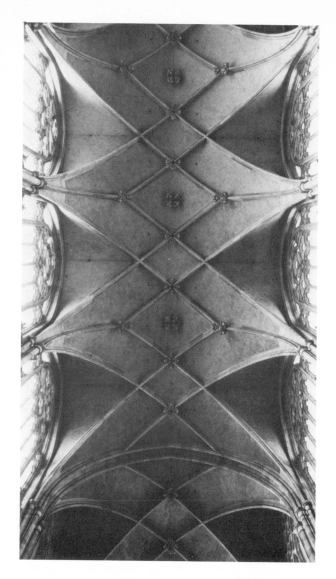

At Prague in 1385 Peter Parler broke the choir vault free of the strict bay formula of the piers by using a simple mesh structure: the chevron vault.

Bohemian architects copied the dramatic flying ribs used in some English churches. South portal, St Viet, Prague

After his successful completion of the choir at Prague, Peter Parler summed up one potential of this new dynamic disposition of the ribs in his design for the choir of the church of St Barbara at Kutna Hora (Kuttenberg) in 1388. This work, built under royal patronage, owed little to the austere discipline and restricted economy of the municipal preaching halls. Here the florid magnificence of the Flamboyant of France and the Rhineland is echoed in the use of a basilican section. In the vaults fans of ribs supported a lattice interspersed with healdic bosses. Elegantly chased and elaborately pinnacled buttresses suggest the elaborate conceits of chivalric fantasy and were ideally suited to the growing pretensions of national monarchies. The roof, capped by pyramidal towers during the sixteenth century, has the same quality of splendid magnificence that we have seen in the Henry VII chapel in England.

The Bohemian tapered, pyramidal roofs and fretted skyline of pinnacles and crockets at Santa Barbara, Kutna Hora, reflect royal patronage and a competitive architecture of display.

Flying buttresses at Kutna Hora (Peter Parler, from 1388) were elaborately cut, pierced and decorated to emphasize the role of the church as a royal chapel.

Throughout the long arc stretching from the Low Countries to the Baltic states a distinctive brick Gothic idiom emerged during the fourteenth century. Hall churches and town halls built of severe planar shells of brick were capped by distinctive gable fronts in which endless changes were rung upon the theme of the pierced decorative gable. Having sacrificed the fretted skyline and staccato accents of pier, pinnacle, and flying buttresses to the exigencies of brick building, the designers concentrated decorative elaboration upon the gabled frontispiece. By translating the complex trusswork of the high-pitched timber roof into a linear fantasy of sculptured accents on the gable, they provided a foil to the simple planar walls of the basic box. Here the idiom evolved from the vernacular house fronting to the street. So successful was this regional style that at the end of the Middle Ages it was carried over to East Anglia in England where it was to have a profound effect upon the emerging Tudor design.

This brick architecture was equally well adapted to civic, ecclesiastical and military functions. At Tangermünde, Lübeck, and Toruń town halls vied with the great churches in the richness of their gable fronts. The masons showed special ingenuity in

Plain brick surfacing was logical structurally, but the eastern European designer continued to recall the decorative potential of frame architecture in the stepped gables. Chapel, fortress of Marienburg (Malbork), Poland

the design of vaulted halls. At Marienburg and Marienwerder the Teutonic knights created military strong points where towering walls of brick and complex systems of defence in depth contained chapels, halls, dormitories, and storehouses modelled upon the prevailing vernacular. In Finland, Denmark, and southern Sweden this translation of the heavy wall of wood into a shell of brick led to a distinctive type of hall parish-church in which brick gables capped heavy walls built of gigantic glacial stones.

So successful was this regional hall-church style, that major basilican churches such as the great Marienkirche at Danzig were rebuilt in the fifteenth century by raising the aisles to the full height of the nave. Throughout the Baltic region, vaults were built with a pronounced domical upthrust. With these steep pitches the vaults could be laid up with little or no centering, a matter of some importance in the agricultural marshlands where the forests had long been cut back. Almost invariably, the ribbing patterns copied English stellar patterns, with the ribs disposed on the domical shell in closely knit decorative stars.

The fortresses of the Teutonic knights were massive constructions of brick dominating the countryside. Marienwerder, Poland, 1300–84

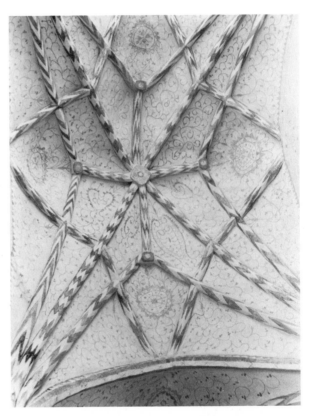

In the Baltic states stellar and lierne vaulting patterns were influenced by English and German masons. Heavy brick piers and walls carried domical brick vaults with the ribs disposed as a decorative star over the surface. Nave vault, Espo, Finland

The demand for the spacious simplicity of the hall
church interior was such that basilican churches
were rebuilt as halls. Marienkirche, Danzig, at the
end of the fourteenth century before north and
south aisles were heightened

North German masons at Danzig evolved a complex
decorative star pattern of ribs. In the reconstructions
since the second world war brick masons built up
domical segments between the ribs.

Gerlach of Cologne built a hall choir from 1400–12
at Linköping cathedral in Sweden in which the ribs

carried strongly bowed or domical vaulting panels,
built largely without centering.

Just after 1300, the nave of the cathedral at Meissen was built as a pillared hall.[1] In a straightforward adaptation of the elements of the French Gothic, quadripartite vaults, heavy transverse arch rings, and shafted piers with caps were disposed over a spacious interior. The ribbed quadripartite vaults with their strongly accented articulation into bays as yet did not take advantage of the new spatial unity possible in the hall. This tendency to break the vault into separate compartments still remains evident in the chapel of St Barbara built by Arnold of Westphalia in 1479 as an entry to the hall nave. The decorative ribbing holds to a stellar pattern rather than the diagonal mesh of Bavaria.

Hans von Burghausen (known as Hans Stethaimer) took the pattern of the star vault, and by introducing subsidiary lierne ribs along the ridge, created a form which adapted the mesh vault successfully to the delicate piers of the hall church. The extraordinary slenderness of the octagonal piers in the Heiligkreuzkirche at Landshut opened the interior to diagonal vistas and equivocal spatial effects quite in contrast to the rigid axiality of the basilican Gothic. The new patterns of vaulting, with relatively flat soft curvatures of the shell and a profuse inter-

The Strasbourg crossing suggested the potential of hall-church spaciousness.

locking of diagonal ribs and liernes, contributed to this spatial unity of the hall.

In Saxony, Silesia, and southern Poland architects evolved a regional variant strongly influenced by the successful brick Gothic idiom of the Baltic. The citizens of these prosperous mining towns took the basic form of the brick-shell hall from the north but in their vaulting favoured a simpler use of the stellar pattern. The four-armed stars, bounded by ribs, subdued the sharp folding of the quadripartite vault but they were not raised into domical segments as were the brick vaults of the Baltic region. Essentially, the masons of this area used barrel vaults in which segments were cut in between the arms of the stars to bring the shell to

point support. In the comparatively narrow aisles a distinctive diagonal placement of the ribs, locally known as 'springgewölben,' broke free of the rigid compartmentation of the Meissen nave. At no time did they use the closely meshed grids which had been introduced in south Germany.

NOTE
1 Paul Frankl *Gothic Architecture* (Penguin Books 1962) 141

At Meissen cathedral the designer of nave and aisle (1300) realized the spatial unity possible in the hall types, though the vaulting pattern was conservative.

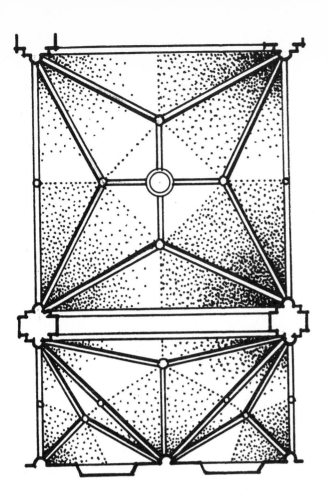

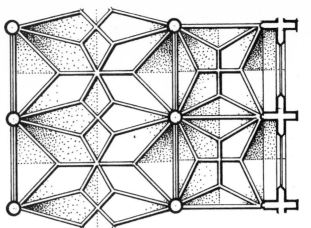

Obviously the precise pattern used in these stellar vaults was a matter of individual choice. In the Heiligkreuzkirche, Landshut, decorative stars were used over the nave and simple stellar patterns in the aisle (1407).

The pointed, star-ribbed vaulting over the nave of the Heiligkreuzkirche, Breslau (Wrocław) of 1341 was a direct and simple answer to the vault problem.

Over the aisles of the Heiligkreuzkirche, Wrocław, the mason devised an ingenious diagonal placement of vaulting segments to suit the narrow compartment.

The hall church – a simple brick envelope carrying mesh or stellar vaults – freed the late Gothic designers of central Europe to embark upon two centuries of regional development in architecture. Along the Danube and to the shores of the Baltic, hundreds of unpretentious hall churches of the fourteenth and fifteenth centuries testify to the success of the combination of spatial unity with structural diversity. An outstanding example is the choir of the friary church at Steinakirchen-am-Forst,

The architect of the galleried hall devised for the choir of the friary church at Steinakirchen am Forst, Austria, intersecting and truncated ribs and domical segments in the elaborate vault.

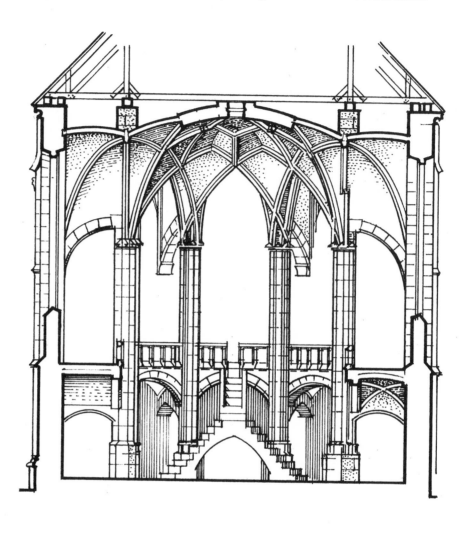

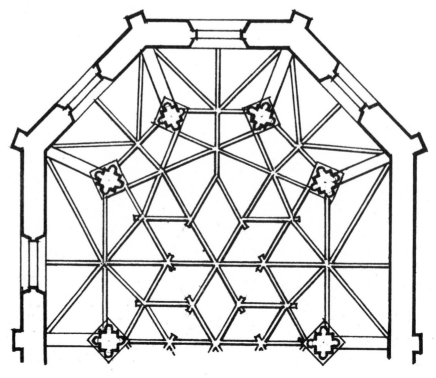

Austria. In this galleried hall the vaulting ribs spring from opposite sides of the pier to cross and cut through one another above the springing. Lines of force intersect and, at the apex of the vault, projecting just beyond the node of intersection to give a flourish akin to the draughtsman's crossing over of lines.

At the very end of the Gothic in Germany, during the second quarter of the sixteenth century, the intricate logic of rib and pier articulation received its classic statement in the Marienkirche at Halle on the Saale. The delicately fluted piers suggest the sharp and linear cutting of wood, where the chisel and scraper cut into the log to create a texture of sharp edged surfaces. The concave facets of the pier slide up and through a branching maze of flying ribs which spring out to brace and stiffen the vaulting rib. Everywhere the ribs are cut and chased to emphasize acute linear accents.

In every detail the art of the woodcarver reigns supreme. In place of the bundle of shafts tied by horizontal rings, as in the early Gothic, the pier becomes a faceted log. Slender flying ribs with concave cuts deny the granulated texture and brittle friability of stone. A lacework of ribs on the vaulted shell gives a theatrical and dramatic expression to the intricate play of forces within the vaulted shell. Everywhere the effort is to deny the weight of stone. The structure is intuitively transmuted to a grid of force and a play of stress. Walls vanish, mass disappears, and even the continuity of the shell is made subservient to a dramatic static diagram.

Indeed, so perfect was the dematerialization of mass, so acute the static intuition, that there was literally nowhere to go from this brilliant summation. Not until the nineteenth century when iron and steel freed the designer from the dictates of heavy mass and ponderous weight, could engineers and architects once again essay the framed cage.

At Halle the designer swung flying ribs from the concave piers to brace the springing of the nave vault.

Sharply cut ribs, more reminiscent of wood than masonry, stiffened the low profile barrel vault of the nave of the Marienkirche, Halle on the Saale.

The monks used medieval ribbing over the choir in the initial work at San Augustin, Acolman, c 1545.

In New Spain, the friars and clergy used a simple and dignified version of the hall church. The Mexican highlands, so similar to the high plateaus of Castile and Andaluzia, proved to be quite suitable to the indigenous architecture evolved in the Spanish peninsula. The conquest was brutal, but the conquistadores did bring with them a firm sense of order in the town, a wealth of architectural innovation, and a host of technical invention. Though they smashed the brilliant, late neolithic culture of the Aztecs, the Mayas, and the Incas, they did not leave the Indians in a cultural vacuum, as did the English to the north. In this brief but widespread flowering of the Gothic on a new continent hundreds of unpretentious friary churches, handsome and structurally sound medieval buildings, were erected throughout the Indian domains, as surrogates and substitutes for the lost riches of the Indian faith.

At Yanhuitlan, between Puebla and Oaxaca, the abandoned convent church is isolated in a wasteland of eroded gulleys and dry arroyos. Repeated corn croppings on hilly sites and the introduction of sheep to a semi-arid land destroyed the economy, but the church remains to attest to the prosperity of the valley in the sixteenth century. Basically a fortress church, with stepped external buttresses, tiny window openings, and ribbed masonry vault, the structure was the centre of a complex conventual plan. The convent functioned as strong point,

The fortress mission churches in Mexico were built as medieval vaulted halls braced by external pier buttresses. Yanhuitlan, Mexico, 1543–

communal focus, school, and civic hall, as the Indian was forcibly remodelled on a European pattern. The Mediterranean pattern of inward facing courtyard planning, with the functioning elements looking in to a sheltered and protected circulation corridor, proved ideally suited to the demands of a fortified teaching complex, and as in Spain was well adapted to the climate.

The vaults of the nave at Yanhuitlan are stellar-ribbed structures which show an assured technical command of the processes of construction. When it is considered that the vaults were constructed by Indian masons who had just turned their hands from pyramids and temples in which the crude corbelled vault was the greatest technical triumph, one cannot but marvel at the competence of the friars and clergy. With the building handbooks of the time, supplemented by the occasional assistance of travelling masons and carpenters, they created structurally sound, aesthetically satisfying, monumental fabrics on the very periphery of the known world. The strength of the medieval tradition of building, its applicability to a wide range of technical problems, and above all its inherent structural logic become evident in the success of these fabrics conceived and built in isolation from the main currents of the European tradition, at Yuriria, Acolman, Actopan, and Huejotzingo, in an arc about Mexico City.

The major cathedrals were designed in imitation of the pillared halls of Andaluzia. For the most part the results are dry and unconvincing, as in Spain, remaining an ill-digested screen of Renaissance detail superimposed upon a Gothic structure. But the architect at Merida achieved some success in fusing the elements of Renaissance and Gothic. He applied a severely rectilinear grid of ribs to the shallow saucer domes over the nave. He avoided copy-book solecisms in the design of the piers leaving them as plain, round cylinders with caps, almost Romanesque in their simplicity. How much this is the result of rigorous economy or how much the effect of a mannered severity in design it is difficult now to tell. But the total effect is fine: a simple vocabulary of design in which the boxy shell of the wall contains the marching cadence of piers and an undulating shell vault.

Despite the bombast and rhetoric of the Churrigueresque Baroque of Spain and Mexico, it rested upon a firm base of structural order inherited from the arts of the medieval mason and the disciplines of the Gothic architect. Peel away the plaster cherubs, cut back behind the gilt crowns and furbelows, and you find the good sense and logic of structural engineering. Indeed much of the spatial dynamics and imaginative play with interpenetrating form which is the special delight of the Baroque emerged because seventeenth-century architects turned away from mere classicism and archaeology to study the structural achievements of medieval masons. Though they decried the 'Gothik' manner they were only too ready to use medieval technology.

The domical vaulted segments over the nave at Merida cathedral, Yucatan, were executed with a regular, rectilinear rib pattern which is a very successful adaptation of the medieval ribbed vault to a Renaissance pattern (1574–98)

Eventually the columned hall of the Iberian Gothic was translated into a Renaissance idiom in which a range of domes and lanterns gave a diffuse over-all light to the interior. Capilla Real, Cholula, Mexico

At Cholula the architect turned back to the old Byzantine structural pattern of pierced dome and lantern.

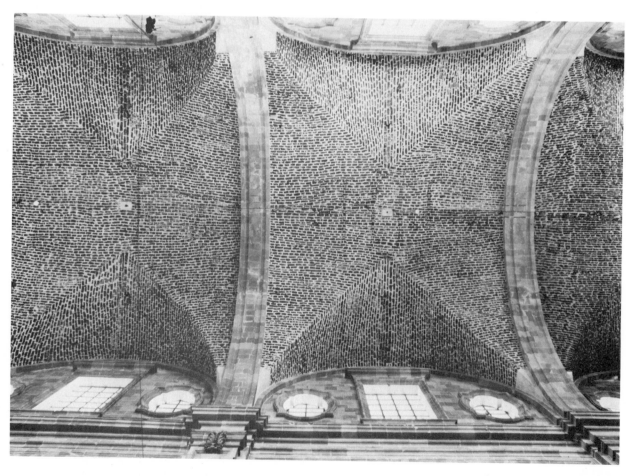

The Baroque architects of the Jesuit church at Guanajuato constructed their vaults of small-stone,

folded and curved plates, exactly in the medieval tradition.

13

CURVILINEAR RIBS:
RESURGENCE OF THE SHELL

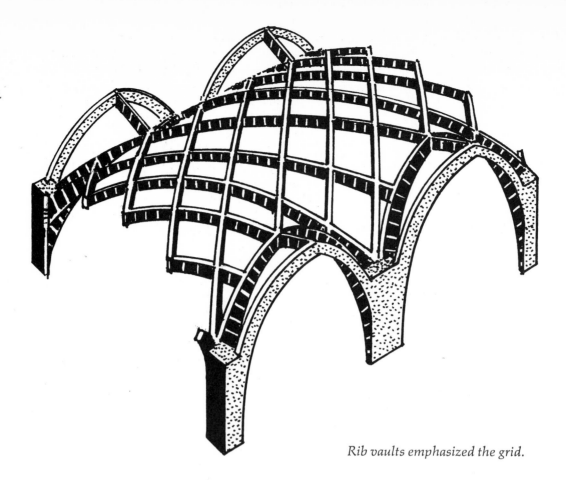

Rib vaults emphasized the grid.

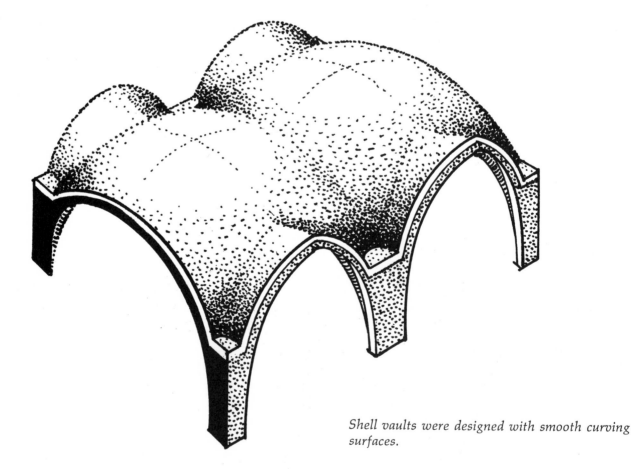

Shell vaults were designed with smooth curving surfaces.

OVERLEAF *Hall nave, Freiburg, Saxony*

In all Gothic masonry building a fundamental tension underlay the design. The varying dispositions of mass, shell, rib, and frame – ranging from region to region and from time to time – could not conceal a basic conflict between the smoothly curved planes of vaulting masonry and the rectilinear grids and space frames created by the ribs, shafts, and flying buttresses. No small part of the dramatic appeal and empathic excitement came from just this apposition of opposites.

The tradition of frame building in timber had led inexorably to lattices of straight elements in wood. Masons had no difficulty in translating this rectangular gridding into bars, shafts, and colonnets locked into open geometries of line in the wall. Indeed in England the Perpendicular designers translated this vocabulary into a consistent structural and aesthetic whole, in which all vertical planes were enlivened by a systematic and repetitive linear pattern deriving precisely from timber-frame techniques.

Only in the vaulting was the parallel more difficult. Because it was necessary to curve the rib in the vertical plane so that it would act as an arched brace, rather than as a straight timber prop or strut, the from of the ribbed vault diverged markedly from the rectilinear panelling of the wall. And so it should have, because the vaulting span had to meet quite different loads and pressures from those of wall or pier. Intuitively recognizing these conflicts and difficulties, medieval structural designers in the fourteenth and fifteenth centuries began to separate analytically the three components of vaulted structure: the rib, the curving shell, and the sharp fold.

The question facing the late Gothic vault designer was one of choice and emphasis. He had a structure – the ribbed quadripartite vault in which the rib, the curved shells of the panels, and the folding of the planes were integrated into a quite satisfactory structural arrangement – but it was a form which dominated the entire fabric by its logic of concentrated loads and sharply accented planes. If he was to free his designs from this rigid formula, he had to choose one or another of the structural components of the vault, the rib, the shell, or the fold, emphasizing one at the expense of the others.

In point of fact the choices were made in sequence, but once made the system continued in use as alternatives up to the very end of the Gothic. As we have seen, in the fourteenth century architects in both England and central Europe chose the rib as the critical element. Lierne, mesh, and stellar grids, often combined with flying ribs, created a whole new vocabulary of lattice structures. Well into the sixteenth century this viable alternative was used, as for example at St George's, Windsor, or in the nave of the Marienkirche at Halle. The concave cutting of profiles, the shallow curvatures of ribs, the sparse rectilinearity of both designs make them final summations of the frame tradition.

Other designers emphasized the continuously curved shell surface as the dominant concept. The flaring conoids of fan vaults in England were a precise statement of this renewed interest in shell geometry. Not prepared to sacrifice the expressive power of the line the architects retained a delicate

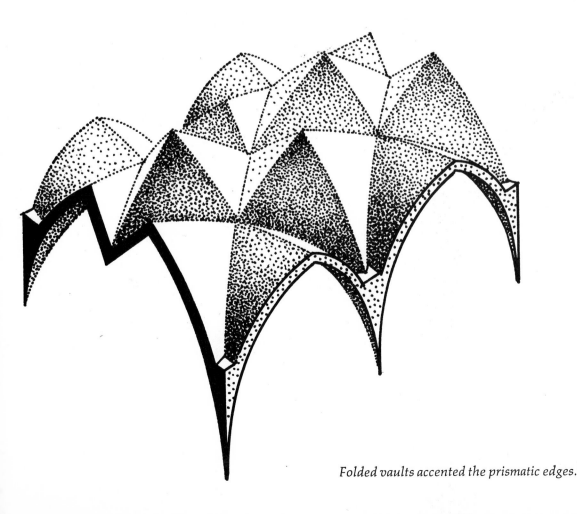

Folded vaults accented the prismatic edges.

surface pattern of ribs to make visual the play of forces over the vaulted shell. In central Europe curvilinear rib vaults do just this.

Those who preferred the sharply folded plates as a structural device turned back to the groin intersection and the folded crown as the keys to design. By so doing they were able to dispense with the rib. Making a decisive break with the skeleton or frame which had been the energizing element of the Gothic they were able to create a quite novel folded-shell structure.

About 1400 the choir vault of St Barbara, Kutna Hora, was built with the stellar pattern of the ribs emphasized. In 1512 Ried created a nave vault which was a curved planar shell in which the ribs evoked the play of stress in the vault.

By 1480 Arnold of Westphalia had simplified the basic theme of the vault by dispensing with the rib and emphasizing the prismatic interlocking of folded plates of brick masonry.

Occasionally vaults were built only as grids of ribs without any panel infill, to let the light pour through the lattice from a lantern, for example, as in the Capilla del Condestable, Burgos cathedral, built from 1482 to 1494.[1] The Spanish examples may derive from Moorish flying-arch constructions like those in the mosque at Cordoba. But in most vaults, no matter how elegantly detailed and structurally complete the ribbed grid, the designer added a continuous shell of masonry. As we have seen, very often the ribbing pattern was quite arbitrary in its arrangement, changing from bay to bay over a standard shell surface. Often the projections of this shell surface obtruded through and cut across the rectilinear mesh of the ribs. Evidently there was a conflict between two quite different concepts of structure. Only when designers elected to design the shell first, and then a pattern of ribs evolving from its statics, could they properly unify the two elements.

Just this occurred in fan vaults. The vertical splay of ribs modelled on the undersurface of the doubly curved concoid gave a visual accent to the compression forces travelling down the arcs of the shell; but, more important, the horizontal hoops or banding rings followed the curvature of the shell, not a straight trace laid out on the construction platform. Once the ribs began to be subservient to the configuration of the vaulted surface, the mason could more easily adapt the shell to the flow of forces. The rigid rectilinearity in plan dictated by the projection of the ribs from a simple linear diagram on the working platform was swept aside to be replaced by a more subtle, if more complex, study of the working of the vaulted shell itself.

In the vestibule to the mihrab in the Al-Hakim II mosque at Cordoba, eight springing points carried flying ribs in an octagonal pattern.

In the crossing vault under the lantern at Burgos, 1540–68, all surface was eroded away.

In the vault over the second mihrab (the capilla de Villaviciosa), 961–76, at Cordoba, decorative vaults were introduced into the panels.

The decorative patterns were derived from Moorish precedents.

In the Silk Exchange at Valencia, built from 1483 to 1498, shallow saucer domes with a reticulated grid of ribs were sprung from piers with twisted shafts; though the rib pattern remained rectilinear, the spiral of the pier was a deliberate attempt to break free of the rigid formulae of the past. At Belém, Portugal, a Hieronymite convent was built from 1499 at the site of Vasco da Gama's return from India. In this celebration of the new horizons opening to Europeans, the plastic and dynamic emphasis upon the shell was used to create a dramatic structure in which faceted conoids supported a decorative mesh of ribs.

The nave of the parish church of Freiberg in Saxony, built from 1484 to 1509, suggests the new primacy of the vaulted shell.[2] Ribs were kept straight in plan and interlaced to form a widely spaced mesh, but the concave modelling of the pier was carried up into the facets of the vault. Where at Halle the pier is braced against an independent mesh of ribs, here pier and vault interlock to create a counterpoint of modelled surfaces. So strong was the total impact that it was relatively simple for designers to follow this theme by using broad concave and convex curvatures in the baroque choir loft and organ.

NOTES
1 John Harvey *The Cathedrals of Spain* (London 1957) 247
2 Paul Frankl *Gothic Architecture* (Penguin Books 1962) 196

A regular interlace of ribs was carried on twisted columns in the silk exchange, Valencia, 1483–98

In the hall nave of the church at Freiberg, Saxony, slender octagonal piers with concave facets emphasized the acutely cut faceting of the late Gothic. In the vaults delicately poised ribs were accented by medieval floral painting on the vault panels.

D. Boitaca and João de Castilho devised an elaborate static configuration of rib and panel in the Hieronymite convent at Belem, Portugal, from 1502–19. Curved ribs and facetted conoids supported a complex ribbed shell.

In earlier vaults warped groins and curved ribs were the results of a failure in technique. Now they became integral parts of the design. Certainly there was no lack of precedents to fall back upon in this revival of the curve. Medieval manuscript-illustrators had long made use of sinuous organic lines. During the fourteenth century window tracery echoed this curvilinear accent in flamboyant or 'flame-like' patterns. The ogee arches and reversed curves of the Bristol masons were applied throughout Europe during the late fifteenth century to door and window heads, as at Danzig. Before the curved rib was used in vaulting, stained-glass designers had suggested the form in decorative canopies where the figures are surrounded by frames of branching trees.

As Gothic masons took advantage of these curvilinear patterns to devise new vaults they often emphasized the obvious parallels between these structural interweaves and the intricate geometry of living forms. Architecture became 'organic' in a deliberate effort to search in the world of nature for structural principles. It was no accident that the first consistent use of doubly curved ribs, over the Simpertus Arch, built in 1492 as a gallery in the church of Saints Ulrich and Afra at Augsburg, the heavily crocketted ribs of the facing suggest an interlace of branches.[1] At St Viet, Prague, in the gallery commissioned by Vladislav II, the ribs were designed as naturalistic boughs with branches. This realistic copying of the superficial aspect of living forms, so akin to the romantic rococo of the eighteenth century, was of little immediate structural importance, but it did free the designers from the restraints of the gridded linear cage.

NOTE

1 Paul Frankl *Gothic Architecture* (Penguin Books 1962) 194

At Freiburg-im-Breisgau Hans Parler used s *curves, intersecting bars, and truncated segments of tracery to emphasize the later Gothic search for effects of structural drama.*

The sinuous, willowy line in Gothic construction: curved ribbed soffit, choir loft, St Georgskirche, Nördlingen

The search for decorative innovation led to a deliberate reversal of static forms. South porch, Marienkirche, Danzig, c 1500

Between 1469–74 the piers of new north aisle of Braunschweig cathedral were built with a twisted spiral. The direction of rotation changed from pier to pier.

Benedikt Ried built the Vladislavs Oratorium in 1490–3 with a dropped pendant vault and ribbing modelled with twigs, knotholes, and bark.

If designers had stopped at these purely superficial uses of 'organic' form, the curved rib vault would be but a minor chapter in the elaborate game of decorative virtuosity in architecture. But they did not stop there. They went on during the sixteenth century to a highly imaginative, if intuitive, study of the forces operating in the vaulted shell.

Model analysis today shows that the lines of pressure and tension in a structure follow, not a lattice, but a curving interlace of isostatic lines. If we place one of these model analysis studies alongside a plan for a sixteenth-century curved rib vault, a startling similarity emerges. In each case sinuous lines interlock in a complex geometry.[1] Or, if a careful sequential series of assumptions is made regarding the behaviour of tiny arbitrary panels within the vaulted surface, these can be linked mathematically to gain a fair approximation of the actual lines of pressure and tension. This technique of indeterminate computation, projecting an assumption through hundreds of contiguous panels to prove or disprove its validity, was of only minor use until the invention of the digital computer. Now, within a few minutes the laborious yet rather simple mathematics can be cleared away. In a 'fine grain' analysis of the behaviour of vaulted shells precisely the same curving lines of pressure and tension appear as those disclosed by model analysis.

From these data the plastic flow or deformation of elements within the design can be studied. Dangerous concentrations of loads can be identified and isolated so that the structure can be redesigned to spread the loads more evenly across a thin shell. Where the designer in linear frame concentrates loads, strengthening these nodal points, in shell surfaces he spreads the loading to save material. Most important, in this progressive step-by-step adjustment and shaping of surface to take the load efficiently with least dead weight of structural material, warped shells and curving interlaces of ribs emerge as the lightest pattern for long spans. They may not be the most economical, because of the expense and difficulty encountered in shaping curved elements, but they are the most efficient in terms of material.

It is evident that these later Gothic designers were turning away from widely spaced linear and skeletal ribs which concentrated loads upon the supports to a more subtle integration of rib and shell. In the place of a lattice or frame of ribs carrying a relatively independent shell, their ribs now were intuitively designed as integral parts of the vault, giving a clear statement of the complex pressures within the shell surface.

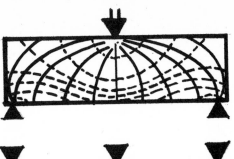
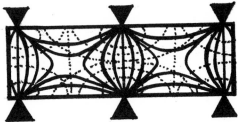

Isostatic lines of pressure and tension trace out sinuous paths in a structural member.

These static traces bear a marked similarity to the curvilinear rib patterns used in sixteenth-century vaults. (after Cavallari-Murat)

In the vault of the Diet hall, Hrad, Prague (1559–63), Bonifaz Wolmuet suggested the static forces in the vault by curving and interlacing the ribs.

Sixteenth-century architects achieved this subtle geometry and engineered precision by applying relatively simple techniques of layout in a step by step progression. It is not necessary to explain the proportions of the church and its detail or the seemingly complex faceting of pier and rib in terms of a theologically inspired numerology. The forms actually derive from the consistent use of the compass and the set square on the drawing board. Piers were laid out by setting squares diagonally within squares to find the points to swing profile arcs from.[2]

In the layout of vault ribbing the architect's primary control was the plan sketch in which the ribs were laid in projection. This small-scale sketch could then be enlarged to full size on the working platform or floor with traces scribed in chalk. When a straight line on this plan was projected up to the desired vaulting profile the result was a rib of single curvature. But when it became customary to curve the layout of ribs in plan the resultant form was doubly curved, giving rise to the dramatic oscillating effect of these curved rib vaults. It was probably inevitable that architects accustomed to work

Nave vault, Marienkirche, Halle: the precise adaptation of shell and rib to load

with the openwork fretted ribs of towers and spires would attempt to cut the rib free of the vaulting plane by introducing changes in depth. Finally they introduced another parameter of variation by twisting the ribs on the surface.

NOTES
1 Augusto Cavallari-Murat 'Static Intuition and Formal Imagination in the Space Lattices of Ribbed Gothic Vaults' *Student Publications of Design* 2, 2 (Raleigh NC: North Carolina State College 1963), translated from an article in *Atti e rassegna technica* (Journal of the Society of Engineers and Architects) (Turin, July 1958)
2 For an illuminating account of these procedures see François Bucher 'Design in Gothic Architecture: A Preliminary Assessment' *Journal of the Society of Architectural Historians* 27, 1 (1968). Professor Bucher is at present working on a manuscript on this subject, based on the examination of over two thousand medieval plans, designs, working drawings, and presentation studies. Such an examination can clarify many of the problems raised in the study of Gothic structures. Certainly it will go far to emphasize the thoroughly professional nature of the architect's discipline in the Middle Ages.

Benedikt Ried was the central figure in this sixteenth century play with vaulted structure. After service as an artilleryman and engineer, he was called from Budapest to Prague by King Vladislav II in 1490 to design the tourney chamber now known as Vladislav Hall, which stands in the Hrad palace complex on the hillside below the cathedral. The Hrad or castle across the Vlatava from Prague had been a typical medieval strong point commanding the crossing to Prague. During the monarchic consolidation of the late fifteenth and sixteenth centuries it was changed to a palatial royal residence, to act as an administrative residential and ceremonial centre for the kingdom of Bohemia.[1] The steep slope presented a difficult planning and structural problem. The equestrian and ceremonial hall required a long span to suit it to armed tourneys and wide entries for the horses which were stabled in the lower vaults.

The vault over the 'jousting area,' spanning 49 feet, had to be supported on piers springing from a base two stories below the main hall. To avoid heavy buttressing Ried used wrought-iron tension bars which cut through the haunching just below the crown of the vault. The tension bars and heavy rectangular ribs on the upper surface of the vault were sufficient to ensure its stability when the roof burned and fell in 1541.

Underneath Ried designed a petaled interlace of curvilinear ribs. The ribs swing from the mass of the pier in long, sweeping curves which cross over one another to create a rosette pattern at the crown. The geometry as laid out on the working platform is a relatively simple affair of arcs of a circle but when projected up to the planes of the vault the ribs assume doubly curved and oscillating movements. The concave faceted piers are cut directly into the plates of the vaulting panels, and below these supports curving ribs are sprung diagonally across the pier faces to meet, pierce, and continue on to complete the petaled pattern.

NOTE
1 Götz Fehr *Benedikt Ried: Ein deutscher Baumeister zwischen Gothik und Renaissance* (Munich 1961) 18

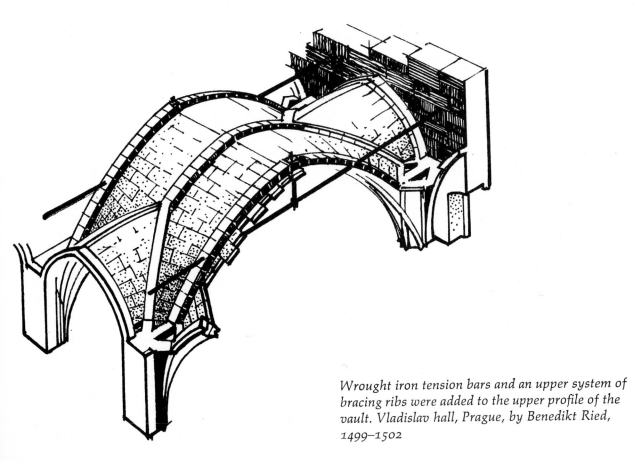

Wrought iron tension bars and an upper system of bracing ribs were added to the upper profile of the vault. Vladislav hall, Prague, by Benedikt Ried, 1499–1502

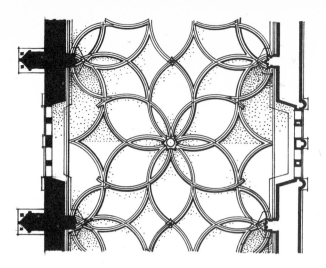

The plan projection of the ribs at Vladislav hall evolve as a sequence of arcs interlocking to create a leafed centrepiece.

At the wall piers Benedikt Ried swung the rib arcs abruptly out of the concave pier facets crossing them one over the other in differing planes. Vladislav hall, Prague

When projected up to the barrel surface of the vault, the ribs assume double curvatures as they swing across the curved surfaces. Vladislav hall, Prague

In the small vault over the Rider's stair at Vladislav Hall, Ried changed the flowing, continuous curvatures and floral patterns of the hall vault to short, staccato, truncated segments.[1] Heavy in profile, the ribs intersect at varying planes. Cutting above and below one another and interweaving in a complex harmony, they establish a curved continuum which has depth as well as surface. He enhanced the effect of a dimensional force-field by abruptly truncating ribs after intersection. The cut, open end of the rib

The short, stacatto segments and intersections in depth create a highly equivocal construct in the Riders Stair.

bleeds lines of force from the vaulted surface. Nothing remains of static and self-contained mass. The vault continually works, giving off energy, yet locked in a tenuous equilibrium.

The open-ended, interweaving rib is truly modern in its rejection of classic balance and contained form. Today, Ried would be a biologist reading structure into the living molecule or a mathematician building indeterminacy into a solid-state computer.

NOTE

1 Götz Fehr *Benedikt Ried: Ein deutscher Baumeister zwischen Gothik und Renaissance* (Munich 1961) 30–1

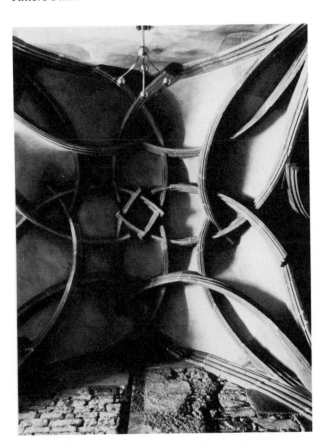

Dropping the formal arrangement used in the hall, Benedikt Ried devised short truncated segments of arcs intersecting in differing planes over the Riders Stair entry to Vladislav hall, Prague, 1500. (after Fehr)

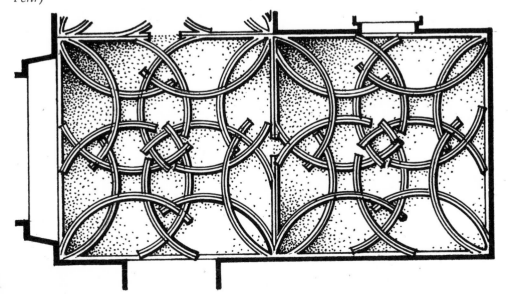

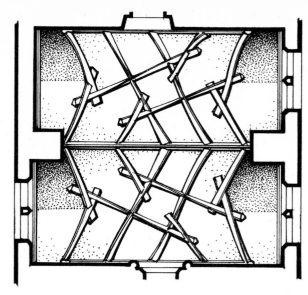

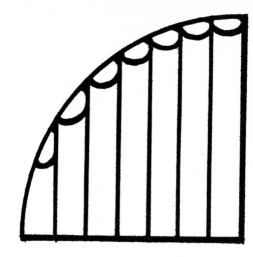

In the vault over the Bohemian chancery of the Ludwigstrakt at Prague, Benedikt Ried added a rotation or twist to the rib profile (1505). (after Fehr)

Nicolas of Oresme: the graphic representation of motion and change, 1350.

In the vault of the Bohemian chancery, added to Vladislav Hall in 1505, Ried again used short truncated ribs overlapping in differing planes but to heighten the effect of movement and organic elasticity, he twisted or rotated the ribs.[1] Evidently in his designs for these vaults he was drawing upon his earlier experience as a gunner. Arguing from the flight of the missile, which was still a matter of heated discussion amongst theorists, he made a parallel between the path of a projectile and the spring of a vaulting rib and, as rifling imparts a rotation to the shot steadying it in flight, he twisted the ribs and so made them an expressive symbol of energy. Though locked in position it could read as the path described by a moving force. It could curve in various planes, overlap, and interweave to give depth and by rotation alter its plane of reference.

In this pulling together of the fields of both dynamics and statics, Ried was very much the child of his age. Since 1350 when Nicolas of Oresme, in the *Tractatus de latitudine formarum*, first gave expression to the changing intensities of a quality, the graphic representation of motion had posed a special problem to geometers.[2] The critical diagram in which the changing quality or state of an object is shown by the two co-ordinates of time and quantity opened the way to all later quantitative graphic analysis. By 1440 Nicolas of Cusa had extended the argument by introducing the concept of infinity. He claimed

'a union of extremes through transitions and middle terms, and of their comprehension by means of the continuity thus effected.' Pointing out that the circle of infinite radius is identical with the straight line, he took the first step to the infinitesimal calculus.[3]

In the sixteenth century the problem of the graphic representation of motion and the interrelation of changing quantities had become critical. There was a purely practical need to devise formulae which could be applied to the flight of the artillery projectile. Astronomers such as Tycho Brahe, with improved observations which could fix planetary orbits, were having difficulties with the old Copernican geometry of ideal forms. In the arts, the perspective studies of Alberti had shown that form and position on the picture plane were factors relative and not absolute. The arts of building needed new formulae which could be used to plot accurately the forces held in equilibrium in a static machine.

Not until 1604 when Kepler published the *Ad vitellionem paralipomena* were these insights fused into a simple and manageable geometry. By arguing from the changing aspects of conic sections he was able to devise a continuity of geometric forms evolving between the line pair and the circle. From line pair, to hyperbola, parabola, ellipse, and circle, an infinite series of geometric curves generated by changing quantities and foci gave a predictable and simple basis for the fall of the apple, the flight of

The trajectory traced out by shot was a problem which engrossed mathematicians in the fifteenth and sixteenth centuries.

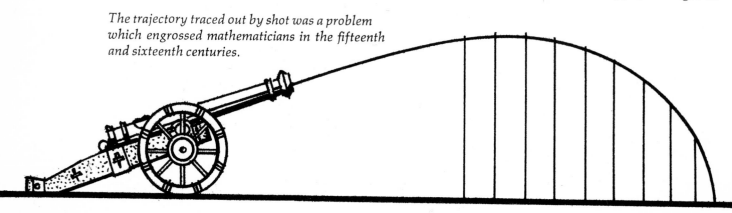

the projectile, and the trajectory of the planets. For the artist, Guidobaldo del Monte's book on perspective in 1600 summarized the changing aspects of quantities in the cone of vision. With these bases, seventeenth-century Baroque art and a Newtonian physics laid the foundations of the modern world.

Benedikt Ried was trapped between the structural expression of the Gothic north and the classicist severities of the Renaissance south. He brought to fruition that long search for expressive structural dynamics which was the motivating force of the Gothic. He used the geometry of the mason and the analytic skills of the architect with such freedom and assurance that during the seventeenth century Prague became a centre for studies in the statics of dome and vault. But, because his geometry was based upon the purely practical application of square and arc, he was unable to grasp or state general observations or conclusions from his technically skilled parallel projections.

With parallel projection it was quite possible to show diagonal walls or surfaces as foreshortened drawings and there was no problem involved in projecting a plan up to a curved vaulting surface. But in this system of projection there was no unifying projection point, a vanishing point on the horizon which would pull all elements of a design into a consistent pattern. Medieval painting and graphic art show this contemporaneity and parallelism of projection to a nicety. Varying projections, indeterminately conic and perspective or parallel and isometric, exist together without being related to a unifying spatial field. By the mid-fifteenth century Alberti in Italy had devised an ingenious construction with string and template (a typical stonecutter's trick) by which he could accurately plot a perspective projection, that is, cut a plane through a conic projection.[4] By 1505 Pelerin at Toul in France had translated the complex string and template technique of Alberti into a problem in elementary plane geometry. This technique seems to have been mis-

Simultaneous views with an independent perspective projection for each structure. Lorenzetti, 1337-40

understood in Germany because Dürer's text, the *Underweysung der messung* of 1525, was an incorrect interpretation. Ried's experiments with stereotomy and projection fall into just this period of play with half-understood principles of projection and the representation of change and motion.

Northern artists only imperfectly grasped the lessons of perspective projection and the architects fumbled with the elements of Roman classic design. Yet so fashionable was the new humanism sweeping in from the south that painters and designers had to introduce Renaissance motifs. No matter how skilled the technique of the practitioner of Gothic design, he had to make a stab at the Italianate. The princely patrons and stylish ecclesiastics who dictated the commissions insisted upon up-to-date and fashionable garb for their buildings. In the case of Vladislav Hall Ried satisfied his royal clients by casing portals, doors, and window frames with curious half-round columns and caps with a classic architrave, though he kept the Gothic stone mullion in the window.

NOTES
1 Götz Fehr *Benedikt Ried: Ein deutscher Baumeister zwischen Gothik und Renaissance* (Munich 1961) 34–5
2 Siegfried Giedion *Mechanization takes Command* (Oxford 1948) 17
3 William M. Ivins, jr *Art and Geometry* (Cambridge 1946) 94–5
4 Ibid 89

Varying perspectives without a unifying projection. Giotto, bf 1300

In the Annenkirche at Annaberg, Saxony, the curvilinear rib vault was carried on slender octagonal piers (1499–1522).

When Benedikt Ried built the nave of Santa Barbara at Kutna Hora from 1512 as a galleried hall he pulled the varying parameters of the rib into a consistent system. Reverting to the petaled interlace of the main Vladislav Hall vault, he strengthened the profile of the ribs, making full use of overlapping and interpenetration.[1] A flatter curvature to the vaulting shell made it more adaptable to the rib system. The clash between shell and rib which confused the design at Vladislav Hall disappeared. All vestiges of compartmentation into rigid bays were suppressed. None of the ribs was swung directly from pier to pier. Instead, they were swept up in intersecting arcs, not from the shafts of the piers but from the concavities between shafts. At the piers this effort to create independent yet interlocking structural systems led to a dramatic interlacing. The ribs of the vault cross over and intersect in depth just before entering the pier. Then, piercing through the shafts and hollows of the pier they emerge again as truncated segments. By this device Ried emphasized the punching or shear forces generated by the rib pressures. The entire structure is vibrant with contained and disciplined force. The diaphanous glass, the free mastery of these webs of stone, and the floating insubstantial elegance of the structural programme make it a royal chapel in direct line of descent from the Sainte Chapelle at Paris.

In these Bohemian works, executed by Benedikt Ried under royal patronage, the theatrical use of structure suited exactly the demands of a burgeoning royal court. As in the Henry VII chapel at Westminster, the heady and extravagant emphasis upon dramatic structural conceits was a testimony to the pageant chivalry of the time. Courtiers may have spoken for classic rigour but what they really wanted was a florid display piece. Throughout Europe the castles and palaces of the sixteenth century provided a perfect setting for the splendid pretentions of the new monarchs and aristocrats of Europe.

But when applied to the sober walling, stark piers, and limewashed interiors of the town churches, the curvilinear rib vault was a dissonant element. This is evident in the Annenkirche at Annaberg in Saxony. Begun in 1499, the walls and sharply faceted piers are typical of the simple planar elements of the burgher's church; on the other hand, the vault, built between 1516 and 1522, was obviously modelled upon the curved rib structures of Bohemia, and it clashes only too obviously with the simple boxy shell of the building. The concave-sided piers punch awkwardly into the saucer dome of the vault and the ribs spring awkwardly from brackets let into the piers. A sharp groin line at each bay projects independently of the ribbing pattern, making it clear that the curvilinear floral pattern of ribs was imposed with little thought upon a predetermined structural shell. Evidently, the late Gothic hall church of the sixteenth century needed a vaulting quite in contrast to the sophisticated dynamics of the curved rib vault and, as shall be seen, the severe prismatic, ribless vault filled this need exactly.

Despite these difficulties, the curved-rib vault continued in occasional use throughout the sixteenth century. In the St Anne chapel of the canonry at Freiberg, for example, it was fused effectively with the concave-sided pier. In such small applications, in tiny chapels and odd corners, the special impact of the curved-rib vault was most effective. Over the spiral staircase of the town hall at Rotenburg-ober-Tauber, there is a vault built well on in the sixteenth century, in a building predominantly Renaissance in detail, which uses many of the motifs invented by Benedikt Ried. These spiral stairs were the special glory of the medieval mason, placing severe demands on stereotomy and layout. Architects continued to use openwork spiral stairs throughout the sixteenth century, emphasizing them as dramatic display pieces opening through to the major halls and courts of the palaces and abbeys. The details are Gothic in the castle at Meissen and Renaissance in the courtyard at Tomar in Portugal, but the structural techniques are identical.

Philibert de l'Orme has long been accounted the first French architect in the sixteenth century to grasp fully the potential of the new Italianate Renaissance flooding in from Italy. And yet his designs, working drawings, and structural sketches were firmly rooted in the long tradition of medieval building. His ingenious systems of wood framing emerge from the Gothic tradition of carpentered frame. The scale and complexity of his designs mirror the staccato skylines and busy complexity of the Gothic, not the serene horizontality of the Mediterranean. In his chapel for the Château d'Anet, where he deliberately accepted the domical central plan of the Mediterranean, the vault is executed with intersecting and curved radial ribs which look back to the

intricate force fields of the late Gothic and as such provide a link between the Gothic and the subtle complexities of the Baroque. In the north, to the early seventeenth century, Gothic structure and Gothic energy insistently intrude, despite the Palladian restrictions brought in from Italy.

NOTE
1 Götz Fehr *Benedikt Ried: Ein deutscher Baumeister zwischen Gothik und Renaissance* (Munich 1961) 36–40

The thin profiles and indeterminate changing curves of the Annaberg vaults obscure the structural flexibility of the curved rib vault (1519–22).

Each bay at Annaberg was designed as a saucer shell independently of the decorative pattern of curved ribs (1519–22).

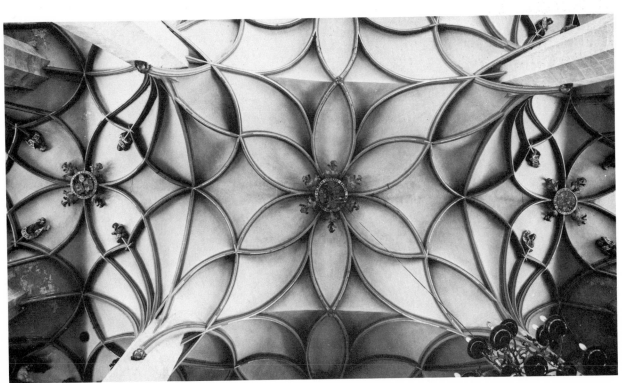

Sixteenth-century concave faceted pier and simple curvilinear rib vault. St Anne chapel, Freiberg, Saxony

Long after the Renaissance had created an accepted idiom, local masons continued to execute skilled Gothic structures: staircase vault, townhall, Rotenburg-ober-Tauber (1572–5).

Openwork spiral stairs became dramatic display pieces during the fifteenth century. Stair, Albrechtsburg, Meissen, by Arnold of Westphalia (1475)

Sixteenth-century design in central Europe alternated between the continuity of the medieval tradition and the novelty of the new Renaissance. False perspective, painted curvilinear ribs, Gothic crockets, and Renaissance forms entwined a window at the castle at Füssen.

During the last quarter of the fifteenth century Spanish designers began to introduce curved lierne ribs into the patterning of vaults. At San Juan de los Reyes, built in Toledo from 1478 to 1492 as a burial chapel for Ferdinand and Isabella (though never used as such), Juan Guas added curvilinear ribs to the stellar pattern of the octagonal vault over the crossing lantern. They are little more than an aesthetic flourish adding verve and style to a ribbed vault. By the sixteenth century the curved rib was being used with more assurance. In the Capilla Real at Granada, also founded as the tomb chapel for the sovereigns, in 1506 Enrique de Egas designed vaults which enliven the shallow domical shell with a playful and delicate filigree of lacework ribbing. Ribs were of single or double curvature and were ornamented with crockets to give exactly that air of exuberant fantasy which so enlivened English Tudor work.

At Salamanca Juan Gil de Hontañon, from 1512 to 1538, designed vaults in which a contrasting and interlocking pattern of short curved ribs cut across the radial and stellar pattern of the tiercerons. In the chevet, completed by 1577, this stellar and curved pattern evolved into a dramatic lobed and petaled interlace of ribs. Between 1513 and 1522 Enrique de Egas brought this Spanish curved-rib construction to its apogee in the sanctuary of the cathedral at Plasencia. Curiously, despite the close linkages evident between Spanish and German masters, in Spain only the secondary lierne ribs were curved. The architects were hesitant to curve the principal tiercerons in plan and there was no rotation, twisting, or overlapping of the ribs as had occurred in Saxony and Bohemia. In Spain the motivation for the use of the curved rib was decorative rather than structural.

In Spain only the secondary ribs were curved in plan. Stair vault, Sala Capitular, Segovia cathedral

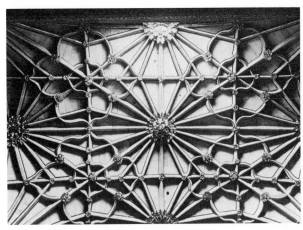

Gold brought from Mexico and Peru enriched the elaborate bosses of the apse vault. Salamanca cathedral

Doubly curved lierne ribs over the crossing of San Juan de las Reyes, Toledo, Spain, 1476.

Over the Capilla Real, Granada, Enrique de Egas used the curved rib to enliven the vaulted surface (1504–21).

Although the wall decoration and door trim were executed with Renaissance detail, Fernan Ruiz built a ribbed vault over the transept at Cordoba, 1523–60.

The interlacing ribbed curve of the late Gothic vault was used as a decorative motif in both architecture and art. Gable, Tábor, Czechoslovakia

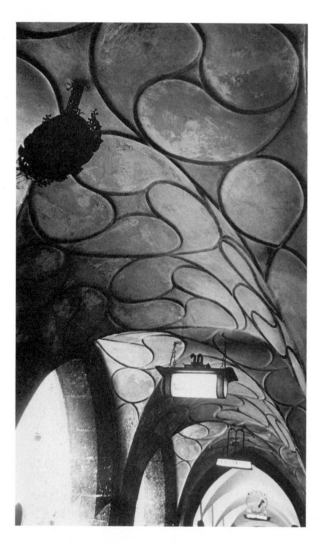

The meandering curve on the vaulted surface began to lose all structural significance but was kept as a decorative plaster line: arcade, Herzog Friedrich Strasse, Innsbruck, Austria.

Baroque architects devised vermiculated rib patterns in which the rib degenerated to a decorative texture. Sagrario, Carthusian monastery, Granada, 1704–20

Even where the rib had long lost all structural significance Baroque designers continued to use it as emphatic accent on the shell surface. San Cayetano, Guanajuato, Mexico, 1788

14

CELLULAR VAULTS:
ELIMINATION OF THE RIB

We have seen how the masons of the twelfth and thirteenth centuries took the rib from its start as a cover or mould for the sharply folded crease of the vault to extend it down the pier as a shaft, over the window opening as bar tracery, and across the aisle as a flying buttress. By the fourteenth and fifteenth centuries the rib was dominant everywhere, spreading in complex meshes over the vaulted surfaces and breaking the massive solidity of the wall into framed panels. Throughout the north, the technique of the carpenter, who created a frame and then filled it in, was the accepted mode of building. The articulate force-diagram of thrust and restraint, pressure and retention, along clearly defined lines of action and reaction had become an entrancing exercise in geometry and analysis, often overriding the logic of material and denying economy of effort. This emphasis upon line broke the rib design free of the shell. In turn the shell, now relatively independent of the gridded pattern of the ribs, changed to an undulating plate of masonry with no folded accents. The curvilinear rib vault of the sixteenth century was the last flowering of this expressive temper in the architecture of the Middle Ages.

But even during the height of the French craze for delicate openwork constructions there were influences and needs countering the trend to frame. Along the Baltic where there was little good building stone, brick was the only economical fireproof material. After a few experiments with light skeletal construction the Baltic builders evolved a characteristic north German mode of building in which available materials were used to better advantage. The plasticity and relatively low strength of the lime mortars used in brickwork demanded continuous surfaces rather than slender supports. The end product, as we have seen, was the planar box of the hall church.

Throughout the south along the Mediterranean littoral the Gothic had always been a foreign style ill-adapted to the climate. By and large the southerners favoured capacious roomy interiors, heavy sheltering walls, and the minimum of window openings. Without the high-pitched roof of the north, not really needing the complex apparatus of buttress and flying arch with wide spans and open bays, and with only narrow slots of windows to receive the tracery, Italian, Catalan, and southern French buildings of the thirteenth and fourteenth centuries were only nominally Gothic. Medieval, but not Gothic except in detail, these structures suggested new patterns of building which could recognize the resurgent dominance of shell surface, planar wall, and heavy mass.

In the heartland of Europe at the end of the fifteenth century the architect was in a difficult position. In place of the well-understood problems of the monks, the clergy, or the townsfolk of an earlier time he had to face the peremptory demands of a new aristocracy anxious to recapture the splendid trappings of Imperial Rome. For a time he had some success with an involved and elaborate display of structural virtuosity. But this flowering was brief, little more than a quarter of a century. To the precious young aristocrats of the court, the subtle complexities of structural play on the vaulted surface were an exercise in tedium. And if the truth be known, what could the architect do to further enrich the vaulted surface? Almost every conceivable geometric figure had been pressed into play. Mere multiplication of ribs led only to greater confusion. The curvilinear rib was one way out of the dilemma but it was so difficult to design and control that only the most astute could achieve satisfactory results.

On the other hand, when the architect worked, not for the royal courts or a princely patron, but for the prosperous tradesmen of the town, he had to design simple and austere buildings suitable for meeting and sermon, rather than pomp or pageantry. Distrusting the new Italianate motifs imported from Rome, and averse to the rich elaboration of subtle detail characteristic of the royal works, these townsmen favoured what might be described as Protestant structures, which were comprehensible, simple, and emphasized a dry logic in the use of materials.

Despite the overwhelming success of the rib as a unifying device in the decorative programme of the Gothic, carpenters and masons gradually turned away from the rib to sharp planar edges. In place of the three-quarter-round rolls and half-round mouldings of the early Gothic, they used sharply angled planes and concave surfaces meeting in hard, crystalline accents on the pier surfaces. By the end of the fifteenth century the masons emphasized the prismatic play of surface, modelling their designs upon the acute angles and accents of woodcuts and block prints. Rather than emphasize the granular texture of stone which favours rounded profiles, they preferred to cut it as if it were wood, with sharp edges and hollowed surfaces. The rib was now a thin rectangular brace. The shaft had died away into the faceted surface of the pier. The planar wall was once again emerging as the dominant vertical element. In the vault, the obvious answer for the mason was to suppress the rib; to turn back to the play of surface. Logical in retrospect, the decision must have entailed a severe wrench away from customary modes of vaulting calculation. After centuries of reliance upon the rib as the key to the statics of the vault, the architects turned to folded plates. Where in England the masons had devised the curved-shell conoid of the fan vault to escape the complex geometry of the lierne vault, in central Europe they created prismatic shells to avoid the heavy texture of the mesh vault or the subtle convolutions of the doubly curved rib.

OVERLEAF *Prismatic cross-groined vault: cloister, St Francis, Bechyně, Bohemia, 1500*

In terms of constructional convenience there was much to be said for dropping the rib. In simple quadripartite vaults of the thirteenth century only the ribs needed heavy wooden centering and they were few and widely spaced. The panels required only a light support at the crown. But with stellar and mesh much of this initial economy in construction formwork was lost: the entire interlace of ribs required extensive wooden centering during construction.

Structurally there was no reason why the rib should not be suppressed. Architects had long been aware of the stiffness and rigidity which acute folding gave to a vaulted surface. They had only to turn to the Romanesque cross vaults of the eleventh century to see that it was entirely possible to build shell surfaces without the complicating extra factor of the rib.

Francisco Baldomar built a ribless vault about 1447 over the large chapel of Santo Domingo in Valencia, Spain. This same type of vault was used by Baldomar in the tower of the convent and in the somewhat later Miguelete passage of the cathedral of Valencia.[1] Pedro Bonfill the younger built a ribless vault in the Puerta de Cuarte in Valencia about 1450.[2]

The vaults were constructed of carefully cut ashlar masonry. At Santo Domingo, Baldomar used a stellar pattern for the groins with the tiercerons modelled on the surface of the vault as projecting groin lines. Between these groins each panel was cut as a smoothly curved concave web. No particular emphasis was placed upon sharp folding or faceting of the vaulted surface; rather, the slightly upset groins were used as a substitute for ribs. These vaults were ribless but not prismatic. They derive more from the local techniques of Catalan vaulting than from new experiments in folding and shaping the shell surface. As such they were part of the widespread reaction against framed design and their geometry makes them precursors of the quadripartite ribless vaults of the Renaissance, as at St Sauveur, Figeac, or the eighteenth-century vaults of the Jesuit church at Guanajuato in Mexico.

During the fourteenth and fifteenth centuries Muslim architects in Egypt, Syria, Turkey, and Iran, devised prismatic surfaces to effect the transition between vault and support. Initially this technique grew from the stepped squinch arches, or honeycomb pendentives used in the khalif's tombs at Cairo.

During the burst of building activity accompanying the expansion of Ottoman influence, wide use was made by Turkish architects of different kinds of prismatically folded surfaces. In the fourteenth-century minaret at Selçuk, Turkey, the transition from octagon to cylindrical shell was achieved by folded planes. In the pendentives of the Murad I mosque at Bursa (1365–85), tiers of prisms made the adjustment to the dome. The systematic use of prismatic surfaces is evident throughout the structure of the Murad II mosque (1424–6) at Bursa. As late as 1557, prismatic pendentive surfaces were used in the Süleimaniye mosque at Istanbul.

In Spain Francisco Baldomar turned back to the ribless vault in which curved surfaces met at a sharp groin. Capilla de San Vicente Ferrer, Santo Domingo, Valencia, 1437–62

In a widespread reaction against ribbed structures the vaults of St Sauveur at Figeac were completed in the seventeenth century without regard to the Gothic rib springings.

Turkish Islamic builders adopted the prismatic folded surface as a transition between geometrically different forms. Minaret, Selçuk, Turkey

Triangular prisms made a useful pendentive surface in the porch vaults. Murat 1 mosque, Bursa, Turkey

Islamic builders used stepped squinches and, later, prismatic folds to make the transition between dome and support. Khalif's tomb, Cairo, c 1400

In regions where sun-dried or fired-clay brick was the customary unit of construction, it was perhaps inevitable that masons would experiment with folded-shell structures. Bricks are most easily laid up in flat planes, and sharply angled intersections allow keying of bricks around the edge. In Iran folded prismatic geometries were used by the masons to great effect in the pendentives marking the transition between dome and rectilinear walling. From the medressah Bibi Quasem of 1340, and the Darb Imam mosque built before 1467, to the Lotfollah mosque of 1603 to 1618, Isfahan's architects evolved a most attractive variant of the prismatic vaulted surface in which a skin of fired and glazed tiles refracted the light. Reconstructions and repairs at Shiraz show that in many cases the prismatic form develops from the intersections of buried ribs or flat tile armatures built into the planes of vaulting. Many of the later prismatic constructions are of tile and plaster quite separate from the brick structural vaults, often quite simple barrel-vault or half-dome structures.

The Mediterranean and the deserts of the Near East were not impermeable barriers separating the two cultures of Islam and Christianity. Monks and pilgrims continued to visit the holy shrines long after the expulsion of the Crusaders. The initial phases of the medieval rebirth of learning and technique in the north owed much to the invigorating currents of Muslim science and technology which swept into the closed and insular world of Europe on the return of the Crusading knights. Certainly the wide travels of clerics and traders through the Muslim and Mongol domains in the fourteenth century make it possible that a returning traveller may have brought back the idea of ribless vault constructions; it is perhaps even likely that this happened along the Balkan frontier, but it is not proven.

NOTES
1 John Harvey *The Cathedrals of Spain* (London 1957) 175
2 Professor Felipe Ma Garin, of the University of Valencia, has emphasized that these vaults derive from an indigenous Spanish source and not from central European ribless vaults. In a letter of 7 April 1961 he writes: 'The Valencian type without ribs is, without doubt, original and a logical result of the technical and aesthetic development of the Gothic of the Spanish Mediterranean.'

In the Middle East markets, caravanseries, dwellings, and mosques were built of sun dried brick shells. Caravanseri, Isfahan, Iran

Muslim builders became fascinated by the potential permutations possible where squinches were stepped out to carry an arcade. Medresseh Chahar Bagh, Isfahan

Combinations of prismatic pendentives, stepped corbels, and squinch arch rings enriched the planar surfacing of the Suleimaniye mosque, Istanbul, 1557.

Bricks were laid up in relatively simple barrels and domes. Then tiles or precast gypsum ribs were set in with flat tiles completing the prismatic folds. Shiraz mosque

The resulting prismatic vaulted surfaces were then accented by painting sharp lines along the folds. Vault reconstruction, mosque, Shiraz, Iran

Masons today still use the combination of a light tile rib used as an armature or centering and thin plates of brickwork disposed in prismatic facets

within the armatures. Octagonal crossing vault, bazaar, Isfahan

At Visby on the island of Gotland, at Linköping cathedral, both in the thirteenth-century nave and in the hall choir built early in the fifteenth century, and in Finnish parish churches such as Sipoo, steeply pitched vaults were built of bricks or small stones. From the underside, the dominant rib pattern tends to conceal the domical form of the vault, but when seen from above, as at Lübeck or Blatná, the essential economy of the technique becomes evident. The high pitched domes of the vaulting look like nothing more nor less than beehive corbel vaults. Evidently the masons took full advantage of the steeply pitched shell and flattened coursing to build the vaults without centering. The ribs were nothing more than decorative linear patterns scribed on the domes in an effort to relate them to the customary mode of Gothic detailing.

These pyramidal or domical shells are very similar to the high domed vaults of the south of France. In both cases the form was a logical response to small-stone or brick construction in which the continuity of the shell surface was more important than the focussing of thrusts and loads along ribs. In each case the steep pitch simplified construction by reducing the need for centering. Throughout the later Gothic the pyramidal vault was an acceptable alternative to the low-pitched lattice of ribs. Hans Stethaimer, for example, built a vault in 1408 over the

Hans Stetheimer used steeply pitched angular vaults over the new choir of the Franziskanerkirche, Salzburg, in 1408.

hall choir of the Franziskanerkirche at Salzburg in which the ribs define very sharply angled panels. In so doing the vault becomes a steeply pitched prismatic fabric relying upon acute folding for its strength.

The upper surface of fifteenth and sixteenth century prismatic vaults shows how the brick shells could be built up without centering. The coursing and beds are relatively flat. Church, Blatná, Czechoslovakia, 1515

226

ARNOLD OF
WESTPHALIA:
INVENTOR
OF THE
PRISMATIC RIB

By the end of the Gothic, the palace began to emerge as the major building form in which architects tried out new techniques and novel structures. Windsor and Hampton Court in England, Wawel in Kraków, the Hrad at Prague, and the Albrechtsburg at Meissen all exhibit this new dependence of the leading architects upon royal patronage. In the Albrechtsburg, started in 1471, the rich variety of vaulting pattern traces the steps which led to an entirely novel vault – the prismatic ribless shell.

The architect, Arnold of Westphalia, designed the Great Hall in 1471, keeping the rib as a dominant element. The concave mouldings and sharp profiles of rib slide out of piers which he chiselled and cut as if he had constructed them of wood and shaped them with an adze. But not resting content with a purely decorative application of these forms, he prismatically shaped and folded each vaulting panel so that the vault as a whole became an exercise in sharply angled planar geometry. In so doing he took the crucial step which translated the smooth curvatures of a vaulted panel into a diamond faceted cell. The terms Zellengewölbe or Diamantgewölbe, used in German to describe these vaults with their stress upon cells or diamonds, emphasize this new planar folding. Where in the typical mesh vault of the fifteenth century it was customary to dome each vaulting panel slightly, as at Maulbronn, Arnold

went further to convert each large panel into a tent-like prism.

Quickly grasping the potential of the steeply pitched prismatic web, Arnold went on to dispense entirely with the cumbersome apparatus of the rib. From 1475, in a series of experiments in the halls and chambers of the Albrechtsburg castle, he created an entirely novel structural expression for the vault. The customary stellar and mesh patterns popular in the late Gothic of Germany were projected up to vaulting surface to create, not interlacing patterns of ribs but prismatic, diamond hard, folded planes which emphasized the structural rigidity of a creased or folded shell. Built with brick shells, the vaults were invariably covered on the underside with a heavy coat of lime plaster to cover minor constructional irregularities. The white plaster surfacing strongly emphasized the crystalline faceting, as each prism caught the light in contrasting tones of reflection and shade.

Cathedral buildings which were part of the Albrechtsburg complex were rebuilt using these new prismatic vaults. In the cloister of the cathedral and in the priory a relatively simple cross-groined form

Arnold of Westphalia, in 1471, designed the Great Hall at Meissen with stepped piers, angular web cutting, and slender ribs with concave mouldings.

of ribless vault was devised in which prisms were set in at the crown. This was to be the source for the sixteenth-century Bohemian experiments with prismatic vaulting. The Bishop's castle on the hill just below the Albrechtsburg has many of these cellular ribless vaults and particular ingenuity was shown in adapting the stellar pattern to polygonal and irregular rooms.

227

ARNOLD OF
WESTPHALIA:
INVENTOR
OF THE
PRISMATIC RIB

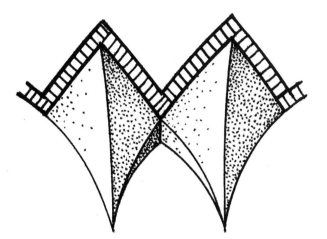

In the Albrechtsburg at Meissen the web was acutely folded to create prisms or cells, 1475–1500.

The cathedral cloister at Meissen was rebuilt about 1480 with cellular vaults in which cross groins were introduced at the crown.

In the bishop's castle at Meissen the ribless cellular vault with a decorative stellar pattern was adapted to polygonal rooms.

Brick and mortar never were well suited to the framed cage of the classic Gothic. As we have seen, plastic flow of the wide mortar joints used in characteristic medieval brick construction led to serious distortions and malformations where brick was used in narrow piers and isolated supports. But brick walling and vaulting were well adapted to structural use if the continuous planar surfaces were so interlocked that the inevitable distortions under load could be absorbed within the shell. Properly used, this elastic deformation of brick shells was a positive advantage, allowing the structure to flex, spreading the loads better across a wide seating.

In the structural diagram the interlocking prismatic brick shells of a typical early mesh cellular vault of about 1480 are shown as they are generated by the projection of a simple diagonal interlace of groin lines on the working platform. For clarity the vertical bounding walls of brick along the sides have been cut away, but it must be remembered that success of the system depended upon edge restraint along the entire side of the structure and this was of course provided by the planar walls of the brick Gothic hall. In its way it is as sophisticated and knowledgeable a structural response as was the curvilinear rib vault, but it is a simpler and more direct structural statement.

At Jüterbog, south of Berlin, the town hall was built from 1498–1507 using ribless cellular vaults in the major rooms.

Brick masons enthusiastically adopted the cellular vault at the turn of the century. Built of brick and mortar with a plaster finish coat, the cellular vault dispensed entirely with the need for expensive stone ribs. Cloister, Jagellon university, Krakow, 1492–7

From 1475 to 1500 mesh cellular vaults at Meissen, Würzen, and Annaberg were designed with large simple prisms springing directly from the side walls. The generating trace in plan was a regular diagonal grid. From 1500 to 1530 mesh cellular vaults at Chomutov, Greinberg, and Würzen were carried on prismatic fans.

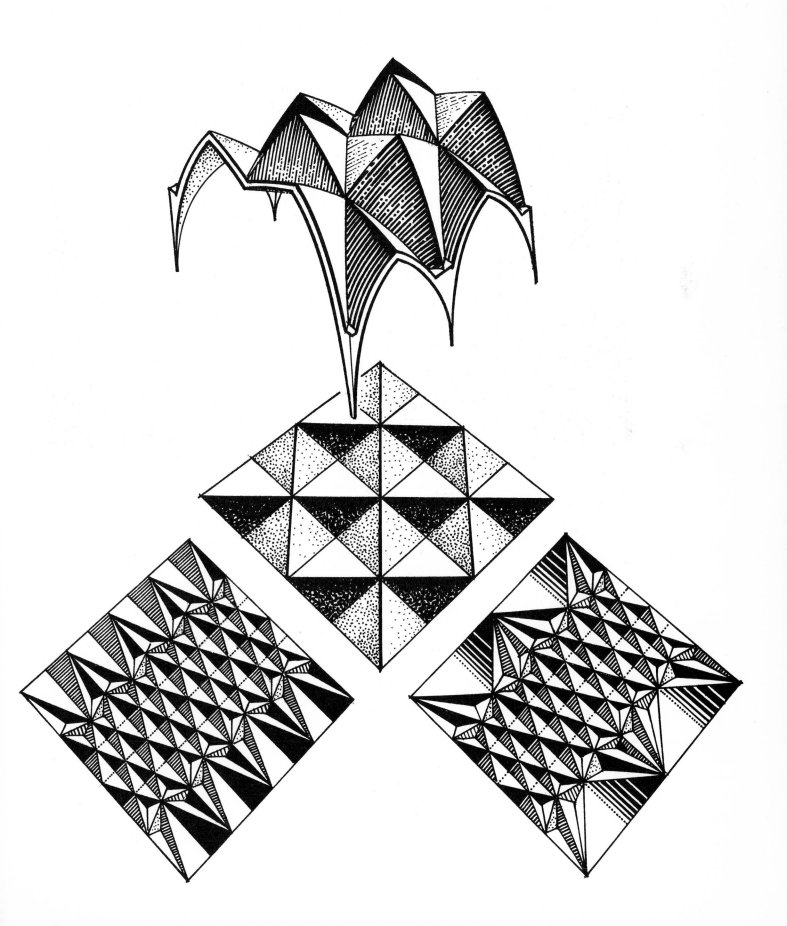

Arnold of Westphalia died in 1480, but well through to the turn of the century prismatic ribless vaulting found wide use in the rich mining towns of Saxony. During this first phase the brick masons emphasized large, acutely folded panels which gave the maximum of structural expression to the shape of the vault. The hard cutting of the shell surface into easily comprehended planar shells seems to have appealed particularly to the prosperous burghers of these inland towns, in its obvious parallel to the angular faceting of wood cuts.

The diagonal mesh used with large simple prisms proved to be well suited to residential applications, as in the house entry at 5 Klostergasse, Annaberg. With continuous restraint along either side of the passage, the regular mesh could abut the wall in closely spaced supports. But where windows or doors were cut in the walling, some means had to be found to support the gridded prism on widely dispersed springings. Before 1500 the prisms were reduced in scale to create a more delicate net which was carried on splays or fans of curving prisms, as in the examples at Wurzen, Chomutov, and Greinberg. Eventually, the difficulties encountered in making a successful transition between folded-fan support and the regular mesh led to a general acceptance of cross groin or stellar plans.

Diagonal mesh with large prisms: 5, Klostergasse, Stradliche Bucherie, entry hall Annaberg, Saxony.

In the Bishop's castle, Wurzen, Saxony, the cellular mesh vault was carried on prismatic fans.

The ribless cellular vault was rare in Austria but at Greinberg on the Danube a regular mesh cellular vault was built, probably by Bohemian masons, 1488–93. (after Clasen)

In the early use of mesh and cross-groin cellular vaults, little difficulty was encountered in the termination of the prismatic folds on the wall surface. The relatively uncomplicated forms could fair away into sharp angles as at Meissen or Annaberg. Occasionally a splayed triangular seating, as in the church at Kadaň, Czechoslovakia, or at the castle at Wurzen, Saxony, provided a broader seating for the folded surfaces.

But, as we saw in the Romanesque, to swing the groin arcs through their long arcs and have them meet precisely at an angled intersection is a tricky problem for the craftsman. At first they introduced wedged prisms to carry the groins. By 1500 the plasterers solved this difficulty by bringing the arcs to a curved apex as at Nezamyslice or Bechyně, Czechoslovakia. In time, the Renaissance pilaster cap began to be used as a bracket from which the folds could spring directly.

Prismatic groins emerged directly from the wall at 5, Klostergasse, Annaberg, Saxony. Later plastering tended to separate the groins.

As the Renaissance column or pilaster cap was introduced a clash developed between the prismatic vault and the static form of the column or pilaster. Nezamyslice, Bohemia

At Kadan monastery in Bohemia prismatic plaster wedges provided a seating for the springing of prismatic fans.

After the initial experiments with mesh patterning of cellular vaults a simple and yet very satisfactory form was devised in which the old geometry of crossed groins in each bay was used to generate a prismatic pattern. Under Renaissance influence, the ribless groin vault was beginning to supersede the ribbed form as in the aisle of the Thomaskirche in Leipzig, built from 1496. When designed to accord with the new Renaissance style each bay of smoothly curved and almost horizontal surfacing was supported by a heavy transverse arch ring.

But, when built as a Gothic structure of folded shells, the two intersecting diagonal groins carried four prisms. The advantages were evident: the mason could create thin brick shells in a folded pattern without heavy centering and cut-stone arch rings. Cross-groin cellular vaults were ideally suited to the narrow spans and short bays required to vault cloister arcades. At Meissen in Saxony, and in the cloisters of the church of St Francis at Bechyně, Czechoslovakia, steeply pitched cross-groin vaults were used in prismatic constructions.

Cellular vaults were ribless and prismatic. In the cross-groin cellular vault four pyramids were introduced at the crown to create the characteristic cross groin and prism pattern.

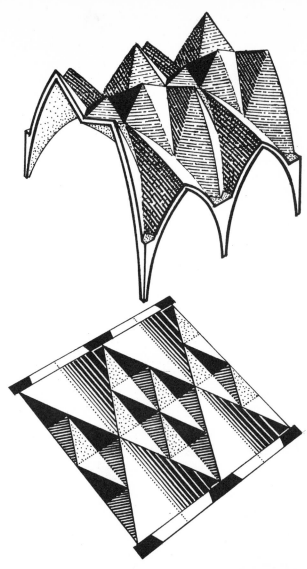

In typical early Renaissance usage groins were slightly exaggerated by giving a double curvature to the vaulting segments in the aisle. Thomaskirche, Leipzig, after 1496

Over square bays with spans longer than those suitable for simple cross-groin vaults, the stellar pattern remained an obvious choice. Substituting a folded fan for a splay of tierceron ribs, the masons intersected the curving prisms to a pattern of crossed groins at the apex. This quadratic star became the favoured pattern in Bohemia. After the disruption and religious strife caused by the Hussite revolts of the fifteenth century the pent-up demand for new building in the towns found in it a satisfactory outlet. Though the courtiers and nobility of Prague favoured the decorative elaboration of the curved rib vault, the dissident sects in the smaller towns of Bohemia and Moravia preferred the geometric rigour of these prismatic forms.

In the new nave added to the church of St Francis, Bechyně, about 1500, the type found its definitive statement. Between the arms of the quadratic star, crossed groins were introduced to create a prismatic texture linking bay to bay. South of Prague, in one of the prosperous burgher towns, Soběslav, the same pattern was used in a more closely modelled pattern. In both, cylindrical columns slide up into the vaulting pattern without the interposition of a column cap. The effect of the cross groins introduced between the arms of the star is to create a diagonal mesh of prisms cutting across the stellar bays.

At Bechyně, slender cylindrical piers carried the vault folding. The curved apex springing brought the folds to a manageable terminus. The plain-wall surfaces, cellular vaulting, and simple piers show a deliberate rejection of the elaborate stereotomy of the late Gothic.

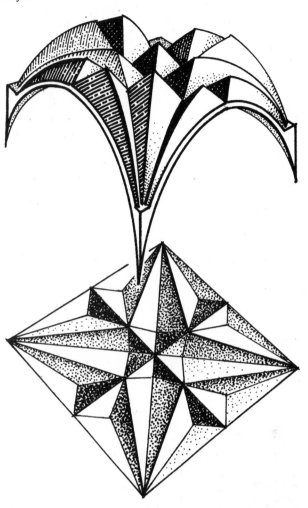

In the star vault four long prismatic compartments intersected at the crown in a crossed groin. Between the legs of this star, subsidiary folds and crossed groins were introduced in varying patterns.

Staněk, in the church at Tábor, Bohemia (1512), used narrow folds in the acutely angled stellar vault of the choir.

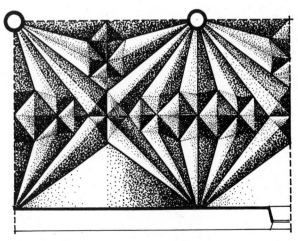

As with ribbed vaults stellar patterns were well suited to long span square compartments. Nave, St Francis, Bechyně, Bohemia, 1491–1520

Over the course of twenty-five years the stellar prismatic vault went through a rapid evolution. The Bohemian brick masons began to decrease the scale of the vaulting panels, using multiform stars in which a sharply creased bundle of folds were swung up from the points of springing. At the church on the town square at Tábor, from 1512, narrow compartments forced the fan of folds from the supports into a sharply angled and acute bundle of facets.

In the new nave of the church at Blatná, the vault designed about 1520 begins to show a weakening of the basic structural form of the cellular vault.

Folding disappears, to be replaced by curved planes. Quadratic stars with cross groins as at Soběslav are used, but, in place of the sharply angled prisms of the earlier work, each panel is a re-entrant curve springing from the caps of piers and pilasters. In the porch, added after 1525, this softening of the initial angularity of the cellular vault is carried to the point where the groin lines are little more than plaster decorations on the underside of a domical vault. Evidently Bohemian designers were beginning to feel the effects of the Renaissance, with its emphasis upon larger and simpler planar surfaces.

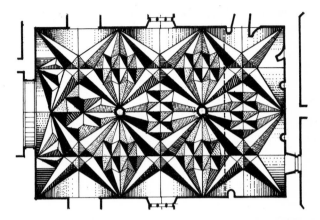

The stellar pattern was modified by introducing cross-groins in place of transverse arch rings. Nave, Saints Peter and Paul, Soběslav

In Saints Peter and Paul, Soběslav, Bohemia, straight sided octagonal piers carried a stellar cellular vault, 1499–1551.

Eventually the cellular vault was to become little more than a curved shell of brick with plaster groins on the surface as in the nave at Blatná after 1515. The plaster groins were swung from Renaissance pilaster caps.

Along the Baltic coast, in Prussia, Poland, Latvia, Esthonia, and Finland, where there was a long tradition of building in brick, the ribless cellular vault was used with particular effect from 1500. Ribbed vaulting in this region had for long been influenced by the English predilection for stellar tierceron vaults executed in tightly meshed, small-scale patterns. Although it is likely that the inspiration for the use of these ribless forms came from Saxony, the Baltic brick masons rarely used the large prisms and high-pitched apices of the Saxon type. Instead, they directly translated the decorative star patterns of their ribbed structures into cellular vaults by suppressing the ribs and erecting small prismatic pyramids on each vaulting panel.

The way in which this was done can be seen clearly in the vaults of the great cathedral of the Marienkirche at Danzig. The vaults in the south transept, constructed in 1446 by Steffens, have decorative ribbed stars at the crown supported by a complex interlace of lierne and tierceron ribs. Essentially, the form of the vault was a shallow saucer dome of brick with a delicate pattern of ribs on the undersurface.

Initially the church had been a basilican structure similar to the cathedral at Lübeck. During the fifteenth century the aisles were raised to the same height as the nave, giving it a hall form. In the south aisle of the nave, Henry Hetzel completed this conversion in 1502 by designing cellular vaulting in which the prisms focus on a decorative prismatic star at the crown.

Over the nave of the Katharinenkirche, Danzig (1503), and at Lomza (1520) this pattern of a decorative prismatic star evolved into a regional variant of cellular vaulting with small angular prisms. So pervasive was the influence of this late Gothic form that it was erected over church interiors which were in every other respect Renaissance in inspiration, indicating that although the architects were willing to use Italianate motifs for the wall detailing, when it came to the serious business of spanning the chamber they preferred to stay with the known and predictable late Gothic structural forms. Here, as in the rest of Europe, the deeply entrenched structural logic of the Gothic masonry vault made it the very last form in the building which succumbed to the new style of the Renaissance.

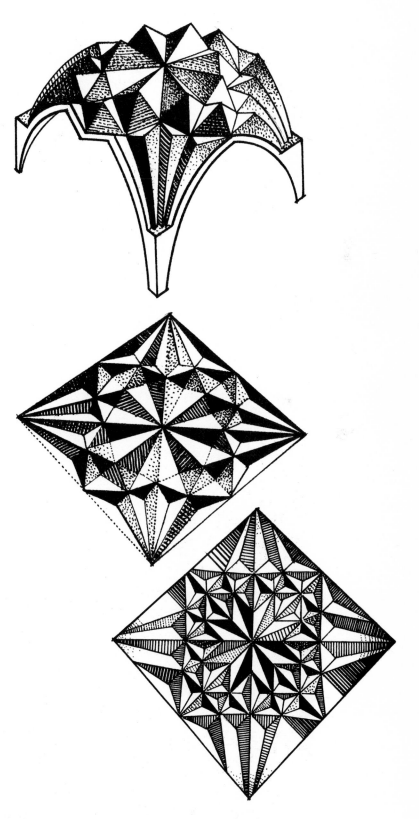

In the decorative star cellular vault an eight-pointed prismatic star was supported by folded supports.

The eight-pointed decorative star gave a dramatic impact to the vault over a square room. Chapel in castle, Telč, Czechoslovakia, 1520

Henry Hetzel raised the south aisle of the Marienkirche, Danzig, to the height of the nave and used a brick decorative star cellular vault, 1498–1502.

In this last flowering of the Gothic during the sixteenth century, architects and designers, masons and craftsmen showed a surprising imagination in their search for forms which could break free of the encumbering formulae and restrictive dogmas of the classic Gothic. Perhaps, just because the Gothic designers felt themselves imperilled by the new emphasis upon classicist tastes and Italianate motifs, they stripped away all of the incidental apparatus of the Gothic to essay novel structural exercises.

We have seen how the English masons in the fifteenth century devised the flaring conoid of the fan vault to give a dramatic expression to the vault as a curved shell surface alone. The fan gave a perfect expression to the search for economy and a visible

logic in the shell structure. Every curve was dictated by the behaviour of doubly curved shells in compression. Each profile was adjusted to the nature of masonry shells rather than being an accidental by-product of the framed masonry cage of ribs.

This triumph of the shell surface was repeated in the evolution of the ribless cellular vault. Starting with the sharply creased folded shells of Meissen, the architects progressively refined the form until it expressed with the utmost economy the behaviour of arched shells of brick.

About 1550, at Slavonice on the Czech-Austrian border, cellular fan vaults were used in several burghers' houses. In these houses on the Market street the cellular vault reaches its ultimate form: a flaring conoid of folds soaring up in identical curves from the springing. By now, mesh and stellar patterning, derived from the earlier ribbed vaults, had been bypassed to devise a form which was a direct and readable expression of the nature of the compression loadings within the shell. The material, brick with a plaster surfacing, dictates the form. By this scrupulous adherence to the logic of the material, the designers of these vaults created the model for a new architecture of shell surface. But the accidents of history and the vagaries of style dictated that these brilliant insights were to be without progeny until, in the later baroque of the seventeenth century, architects began once again to relearn the structural lessons of the Gothic. Indeed, not until our own century, with the renewed interest in economical shell construction brought about by the introduction of ferroconcrete, do we find structures which can compare with these brilliant innovations of the later Gothic designers.

In time the masons reduced the decorative star to a rosette at the crown and emphasized the supporting fan of folded surfaces. House, Marktstrasse, no. 46. Slavonice, Czechoslovakia

In the entry to another Marktstrasse house in Slavonice, the folded fans spring from a pier capped by a free rendition of a Renaissance entablature.

Four splendid centuries of architectural innovation carried building in northern Europe from the indigenous timber barn and framed hall to a dramatic evocation of space and light in the great cathedrals. Arguing from local modes of building and from sensible adaptations to a continental northern climate, carpenters and masons created a new architecture peculiarly suited to the psychological tensions implicit in the Christian faith. Bourgeois councillors, hard-headed abbots, and the clerical elite collaborated in this effort to create a suitable man-made environment for the pan-European aspirations of the church and the restless vigour of prospering communities.

The discipline of the vault, the static balance of heavy loads, the management of public funds in great building enterprises enforced a new role upon the builder. No longer was a craftsman concerned only with the execution of parts of the work; more and more he began to participate in the process of decision and plan. Only he could speak with authority of the play of structure and the stability of the fabric. This professional expertise and technical command assured the architect a new status in late medieval society. Despite society's ingrained disdain for the mechanical arts, a heritage from the slave economy of Rome, the architect entered the palace by the back door and emerged, resplendent in new robe and chain of office, leaning on the arm of the prince or prelate.

Yet this new status and heady sense of power was dangerous. By the sixteenth century the architect had lost much of his contact with the basis of his craft. Rejecting the bumbling parsimony of guild professionals and municipal councillors, turning away from the tiresome and rigorous demands of ecclesiastical patrons, he committed himself to the adventurous freedom of work with the condottiere and princelings of a new Europe. Now, more artist than craftsman, more courtier than consultant, the architect found his metier in the arts of display. Mannered affectations and a complex sophisticated geometry took the place of reasoned structure and logical function. To legitimize their abrupt seizure of power, the new nobility of the Renaissance demanded splendid masques, elaborate follies, and dramatic effects. The architects collaborated only too willingly, turning their skills and talents away from the real problems of the towns and cities to the opulent display of villas, gardens, and gay palaces. A pseudo-chivalric fantasy of pleasure and power based upon geometric and abstract plans made possible a new scale of architectural organization, but it was one which was effectively divorced from the roots of building and the logic of structure.

It was no accident that Gothic became a term of disdain; the new mode needed a rewriting of the immediate past. Manetti, with only a vague account of the thousand years since the fall of Rome as source, wrote that Vandals, Goths, Lombards, and Huns had brought their own architecture with them to replace the glories of classical architecture. Gothic was modern, rustic, coarse, northern, or transalpine. Filarete wrote 'cursed be the man who introduced "modern" architecture.'

In an attempt to find a logical explanation for this 'maniera tedescha,' the German style, the pseudo-Raphael first mentioned the forests of the north as the inspiration for the Gothic. Arguing that the verticality of the Gothic came from the example of the closely spaced columns of trees in forests, he went on to suggest that the pointed arch and the rib were the result of tying together tree branches. An ingenious hypothesis; one of those lucky near misses which cause so much trouble. As late as the nineteenth century this romantic emphasis upon verdant forests and interlacing branches led to the buildings typical of the Victorian Gothic revival. These murky, dark, green, purple, and mysterious caves are in complete contrast to the crisp and engineered clarity of the real Gothic.

As we have seen, the essence of the Gothic was to be found in the term 'modern' used by Filarete. It was a hard-headed yet imaginative and novel effort to concentrate upon artificially shaped structural elements, a systematic analysis of the process of erection, and an empirical adjustment to structural need. In truth the Gothic was neither more nor less romantic than a steam engine or a rocket.

15
EPILOGUE

240

RENAISSANCE,
BAROQUE,
AND THE
NINETEENTH-
CENTURY

By the sixteenth century, the central plan, the dome, and the massive pierced wall, all elements indigenous to the Mediterranean basin, began to replace the linear plans, ribbed vaults, and skeletal walls of the north. Almost a century of experiment was necessary before these southern motifs could be adapted with any success to the demands of the northern climate. In England, France, and Germany classical detail was applied to buildings which remained medieval in inspiration and concept. Well into the early seventeenth century, a chaotic play with decoration concealed the logic of building and the purpose of architecture. Splendid conceits and follies cast a patina of romantic excitement over the walls of buildings. Buildings became façade screens composed and ordered without regard to the structural logic of the spans and without relation to the new complexities of plan in the interior. Grandiose and overworked decoration spread like an ivy or fungus concealing the ordered simplicity of good design.

In truth, not until Italian architects during the first half of the seventeenth century invented the Baroque could there be a real advance once again into problems of structure and space. The boxy and geometric regularity of the wall based upon ideal figures gave way to a plastic manipulation of the surface. In place of the hemispherical lantern dome, elliptical and folded shells not dissimilar to the shell structures of the Gothic freed the Baroque designer to adapt his mass and shell constructions to the new dramatic appeal of the Counter Reformation. Guarino Guarini in Italy turned back to Gothic and Islamic sources for forms which revitalized the tired cliches of the classically inspired Renaissance.

Concealed behind the florid cherubim and vacuous angels of the plastered, gilded, and painted sculpture, the thin brick shells of the Baroque were worthy successors to the empirical vaults of the Gothic. Tension girdles of bolted timbers and wrought iron chains and rods took tensile stresses, timber trusses were devised as triangulated rigid figures, and the developing technology of static analysis gave an economical and predictable basis to the art of building. Perhaps the most significant structures of the Baroque age of Enlightenment were not the florid churches and grand palaces but the utilitarian fabrics devised by engineers and artisans. Military structures using every trick of cramped, interlocked, and vaulted masonry to withstand gunfire, furnaces in foundries, vast conical shells of brick over glassworks, and ingenious hydraulic engineering in the locks and gates of canals showed the way to a new architecture where the dramatic and evocative power of a structural statement gave proper emphasis to the art and science of the builder.

By the nineteenth century, the imperative need for economy and fitness for purpose in these large utilitarian fabrics led to an entirely new interpretation of frame executed in cast and wrought iron. In truth, the engineers who built the lacy iron and glass halls and stations of the mid-nineteenth century, and the bridge builders who flung latticed and bolted iron across the rivers of Europe and America were the true inheritors of medieval tradition – not the eclectic decorator-architects who copied the detail and missed the structural import of the Gothic. Today we stand at the end of a century and a half of experiment with metallic framed structures. So strong has been the influence of this new skeleton tradition, the opus francigenum of our time, that financiers, developers, and architects impose the steel-framed, glass-walled skyscraper as the image of the future without regard to climate, social need, or economic logic. We buy curtain walling by the acre. Extruded aluminum, plastic gaskets, and plate glass substitute for structural logic and intelligent adaptation to climate and use.

Not surprisingly, a new generation of architects has recoiled from this mindless application of frame and panel. The brutal strength of mass walling, the imperatives of shell surfacing in ferroconcrete, twisting and contorting to best meet and counter the pull of gravity are the motifs which stimulate and energize imagination today. At its worst this has led to an affected virtuosity in design; at its best, to a sense of structure and economy of material peculiarly suited to meet the regional demands of our global community.

OVERLEAF *Nineteenth-century iron frame: the Crystal Palace, London, Joseph Paxton, 1851*

Wall and window in the sixteenth century.

241

RENAISSANCE,
BAROQUE,
AND THE
NINETEENTH-
CENTURY

Baroque parish churches continued to be built with cross vaults, but the groins were concealed by plaster clouds and angels. Augustine church, Rohr, Bavaria, by Egid Quirin Asam, 1718–25

The hall church of the sixteenth century evolved into the Baroque plastic shell of the eighteenth. Church at Wies, Bavaria

In the ambulatory of St Eustache, Paris, the ribs, bosses, shafts, and the capitals of the Gothic were translated into Renaissance motifs, 1532–89.

242

RENAISSANCE,
BAROQUE,
AND THE
NINETEENTH-
CENTURY

During the Baroque the structural achievements of
Gothic masons became the source for the dynamic
engineering of folded and warped surfaces in the
dome. St Ivo della Sapienza, Rome, 1642–50

Precise planning and cutting of large stones in the
vaulting webs replaced rough-and-ready coursing
of small stones or bricks. St Nicolas-des-Champs,
Paris, c 1600 rebuilding

The light and delicate cast iron and plaster fabrics
of the early nineteenth century were modern
expressions of frame architecture. Reading room,
Library of Ste Genevieve, Paris, by Henri Labrouste,
1843–50

243

RENAISSANCE,
BAROQUE,
AND THE
NINETEENTH-
CENTURY

Steel, thin-shell construction in shipbuilding, and in tubular bridges used the rigidity of curved planes in a new material. Firth of Forth Bridge, Scotland, 1882–90, Benjamin Baker and John Fowler

Antoni Gaudi used a thin shell construction of tile braced by interlocking ribs in the church of the Colonia Guëll, Barcelona in 1914.

Pier Luigi Nervi makes ingenious use of precast warped plane concrete units to span hundreds of feet. Exhibition Hall, Turin

The combination of shell surface with framed elements in Nervi's structures is precisely akin to Gothic engineering. Casino, Chiacano

OTHER SOURCES · GLOSSARY · INDEX

OTHER SOURCES

MARCEL AUBERT 'Croisees d'ogives' *Bulletin monumental* (Paris 1934)

L. TORRES BALBAS *La Mezquita de Cordoba* (Madrid 1952)

JULIUS BAUM *Romanesque Architecture in France* (2nd ed, London 1928)

JULIUS BAUM *German Cathedrals* (London 1956)

FERNAND BENOIT *L'art roman en France: Provence* (Paris 1961)

BERNARD BEVAN *History of Spanish Architecture* (London 1938)

FRANZ BOAS *The Kwakiutl Indians* (Report of US National Museum, Washington 1895)

DANIEL PAULK BRANCH *Folk Architecture of the East Mediterranean* (New York 1966)

ALAN HOUGHTON BRODRICK 'Grass Roots, Huts, Igloos and Wigwams' *Architectural Review* 686 (February 1954) 101–11

A. BULLEID and H.ST.G. GRAY 'Glastonbury Lake Village' *Glastonbury Antiquarian Society* (1911–17)

HARALD BUSCH and BERND LOHSE *Romanesque Europe* (London 1960)

J. PUIG. I. CADAFALCH *L'art wisigothique et ses survivances* (Paris 1961)

AUGUSTO CAVALLARI-MURAT 'Static Intuition and Formal Imagination in the Space Lattices of Ribbed Gothic Vaults' (translated from an article in *Atti e rassegna technica* (Journal of the Society of Engineers and Architects) Turin, July 1958) *Student Publications of the School of Design* (Raleigh NC. North Carolina State College 1963) 2, 2

V. GORDON CHILDE *What Happened in History* (Penguin Books 1942) 48–52

AUGUSTE CHOISY *L'art de batir chez les Romains* (Paris 1873)

AUGUSTE CHOISY *L'art de batir chez les Byzantins* (Paris 1883)

AUGUSTE CHOISY *Histoire de l'architecture* (Paris 1899) II

W. COXE *Travels in Poland, Russia, Sweden and Denmark* (London 1784) I, 348

K.A.C. CRESWELL *Early Muslim Architecture* (2 vols, Oxford 1932–40)

K.A.C. CRESWELL *A Short Account of Early Muslim Architecture* (Penguin Books 1958)

F.H. CROSSLEY *The English Abbey* (London 1949)

GLYN DANIEL *The Megalith Builders of Western Europe* (Hutchinson 1958; Penguin Books 1963)

W.B. DINSMOOR *The Architecture of Ancient Greece* (London 1950)

FRANZ DISCHINGER 'Schalen und Rippenkuppeln' *Handbüch für den Eisenbetonbau* edited by F. Emperger (3rd ed, Berlin 1928) XII

PHILIP DRUCKER *Indians of the Northwest Coast* (New York: American Museum of Natural History 1955) 67–70

PHILIP DRUCKER *Cultures of the North Pacific Coast* (San Francisco 1965) 25–7, 119–21, 145–9

I.E.S. EDWARDS *The Pyramids of Egypt* (Penguin Books 1947)

W.B. EMERY *Excavations at Sakkara, Great Tombs of the First Dynasty* (London 1958) III

C. ENLART *Manuel d'archeologie française* (5 vols, Paris 1919–32)

JOAN EVANS *The Romanesque Architecture of the Order of Cluny* (Cambridge 1938)

H.G. FENTIMAN 'Opening New Horizons' *Architectural Association Journal* 41, 10 (October 1964)

JOSEF FINK 'Die Kuppel über dem Viereck' in *Festschrift für Carl Weickert* (Berlin 1955) 25–40

A.F. FREZIER *La théorie et la pratique de la coupe des pierres et des bois* (Paris 1769) III, 348

A. GAYAT *L'art arabe* (Paris 1893)

SIEGFRIED GIEDION *The Eternal Present* (New York 1964) I, II

M. GOMEZ-MORENO 'Iglesias mozarabes' *Arte espanol de los siglos ix a xi* (Madrid 1919)

OLEG GRABAR 'The Islamic Dome, Some Considerations' in *Journal of the Society of Architectural Historians* 22, 4 (December 1963) 191–8

E.A. GUTKIND *Urban Development in Central Europe* (London 1964) I, app 3 'The Morphology of a Wurt,' 457–60

S.B. HAMILTON 'Building and Civil Engineering Construction' in Singer, Holmyard, Hall, and Williams *A History of Technology* (Oxford 1958) IV, 442–6

TALBOT HAMLIN *Forms and Functions of Twentieth Century Architecture* (New York 1952) II, 312–424

I.B. HART *The Mechanical Inventions of Leonardo da Vinci* (London 1925)

JOHN HARVEY *The Gothic World* (London 1950)

LOUIS HAUTECOEUR *Les mosquées du Caire* (2 vols, Paris 1932)

DEREK HILL and OLEG GRABAR *Islamic Architecture and its Decoration A.D. 800–1500* (London 1964)

JOHN D. HOAG *Western Islamic Architecture* (New York 1963)

WALTER HORN 'The Great Tithe Barn of Cholsey, Berkshire' *Journal of the Society of Architectural Historians* 22, 1 (1963) 23–32

M.R. JAMES *Abbeys* (London 1925)

JURGEN JOEDICKE *Shell Architecture* (New York 1963)

G.G. KING *Pre-Romanesque Churches of Spain* (Bryn Mawr 1927)

SPIRO K. KOSTOF *The Orthodox Baptistery of Ravenna* (Yale 1965)

WITOLD KRASSOWSKI *Architektura Drewniana w Polsce* (Warsaw 1961) 17–22

GEORGE KUBLER 'A Late Gothic Computation of Rib Vault Thrusts' *Gazette des Beaux Arts*, series 6, 26 (1944) 135–48

GEORGE KUBLER *The Art and Architecture of Ancient America* (Penguin Books 1962)

E. LAMBERT 'Les voutes nervées hispano-musulmanes du xie siècle' *Hesperis* 8 (Paris 1928)

PAUL LEON *L'art roman* (Paris 1917)

GIOVANNI LILLIU 'The Proto-Castles of Sardinia' *Scientific American* 201, 6 (1959) 63–9

Z. S. MAKOWSKI 'Double-Layer Grid Structures' *Architectural Association Journal* 76, 850 (1961)

ALEXANDER VAN MILLIGEN *Byzantine Churches in Constantinople* (London 1912)

PIER LUIGI NERVI *Structures* (translated from *Construire Corretamente* [Milan 1955]) (New York 1956)

RONALD L. OLSON *Adze, Canoe and House Types of the Northwest Coast* (Seattle 1955)

NIKOLAUS PEVSNER *An Outline of European Architecture* (Jubilee edition, Penguin Books 1960)

ALF PFLÜGER *Elementary Statics of Shells* (translated from *Elementare Schalenstatte* [Berlin 1957]) (New York 1961)

HUGH PLOMMER 'Ancient and Classical Architecture' *Simpson's History of Architectural Development* I (rev. ed, London 1956)

ARTHUR KINGSLEY PORTER *The Construction of Lombard and Gothic Vaults* (New Haven 1911)

ARTHUR KINGSLEY PORTER *Lombard Architecture* (4 vols, New Haven 1915–17) note plate 202

AMOS RAPOPORT *House Form and Culture* (Englewood Cliffs NJ 1969)

DAVID TALBOT RICE *English Art, 871–1100* (Oxford 1952)

DAVID TALBOT RICE *Byzantine Art* (Penguin Books 1954)

G.T. RIVOIRA *Lombardic Architecture, its Origin, Development and Derivatives* (2 vols, Oxford 1934)

F.H.H. ROBERTS, JR 'Shabik'eschee Village, a Late Basketmaker Site in the Chaco Canyon, New Mexico' *Bulletin 92, Bureau of American Ethnology* (1929)

D.S. ROBERTSON *A Handbook of Greek and Roman Architecture* (Cambridge 1943)

BERNARD RUDOFSKY *Architecture without Architects* (New York 1964)

MARGUERITE RUMPLER *La coupole dans l'architecture byzantine et musulmaine* (Strasbourg 1956)

A.L. SADLER *A Short History of Japanese Architecture* (Tokyo 1962) 8–14

R.W. SCHULTZ and S.H. BARNSLEY *The Monastery of Saint Luke of Stiris in Phocis* (London 1901)

ANDRE SIEGFRIED *The Mediterranean* translated by Doris Heming (New York 1947)

E. BALDWIN SMITH *The Dome* (Princeton 1950)

H.H. STATHAM *A History of Architecture* (rev. ed, London 1950)

CECIL STEWART *Early Christian, Byzantine, and Romanesque Architecture: Simpson's History of Architectural Development* II (rev. ed, London 1954)

JOSEF STRZYGOWSKI *Early Church Art in Northern Europe* (London 1928)

WILFRED THESIGER *The Marsh Arabs* (Penguin Books 1967) 26–9

BEHCET UNSAL *Turkish Islamic Architecture* (London 1959)

E. VIOLLET-LE-DUC *Dictionnaire raisonné de l'architecture française du onzième au seizième siècle*: I, *Architecture*; IV, *Construction*; IX, *Voute* (Paris 1858–68)

JAMES WALTON *African Village* (Pretoria 1956) 127–41

J.B. WARD-PERKINS 'The Italian Element in Late Roman and Early Medieval Architecture' *Proceedings of the British Academy* 32 (1947) 169

MORTIMER WHEELER *Roman Art and Architecture* (New York 1964) 147

WALTER MUIR WHITEHILL *Spanish Romanesque Architecture of the Eleventh Century* (Oxford 1941)

D. WILBER *The Architecture of Islamic Iran: The Ilkhanid Period* (Princeton 1955)

H.H. WORMINGTON *Prehistoric Indians of the Southwest* (Denver Museum of Natural History 1951)

SUUT KEMAL YETKIN *L'architecture turque en Turquie* (Paris 1962)

SECTION 2 : FRANCE

POL. ABRAHAM 'Les données plastiques et fonctionelles du problème de l'ogive,' *Recherche no. 1: Le problème de l'ogive* (Centre international des Instituts de recherche (Paris 1939) 29–51, 7 figs

FRANCIS B. ANDREWS *The Medieval Builder and his Methods* (Oxford 1925)

MARCEL AUBERT *L'architecture cistercienne en France* (2 vols, Paris 1943)

MARCEL AUBERT *L'art français a l'epoque romane: architecture et sculpture* (4 vols, Paris 1929–32–50)

MARCEL AUBERT 'Les plus anciennes croisées d'ogives: leur rôle dans la construction' in *Bulletin monumental 93* (1934)

MARCEL AUBERT *Notre-Dame de Paris, sa place dans l'histoire de l'architecture du xii et xvi siècle* (Paris 1920)

CARL F. BARNES, JR 'The Cathedral of Chartres and the Architect of Soissons' *Journal of the Society of Architectural Historians* 22, 2 (1963)

ANATOLE DE BAUDOT and A. PERRAULT-DABOT *Les cathédrales de France* Archives de la commission des monuments historiques (5 vols, Paris 1898–1904)

J. BAUM *Romanesque Architecture in France* (London 1928)

FRANCIS BOND *English Church Architecture* (Oxford 1913) I, II

THEODORE BOWIE *The Sketchbook of Villard de Honnecourt* (Bloomington 1959)

ROBERT BRANNER 'Villard de Honnecourt, Archimedes, and Chartres' *Journal of the Society of Architectural Historians* 19, 3 (1960)

HARALD BUSCH and BERND LOHSE *Gothic Europe* (London 1959)

FRANÇOIS CALI and SERGE MOULINIER *L'ordre ogival: Essai sur l'architecture gothique* (Paris 1963)

AUGUSTE CHOISY *Histoire de l'architecture* (Paris 1899)

C. ENLART 'Les eglises a coupoles d'Aquitaine et de Chypre' *Gazette des Beaux-Arts*, 13 (1926)

JULES FORMIGÉ *L'Abbaye royale de saint-Denis: Recherches nouvelles* (Paris 1960)

ERNST GALL *Die gotische Bankunst in Frankreich und Deutschland* (Braunschweig 1955)

T.G. JACKSON *Gothic Architecture in France, England and Italy* (Cambridge 1915)

HANS JANTZEN *High Gothic* English translation by J.C. Palmes (Letchworth 1962)

C. MARTIN and C. ENLART *L'art gothique en France* (2 vols, Paris 1913–25)

CHARLES H. MOORE *Development and Character of Gothic Architecture* (2nd ed, New York 1906)

ANDRÉ MUSSAT *Le style gothique de l'ouest de la France* (Paris 1963)

IRWIN PANOFSKY *Abbot Suger on the Abbey Church of St. Denis and its Treasures* (Princeton 1946)

IRWIN PANOFSKY *Gothic Architecture and Scholasticism* (Latrobe 1951)

ARTHUR KINGSLEY PORTER *Medieval Architecture, Its Origins and Development* (New York 1909)

ARTHUR KINGSLEY PORTER *The Construction of Lombard and Gothic Vaults* (New Haven 1911)

HANS REINHARDT *La cathédrale de Reims* (Paris 1963)

A. RENGER-PATZCH and W. BURMEISTER *Norddeutsche Backsteindome* (Berlin 1930)

CECIL STEWART *Gothic Architecture* (London 1961)

JOSEF STRZYGOWSKI *Early Church Art in Northern Europe* (London 1928)

ALLAN TEMKO *Notre Dame of Paris* (New York 1955)

MAX THIBAUT *Église gothique en France* (Paris 1956)

CLARENCE WARD *Medieval Church Vaulting* (Princeton 1915)

GEOFFREY WEBB *Architecture in Britain in the Middle Ages* (Penguin Books 1956)

SECTION 3 : ENGLAND

T.D. ATKINSON *Local Style in English Architecture* (London 1947)

JOHN BILSON 'Durham Cathedral: the Chronology of its Vaults' *Archaeological Journal* 79 (1922) 101

FRANCIS BOND *An Introduction to English Church Architecture from the Eleventh to the Sixteenth Century* (2 vols, Oxford 1913)

ROBERT BRANNER 'Westminster Abbey and the French Court Style' *Journal of the Society of Architectural Historians* 23, 1 (1964) 3–18

HARALD BUSCH and BERND LOHSE *Gothic Europe* translated by P. Gorge (London 1959)

A.W. CLAPHAM *English Romanesque Architecture before the Conquest* (Oxford 1934)

A.W. CLAPHAM *Romanesque Architecture in England* (London 1950)

G.H. COOK *Mediaeval Chantries and Chantry Chapels* (London 1947)

F.H. CROSSLEY *The English Abbey* (3rd ed, London 1949)

F.H. CROSLEY *Timber Building in England* (London 1951)

JOAN EVANS *English Art 1307–1461* (Oxford 1949)

BANISTER FLETCHER *A History of Architecture on the Comparative Method* (17th ed, revised by R.A. Cordingley, London 1961)

JOHN HARVEY *Henry Yevele* (London 1944)

JOHN HARVEY *An Introduction to Tudor Architecture* (London 1949)

FRIEDRICH HEER *The Medieval World: Europe from 1100 to 1350* (London 1961)

WALTER HORN 'The Great Tithe Barn of Cholsey, Berkshire' *Journal of the Society of Architectural Historians* 22, 1 (1963) 13–23

F.E. HOWARD 'Fan Vaults' *Archaeological Journal*, 68; second series, 18 (1911)

BJÖRN LANDSTRÖM *The Ship* (New York 1961)

PETER MEYER and MARTIN HÜRLIMANN *English Cathedrals* (London and New York 1950)

NIKOLAUS PEVSNER 'Bristol, Gloucester and Troyes' *Architectural Review* (1953) 89ff

NIKOLAUS PEVSNER *The Englishness of English Art* (London 1955)

NIKOLAUS PEVSNER *An Outline of European Architecture* (Jubilee edition, Penguin Books 1960)

DAVID TALBOT RICE *English Art 871–1100* (Oxford 1952)

H. HEATHCOTE STATHAM *A History of Architecture* (rev. ed, London 1950)

CECIL STEWART *Gothic Architecture: Simpson's History of Architectural Development* III (rev. ed, London 1961)

JOSEF STRZYGOWSKI *Early Church Art in Northern Europe* (London 1928)

ROBERT WILLIS 'On the Construction of the Vaults of the Middle Ages' *Transactions of the Royal Institute of British Architects* 1 (1842) 1–69 (reprinted 1910)

SECTION 4 : CENTRAL EUROPE

JULIUS BAUM *German Cathedrals* (London 1956)

WALTHER BUCHOWIECKI *Die Gotischen Kirchen Osterreichs* (Vienna 1952)

HARALD BUSCH and BERND LOHSE *Gothic Europe* translated by P. Gorge (London 1959)

KARL HEINZ CLASEN 'Deutschland Anteil am Gewölbebau der Spätgotik' in *Zeitsschrift des deutschen vereins für kunstwissenschaft* (1937)

KARL HEINZ CLASEN *Deutsche Gewölbe der Spätgotik* (Berlin 1958)

GEORG DEHIO *Geschichte der deutschen Kunst* II (Berlin and Leipzig 1921)

ZBIGNIEW DMOCHOWSKI *The Architecture of Poland* (London 1956)

WILLI DROST *Die Marienkirche in Danzig und ihre Kunstschätze* (Stuttgart 1963)

URSULA DZECZOT *Die Albrechtsburg Meissen* (Meissen 1963)

LAZLO GERO *Magyar Epiteszet, a xix szazad vegeig* (Budapest 1954)

CORNELIUS GURLITT 'Burg Meissen' in *Kunstdenkmaler Sachsen* (1919)

E.A. GUTKIND *Urban Development in Central Europe* (New York 1964)

JOHN HARVEY *The Gothic World 1100–1600* (London 1950)

BRIAN KNOX *Bohemia and Moravia* (London 1962)

HANS KOEPF *Die Baukunst der Spätgotik in Schwaben* (Stuttgart 1958)

ANDRZEL KRAUZE *The Sacral Art in Poland* (Warsaw 1956)

ERNST-HEINZ LEMPER *Die Thomaskirche zu Leipzig* (Leipzig 1954)

DOBROSLAV LÍBAL *Gotická Architektura v Čechách a na Moravě* (Prague 1948)

BERND LOHSE and HARALD BUSCH *Art Treasures of Germany* (London 1958)

VACLAV MENCL *Czech Architecture of the Luxembourg Period* (Prague 1955)

HERMAN MEUCHE 'Das Zellengewölbe' (unpublished doctoral dissertation, Kunsthistorischen Institut, University of Greifswald 1958)

FRIEDRICH and HELGA MÖBIUS *Sakrale Baukunst* (Würzburg/Vienna 1964)

K. MOHRMANN *Lehrbuch der gotischen Konstruktionen* (Leipzig 1890)

HANS-JOACHIM MRUSEK *Meissen* (Dresden 1957)

A. RENGER-PATZCH *Norddeutsche Backsteindome* (Berlin 1938)

OSWALD SCHMIDT *Die St. Annenkirche zu Annaberg* (Leipzig 1908)

OSKAR SCHÜRER and ERICH WIESE *Deutsche Kunst in der Zips* (Leipzig 1938)

EVA STRNADOVÁ 'Bohemian diamond vaults' (draft for unpublished study, Prague 1959)

H.J.W. THUNNISSEN *Gewelven, hun constructie en toepassing in de historische en heidendaagse Bouwkunst* (Amsterdam 1950)

LE BARON VERHAEGEN *Les églises de Gand* (Brussels 1937)

ZDENĚK WIRTH *Kutna Hora* (Prague 1912)

ABUTMENT the support which takes the thrust and weight of an arch or vault

AEDICULE a niche or recess designed to take a statue

AMBULATORY the aisle surrounding the apse of a church, which gives access to altars and chapels

APSE the circular or angular projection of the church sanctuary

ARCH a structure of wedge-shaped blocks which lock into position under gravity loads

ARCHED BRACE a long curved blade of timber used in a roof structure: cruck

BASTIDE a fortified building or town in the south of France

BASTION a projecting tower or earthwork in a system of fortification

BAY one main compartment of vaulting

BENT a transverse frame forming an integral part of a structural system

BORI rectangular huts of corbelled flagstones built in Provence

BOSS a projecting block of stone, carved with ornament, at the junction of vaulting ribs

BRACE the curved or straight diagonal member, introduced to make a rectangular wooden frame rigid

BUTT JOINT the meeting of two pieces of wood which do not overlap

BUTTRESS any considerable projection from the face of a wall, built to resist overturning

CANTED COURSING rings of masonry or brick in a vault, built without centering, at a moderate pitch

CANTILEVER a projecting beam rigidly fixed at one end

CAPITAL the crowning member of a pier or column

CARRACK a fifteenth-century Mediterranean two-masted ship

CATALAN VAULT brick vaulting built without temporary support with canted coursing

CASEMATE a vaulted chamber built in a system of fortification

CATENARY CURVE the shape taken by a heavy uniform cable or chain freely suspended at its ends

CEMENT A finely powdered substance composed largely of silicon and calcium oxides which, on the addition of water, will set up to a hard stoney binder. Produced artificially by burning clays and limestones. Near Naples the pozzuolanic earths and volcanic tuffs were used as a natural cement in Roman times.

CENTERING a temporary construction of timber used to hold up masonry or brick during the process of erection

CHAPTER HOUSE the place of assembly for abbot, prior, and members of a monastery, or other religious community

CHEVET in French cathedrals, an apse with ambulatory and surrounding chapels

CHOIR the area for clergy and choir, separated by a screen from the main body of the church, presbytery, or chancel

CLERESTORY an upper stage in a building, projecting above adjacent roofs; particularly in a church, the projection of nave above aisle

CLOISTER covered passages about an open court used for circulation in abbey or church property

COG a fourteenth-century ship with rudder and single sail

COLLAR a horizontal tie beam near the top of a truss

CONCRETE a mixture of water, sand, gravel, and cement poured into position

CONOID having the form of a cone, particularly in vaulting

CORBEL a masonry bracket projecting from a wall; a short cantilever

CORBELLED COURSING horizontally projected courses of masonry stepping out one over another

CRENELLATION notched openings in the upper part of a parapet

CROSS VAULT the shell form created by the intersection of two cylinders

CROCKET a projecting spur of stone, carved with foliage, used to decorate a gable or spire

CRUCK *see* arched brace

CRYPT a burial chamber below the choir of a church

CURTAIN WALL a sheathing hung from a structural frame

CUSP a point formed by the meeting of small intersecting arches

DEFORMATION the change in shape of a structure under stress. The amount of deformation is described as strain, and permanent deformation, as set

DIAGONAL RIB the rib at the folded edge of a cross vault, cutting diagonally across a bay of vaulting

DIAGRID a diagonally intersecting mesh of ribs

DIAMOND VAULT a ribless prismatic vault of brick-shell construction

DIAPER ORNAMENT any small pattern repeated continuously over a wall surface

DOME a hemisphere or doubly curved shell of masonry traced out by the rotation of a curved template

DOMICAL CROSS VAULT an intersecting cross vault in which the crown is raised so that the shape approximates to a dome. In this case, the diagonal groin traces out a semicircle

DOVETAIL JOINT a joint formed by a tenon shaped as a splay or reversed wedge which locks into a mortise, designed to take tensile stresses

DOWEL a wooden peg used to pin together the elements of a trussed roof

EARTH LODGE round neolithic hut constructed of cut poles

ELASTIC DEFORMATION reversible change of shape under stress

ELEVATION the drawing of the front or face of a building: vertical plane projection

ENCEINTE a fortified enclosure

FAN VAULT in English Gothic, an inverted conoid shell in which the regular ribs are purely decorative

FERROCONCRETE see reinforced concrete

FINIAL the upper portion of a pinnacle or spire

FLAMBOYANT late French Gothic detailing, characterized by s curves and waving curvatures

FLÈCHE a slender wooden spire on a roof

FLYING RIB a rib in vaulting, free of the masonry shell

FLYING BUTTRESS an exposed arch ring which carries the trust of the vaulting over the aisle roof to an external buttressing pier

FRESCO painting applied to a wet plaster surface

FRIEZE a long horizontal decoration high on a building

GABLE the triangular walling terminating a high-pitched roof

GALLERY in a Romanesque church, the passage above the aisle vaulting

GARGOYLE a waterspout projecting from a parapet and carved in a human or animal likeness

GEOMETRIC thirteenth-century Gothic tracery laid out in regular arcs or circles

GLACIS a sloping earth bank in a fortification

GROIN the intersecting edge of two vaulting surfaces; a folded surface

GROUT sand and lime mortar used as a surfacing or fill

GUILD an association of craftsmen, tradesmen, or merchants

HALL CHURCH a pillared hall in which nave and aisle are equal in height

HAMMERBEAM a timber cantilever projecting from the top of a wall to carry an arched blade and strut

HAUNCH the portion of an arch or vault immediately above the springing

HIP the sloped end of a roof

HYDRAULIC CEMENT silicon and calcium oxides which set up to a hard stoney binder on the addition of water. This hydration does not require air (as lime mortar does).

IMPOST a point from which an arch springs

INFILL PANELS the masonry shell of the vault between the ribs

ISOSTATIC LINES lines of pressure and tension in a structure

JAMB the sides of a door or window opening

KEEP the strong central tower of a defensive complex

KING POST the central vertical post in a truss

KIVA Pueblo Indian ceremonial chamber

LANTERN a turret with windows placed over a dome or vault

LAGGING strips of wood covering a wall

LASHING cordage or fibres used to tie together a wooden frame

LATTICE a closely interwoven mesh of struts or ribs

LANCET ARCH a steeply pointed early Gothic arch

LIERNE RIB secondary rib which links diagonals, tiercerons, and ridge ribs to create stellar or mesh patterns

LIME MORTAR the mixture of sand and lime (calcium carbonate) used to bind together the stone or brick of masonry construction

LINTEL the beam bridging an opening

LONGHOUSE a rectangular primitive communal dwelling

MACHICOLATION the projection of a floor and parapet on corbels over a wall, with openings for defensive use

MIHRAB the prayer niche on the Mecca side of a mosque

MITRE a joint at 45° to create a rightangled connection

MORTISE a socket in timber cut to receive the projecting tenon of another timber

MULLION vertical members dividing a window into two or more lights

NARTHEX a shallow porch extending the width of the west front of a church

NAVE the major public area of a church

NICHE an arched recess in a wall

OGEE an arch with an s curve; made of convex and concave curvatures

PARAPET the protective wall above a roof gutter

PENDANT a decorative projection hung from an arch or vault

PENDENTIVE the triangular vaulted shell surface which makes the transition between a dome and a square or polygonal compartment

PIER a mass of masonry, as distinct from a column

PILASTER a shallow engaged pier, usually rectangular in plan

PINNACLE the small spire or turret on top of a buttress

PITCH the inclination or angle of a roof

PLATE TRACERY early window tracery in which geometric openings are cut through a panel of masonry

PLOUGH-SHARE TWIST the twisted surface in a vault created by the intersection with a vertical window jamb

PORTAL FRAME a rigid arched frame or bent set across a structure

POZZUOLANIC EARTH volcanic earth from Pozzuoli near Naples, used in Roman hydraulic cements

PRESBYTERY the sanctuary or choir, reserved for the clergy, at the eastern end of the church

PRISMATIC VAULT ribless fifteenth- and sixteenth-century vault of brick built with folded panels in central Europe

PURLIN horizontal beams in a roof which are fastened to the trusses or principal rafters and carry the outer rafters

PUTLOG HOLES square holes which carried the scaffolding used during the construction

QUADRANT ARCH RING a quarter circle brace which carries thrusts from vault to external buttresses; sometimes concealed under the triforium roof

QUADRANT BARREL a continuous quarter circle vault which abuts at the nave barrel vault and transfers its thrust to the outer wall

QUADRIPARTITE VAULT the simplest form of cross vaulting in which two transverse arches, two diagonal ribs, and two wall ribs divide the vault into four compartments

QUASI-SEXPARTITE VAULT a quadripartite vault divided into six compartments by the addition of a transverse bracing rib

QUEEN POST TRUSS a truss with two vertical struts linking principal rafters and tie beam

QUOIN large stones at the angle of a building

RAFTER the sloping beams which form the upper structure of a roof and which are intermediate supports for the roofing

RAKE the angle of a rafter or brace

RAKING STRUT braces set in a trussed frame at an angle which often parallels the rafters

RATHAUS town hall (German)

REINFORCED CONCRETE or ferroconcrete. A composite concrete structure of frame or shell in which steel bars are introduced to hold the concrete together against cracking under tension stresses

RETROCHOIR the part of the chancel behind the high altar

RIDGE the apex to a roof

RIDGE RIB the horizontal rib at the crown of the vault

ROOD SCREEN a screen dividing the chancel from the nave, surmounted by a cross

ROSE WINDOW a circular window with patterned tracery

RUBBLE masonry of rough, undressed stones

SAUCER VAULT a shallow dome

SCAFFOLDING a temporary structure of working platforms used during the process of erection

SCISSORS TRUSS a truss in which two long raking strutts lap over and intersect to brace the rafters

SECTION the representation of a vertical plane cut through the structure of a building. A horizontal section is known as a plan

SET permanent deformation under load

SEVERY the panel or compartment of a vault

SEXPARTITE VAULT a square bay of ribbed vaulting in which an additional transverse rib divides the vault into six compartments

SHAFT a small column attached to a pier or a pronounced vertical moulded projection on a pier

SHEAR a sliding fracture of an object under stress

SHELL a plate of masonry, usually curved, which is relatively thin in proportion to its span: to be

contrasted with a linear or framed structure

SHORING a temporary structural prop

SILL the lowest member of a frame or structure; a horizontal timber carrying a roof structure

SOFFIT the finished underside of an architectural member

SOLE PIECE the short horizontal member set across the wall plates forming the base of a small triangular truss supporting the rafters

SPIRE a lofty pointed termination to a tower

SPRINGING the point or level at which the actual curve of an arch or vault begins

STAVE CONSTRUCTION vertical post construction, particularly in Scandinavia

STEREOTOMY the cutting of solids. In masonry, the shaping of blocks for use in wall, arch, or vault

STILTING where an arch springing is raised above its base on vertical segments

STRAIN the elastic deformation of a member under stress

STRAINER ARCHES bracing arches introduced to resist the deformation of piers under stress

STRESS the quantitative expression of the condition within an elastic object occasioned by external forces

STRING COURSE a projecting horizontal moulding running along the face of a wall

STRUT a secondary structural member subject to compression longitudinally

STUCCO a hard plaster usually used on the exterior

STUGA Scandinavian timber farmhouse

TAS-DE-CHARGE the lower courses of a ribbed vault, laid with horizontal joints

TAKAYUKA HUT the elevated platform-hut of the southern Japanese islands

TATEANA HUT the conical earth lodge of northern Japan

TEMPLATE a pattern or guide used to shape a profile

TENON a projection on a piece of wood designed to fit into a mortised cut. The tenon is secured by a peg.

TENSION pulling forces or stresses tending to crack or separate material

THATCH overlapping leaves, grasses, or rushes used as a roofing cover

THOLOS a general name for circular buildings in Greek architecture; applied to corbel domed tombs

TIE BEAM the main horizontal timber of a truss

TIERCERON an intermediate rib in a vault which rises from the springing to the crown

TIERSPOINT a pointed arch in which the arcs are swung from third points on the base line

TIPI temporary lodge of the Plains Indian: a cone of poles with a hide cover

TRACERY ornamental stonework at the head of a window

TRANSEPT either of the lateral arms in a church of cruciform plan

TRANSVERSE ARCH RING an arch spanning at right angles to the walls

TRIFORIUM the area between gallery and clerestory which is normally blanked out by the single-pitch roof over the aisle

TRULLI conical houses of stone corbelled construction built in Apulia, Italy

TRULLO CONSTRUCTION corbelled horizontal coursing applied to a masonry cone with an outer sheathing of slightly pitched flagstones

TRUSS a triagulated frame composed of light tension and compression members used for long-span structures

TUNNEL VAULT a half-cylindar barrel vault

TYMPANUM the slab or walling filling the space enclosed by an arch over the lintel of a door

UNDERCROFT vaulted chambers under the principal structure

VAULTING an arched masonry covering of stone or brick. *See for types* arch, barrel, canted, catalan, cellular, tunnel, cross, curvilinear, diamond, fan, groin, lierne, mesh, prismatic, quadripartite, rib, sexpartite, stellar, tierceron

VOUSSOIR one of the wedge-shaped blocks that make up an arch or vault

WEB the shell of the vault as opposed to the ribbed framework

WIGWAM an eastern Indian longitudinal lodge built of lashed poles and bark

WINDLASS a device for raising loads by winding a rope about a spindle

YURT central Asian nomadic dwelling with lattice frame and felt cover

---

In general, architectural terms are indexed to their definition, or principal reference; other references may or may not be included. When no building is listed following a place name, it is generally the cathedral or major ecclesiastical building to which reference is made. Italicized numbers indicate pages on which an illustration appears. Vault types are not indexed as the location of the major discussion of each type is indicated in the chapter titles.

This book
was designed by
WILLIAM RUETER
under the direction of
ALLAN FLEMING
and was printed by
University of
Toronto
Press